THE PELOPONNESIAN WAR

Lawrence Tritle

Greenwood Guides to Historic Events of the Ancient World
Bella Vivante, Series Editor

GREENWOOD PRESS
Westport, Connecticut • London

Library of Congress Cataloging-in-Publication Data

Tritle, Lawrence A. 1946–
    The Peloponnesian War / Lawrence Tritle.
       p. cm.—(Greenwood guides to historic events of the ancient world)
    Includes bibliographical references and index.
    ISBN 0–313–32499–9 (alk. paper)
       1. Greece—History—Peloponnesian War, 431–404 B.C.   2. Greece—History—
    Peloponnesian War, 431–404 B.C.—Sources.   I. Title.   II. Series.
    DF229.T75   2004
    938'.05—dc22   2004047506

British Library Cataloguing in Publication Data is available.

Copyright © 2004 by Lawrence Tritle

Library of Congress Catalog Card Number: 2004047506
ISBN: 0–313–32499–9

First published in 2004

Greenwood Press, 88 Post Road West, Westport, CT 06881
An imprint of Greenwood Publishing Group, Inc.
www.greenwood.com

Printed in the United States of America

The paper used in this book complies with the
Permanent Paper Standard issued by the National
Information Standards Organization (Z39.48-1984).

10 9 8 7 6 5 4 3 2 1

For

Robert C. Tritle, Jr.
(1924–2002)

pater dilectissimus

vir fortissimus

CONTENTS

SERIES FOREWORD

As a professor and scholar of the ancient Greek world, I am often asked by students and scholars of other disciplines, why study antiquity? What possible relevance could human events from two, three, or more thousand years ago have to our lives today? This questioning of the continued validity of our historical past may be the offshoot of the forces shaping the history of the American people. Proud of forging a new nation out of immigrants wrenched willingly or not from their home soils, Americans have experienced a liberating headiness of separation from traditional historical demands on their social and cultural identity. The result has been a skepticism about the very validity of that historical past. Some of that skepticism is healthy and serves constructive purposes of scholarly inquiry. Questions of how, by whom, and in whose interest "history" is written are valid questions pursued by contemporary historians striving to uncover the multiple forces shaping any historical event and the multilayered social consequences that result. But the current academic focus on "presentism"—the concern with only recent events and a deliberate ignoring of premodern eras—betrays an extreme distortion of legitimate intellectual inquiry. This stress on the present seems to have deepened in the early years of the twenty-first century. The cybertechnological explosions of the preceding decades seem to have propelled us into a new cultural age requiring new rules that make the past appear all the more obsolete.

So again I ask, why study ancient cultures? In the past year, after it ousted that nation's heinous regime, the United States' occupation of Iraq has kept that nation in the forefront of the news. The land base of Iraq is ancient Mesopotamia, "the land between the rivers" of the Tigris and Euphrates, two of the four rivers in the biblical Garden of Eden (Gen. 2). Called the cradle of civilization, this area witnessed the early development of a centrally organized, hierarchical social system that utilized the new technology of writing to administer an increasingly complex state.

Is there a connection between the ancient events, literature, and art coming out of this land and contemporary events? Michael Wood, in his educational video *Iraq: The Cradle of Civilization*, produced shortly after the 1991 Gulf War, thinks so and makes this connection explicit—between the people, their way of interacting with their environment, and even the cosmological stories they create to explain and define their world.

Study of the ancient world, like study of contemporary cultures other than one's own, has more than academic or exotic value. First, study of the past seeks meaning beyond solely acquiring factual knowledge. It strives to understand the human and social dynamics that underlie any historical event and what these underlying dynamics teach us about ourselves as human beings in interaction with one another. Study of the past also encourages deeper inquiry than what appears to some as the "quaint" observation that this region of current and recent conflict could have served as a biblical ideal or as a critical marker in the development of world civilizations. In fact, these apparently quaint dimensions can serve as the hook that piques our interest into examining the past and discovering what it may have to say to us today. Not an end in itself, the knowledge forms the bedrock for exploring deeper meanings.

Consider, for example, the following questions. What does it mean that three major world religions—Judaism, Christianity, and Islam—developed out of the ancient Mesopotamian worldview? In this view, the world, and hence its gods, were seen as being in perpetual conflict with one another and with the environment, and death was perceived as a matter of despair and desolation. What does it mean that Western forms of thinking derive from the particular intellectual revolution of archaic Greece that developed into what is called rational discourse, ultimately systematized by Aristotle in the fourth century B.C.E.? How does this thinking, now fundamental to Western discourse, shape how we see the world and ourselves, and how we interact with one another? And how does it affect our ability, or lack thereof, to communicate intelligibly with people with differently framed cultural perceptions? What, ultimately, do we gain from being aware of the origin and development of these fundamental features of our thinking and beliefs?

In short, knowing the past is essential for knowing ourselves in the present. Without an understanding of where we came from, and the journey we took to get where we are today, we cannot understand why we think or act the way we do. Nor, without an understanding of historical development, are we in a position to make the kinds of constructive changes necessary to advance as a society. Awareness of the past gives us the resources necessary to make comparisons between our contemporary world and past times. It is from those comparisons that we can assess both the advances we have made as human societies and those aspects that can still benefit from change. Hence, knowledge of the past is crucial for shaping our individual and social identities, providing us with the resources to make intelligent, aware, and informed decisions for the future.

All ancient societies, whether significant for the evolution of Western ideas and values, or whether they developed largely separate from the cultures that more directly influenced Western civilization, such as China, have important lessons to teach us. For fundamentally they all address questions that have faced every human individual and every human society that has existed. Because ancient civilizations erected great monuments of themselves in stone, writings, and the visual arts— all enduring material evidence—we can view how these ancient cultures dealt with many of the same questions we face today. And we learn the consequences of the actions taken by people in other societies and times that, ideally, should help us as we seek solutions to contemporary issues. Thus it was that President John F. Kennedy wrote of his reliance upon Thucydides' treatment of the devastating war between the ancient Greek city-states of Athens and Sparta (see the volume on the Peloponnesian War) in his study of exemplary figures, *Profiles in Courage*.

This series seeks to fulfill this goal both collectively and in the individual volumes. The individual volumes examine key events, trends, and developments in world history in ancient times that are central to the secondary school and lower-level undergraduate history curriculum and that form standard topics for student research. From a vast field of potential subjects, these selected topics emerged after consultations with scholars, educators, and librarians. Each book in the series can be described as a "library in a book." Each one presents a chronological timeline and an initial factual overview of its subject, three to five topical essays that examine the subject from diverse perspectives and for its various consequences, a concluding essay providing current perspectives on the event, biographies of key players, a selection of primary documents, illustrations, a glossary, and an index. The concept of the series is to provide ready-reference materials that include a quick, in-depth examination of the topic and insightful guidelines for interpretive analysis, suitable for student research and designed to stimulate critical thinking. The authors are all scholars of the topic in their fields, selected both on the basis of their expertise and for their ability to bring their scholarly knowledge to a wider audience in an engaging and clear way. In these regards, this series follows the concept and format of the Greenwood Guides to Historic Events of the Twentieth Century, the Fifteenth to Nineteenth Centuries, and the Medieval World.

All the works in this series deal with historical developments in early ancient civilizations, almost invariably postdating the emergence of writing and of hierarchical dynastic social structures. Perhaps only incidentally do they deal with what historians call the Paleolithic ("Old Stone Age") periods, from about 25,000 B.C.E. onward, eras characterized by nomadic, hunting-gathering societies, or the Neolithic ("New Stone Age"), the period of the earliest development of agriculture and hence settled societies, one of the earliest dating to about 7000 B.C.E. at Çatal Höyük in south-central Turkey.

The earliest dates covered by the books in this series are the fourth to second millennia B.C.E. for the building of the Pyramids in Egypt, and the examination of the Trojan War and the Bronze Age civilizations of the eastern Mediterranean. Most volumes deal with events in the first millennium B.C.E. to the early centuries of the first millennium C.E. Some treat the development of civilizations, such as the rise of the Han Empire in China, or the separate volumes on the rise and on the decline and fall of the Roman Empire. Some highlight major personalities and their empires, such as the volumes on Cleopatra VII of Ptolemaic Egypt or Justinian and the beginnings of the Byzantine Empire in eastern Greece and Constantinople (Istanbul). Three volumes examine the emergence in antiquity of religious movements that form major contemporary world systems of belief—Judaism, Buddhism, and Christianity. (Islam is being treated in the parallel Medieval World series.) And two volumes examine technological developments, one on the building of the Pyramids and one on other ancient technologies.

Each book examines the complexities of the forces shaping the development of its subject and the historical consequences. Thus, for example, the volume on the fifth-century B.C.E. Greek Peloponnesian War explores the historical causes of the war, the nature of the combatants' actions, and how these reflect the thinking of the period. A particular issue, which may seem strange to some or timely to others, is how a city like Athens, with its proto-democratic political organization and its outstanding achievements in architecture, sculpture, painting, drama, and philosophy, could engage in openly imperialist policies of land conquest and of vicious revenge against any who countered them. Rather than trying to gloss over the contradictions that emerge, these books conscientiously explore whatever tensions arise in the ancient material, both to portray more completely the ancient event and to highlight the fact that no historical occurrence is simply determined. Sometimes societies that we admire in some ways—such as the artistic achievements and democratic political experiments of ancient Athens—may prove deeply troublesome in other ways—such as what we see as their reprehensible conduct in war and brutal subjection of other Greek communities. Consequently, the reader is empowered to make informed, well-rounded judgments on the events and actions of the major players.

We offer this series as an invitation to explore the past in various ways. We anticipate that from its volumes the reader will gain a better appreciation of the historical events and forces that shaped the lives of our ancient forebears and that continue to shape our thinking, values, and actions today. However remote in time and culture these ancient civilizations may at times appear, ultimately they show us that the questions confronting human beings of any age are timeless and that the examples of the past can provide valuable insights into our understanding of the present and the future.

Bella Vivante
University of Arizona

PREFACE

The Peloponnesian War among the ancient Greek cities was a conflict that bears comparison with the more familiar conflicts of the twentieth century and its world wars. As the modern world wars were global, so too was the Peloponnesian War that reached across the Greek world—from the western Mediterranean island of Sicily, where Athens' great effort to expand its empire ended disastrously, to western Asia Minor (today's Turkey), where the once feared and even despised enemy of all Greeks, the Persians, intervened and made possible a Spartan victory. The similarity suggested here is seen further in the personalities of the war. The twentieth-century world wars had their Wilsons, Eisenhowers, and Pattons, and so did the Peloponnesian War. In Athens there was the great statesman Perikles, who inspired the Athenians to make bold ventures, literally to risk all in the interests of empire and power. There were great generals who inspired friends and foes alike—men like the Spartan Brasidas, who marched into northern Greece and there ended, at the cost of his own life, Athenian influence. There was the enigmatic Sokrates, a man who challenged everyone he met to think about the consequences of their actions and who in many ways became the founder of Western philosophy.

The Peloponnesian War lasted from 431 to 404 B.C.E., but this is more obvious perhaps to historians today than to those who lived through the events. The idea of creating a unified conflict out of a series of events not necessarily connected belongs to the historian Thucydides, who lived through the war and wrote its history. What Thucydides aimed to do was create a rationalized explanation of conflict modeled on the first major epic poem of Greek antiquity, Homer's *Iliad* (see the Trojan War volume in this series). Homer's war as described in the *Iliad* was mythic, whereas Thucydides' war was real. Homer's war explained events with tales of divine intervention; Thucydides did the same with reason and rationality. But there is no mistaking the imprint of Homer's influence on the "History" that Thucydides would write.

As this great struggle went on, there occurred at the same time in Athens (and to a lesser extent elsewhere) a blossoming of culture and intellectual achievement such as the world has rarely seen. Tourists by the millions still flock to the acropolis in Athens to gaze on the Parthenon and other great buildings from the era of the Peloponnesian War. Literary accomplishments by Sophocles and Euripides dazzled audiences around the Greek world. In the aftermath of the Sicilian Expedition, Athenian prisoners of war earned their freedom through their ability to recite lines from the latest plays of Euripides, certainly a reflection of that poet's popularity. No less remarkable was the satiric and biting comedy of Aristophanes, a critic whose sharp eye missed nothing. No less important were the debates of the world's first philosophers, not only Sokrates, but also thinkers from around the Greek world such as Protagoras of Abdera and Gorgias of Leontini. Athens was the focal point of their activities, made possible by a combination of democracy and wealth, much of it created by the empire that Athens ruled over with an iron fist. This was not the first—or last—time that democracy and imperial power would go hand in hand.

In his famous drama *Oedipus the King*, Sophocles said that "pride breeds the tyrant" (line 873). So, too, does pride breed the power of imperialism, and with that political ambition comes war and violence. Today in the twenty-first century, the peoples of the world are accustomed to violence and its terrible consequences. The experience with violence in the Greek world of the Peloponnesian War era was no different. This conflict witnessed the death of cities, the enslavement of Greeks by Greeks, the rape of women, and the murder of children. Those authors who recorded and wrote while the war raged reflected in many instances on this legacy of violence. In the discussions to follow, this theme of violence will provide a connecting thread as the events and personalities of the great Peloponnesian War are unraveled and presented.

Lastly a word on spelling. Greek names—both those of persons and places—sometimes present difficulties for students whether in spelling or pronunciation. Yet it remains useful for students to see what these look like in transliteration. Although no system of spelling Greek names in English is foolproof, I have preferred Greek forms except for well-known places (Athens, Corinth, Syracuse) and authors (Thucydides, Sophocles). Similarly, titles of Greek texts cited here are referred to in their more familiar latinized or anglicized versions so that student readers may find them more readily.

ACKNOWLEDGMENTS

This work was written during a sabbatical year (2002/3) during which I wrote several other pieces, all shorter but focusing on Herodotus and Thucydides and fifth-century B.C.E. Greek history. A paper on war, peace, and reconciliation was part of a colloquium on that subject at Brown University (March 5–6, 2003), and discussions there with Kurt Raaflaub and others participating in that program actually helped with this study of the Peloponnesian War. I would also like to thank my friend Professor Waldemar Heckel (University of Calgary, past managing editor of the *Ancient History Bulletin*), who read much of this work and offered numerous suggestions that improved the text. Professor Catie Mihalopoulos, my colleague in art history and a specialist in late fifth-century B.C.E. Greek art and culture, also read the chapters dealing with those subjects, as well as that on women, and gave a helpful critique. I would also like to thank my colleague Peter Hoffman, who prepared the maps illustrating various key places in the Greek and Mediterranean world that figure in the events of the Peloponnesian War. My research assistant Christy Cummings read the entire manuscript and helped ensure that students would be able to understand the sequence of events and the nature of the classical Greek world explored here.

Thanks are also due to the staff at Art Resource in New York, especially researcher Humberto DeLuigi, for assistance in gathering a number of the photographs used in this book. I would also like to thank Sharika Sharma of the Penguin Group (London) and the staff of the University of Chicago Press for permission to use the translations of Plato and Euripides reproduced here.

Finally, I am grateful to Professor Bella Vivante for asking me to write this book and for her many helpful suggestions and criticisms, and especially Professor Carol Thomas for her support and encouragement over a personally difficult three years.

CHRONOLOGY
OF EVENTS

Please note: all three-digit dates are B.C.E. *(Before the Common Era);
fifth century and fourth century refer to fifth century and fourth century*
B.C.E., *respectively.* C.E. *(Common Era) designates dates also referred
to as* A.D.

490–478	Era of Persian Wars
490	Battle of Marathon: Athens defeats invading Persian army
480	Battles of Thermopylai/Artemision, Salamis: Greeks defeat Persians on land and sea
	Athens burned by invading Persians
479	Battles of Plataia, Mykale: Persian defeat complete
478/7	Establishment of Delian League, with Athens as its leader
469/8	Battle of Eurymedon
466/5	Revolt and suppression of Naxos by Athens
451/0	Five Years Truce (Athens and Peloponnesian League); Perikles' law restricting Athenian citizenship
449(?)	Peace of Kallias (end of war with Persia)

446/5	Revolt and Reconquest of Euboia
	30 Years Peace, ending "First" Peloponnesian War
440/39	Revolt and suppression of Samos by Athens
435	Outbreak of hostilities between Corinth and Corcyra
433/2	Megarian Decree enacted by Athens
	Dispute between Corcyra, Corinth, and Athens (battle of Sybota)
	Two Congresses at Sparta: Sparta and its allies vote that Athens had broken the 30 Years Peace; they decide on war with Athens
	Spartan embassies (at least four) to Athens seeking negotiations
431, Spring	Theban Attack on Plataia leads to outbreak of Peloponnesian War, called the Archidamian War; final embassy of Sparta (Melesippos) to Athens; first of annual Peloponnesian invasions of Attika begins
430–428	Plague in Athens; death of Perikles
427	Civil war in Corcyra
	Revolt of Mytilene on Lesbos
	Rise to prominence of Athenian statesman Kleon
425	Athenian victory at Pylos/Sphakteria
	Brasidas marches into northern Greece
424	Failure of the Athenian general Thucydides in northern Greece; his life in exile and as historian of the war begins
422/1	Death of Brasidas and Kleon at Amphipolis
	Peace of Nikias ends the Archidamian War
419	Athenian alliance with Argos and allies

418	Battle of Mantineia
416	Athenian attack on Melos—its destruction follows
415	Mutilation of the *Hermai* in Athens
	Profanation of the Mysteries in Athens
	Athenian Expedition sails for Sicily
	Alkibiades recalled from Sicily to Athens
413	Collapse and defeat of Athenian forces in Sicily
	Spartan king Agis invades Attika, seizes Dekeleia
	Thousands of slaves flee to Spartan base at Dekeleia
412	Revolt of Khios, Athenian ally
	Athens opens the "iron fund," a cash reserve on the acropolis
	Persians begin to intervene in Greek war
411	New phase of war erupts, called the Ionian War
	Athenian naval victory at Kynossema; recovery of base at Kyzikos
	Alkibiades active in northern Aegean; intrigues with Athenian fleet at Samos
	Coup at Athens leads to oligarchic takeover, "the 400"; "terror" in Athens
411/10	Counter-revolution in Athens overthrows "the 400"; democracy restored
408	Capture of Byzantion
407	Alkibiades returns in triumph to Athens, elected general
406	Athenian defeat at Ephesos; Alkibiades falls from power
406/5	Athenian victory at Arginusai Islands

	Athens rejects Spartan peace overtures
405/4	Spartan commander Lysander takes command in northern Aegean
	Spartan naval victory at Aigospotami; Athenian fleet destroyed
	Athens besieged, surrenders
	Athens becomes member of Sparta's Peloponnesian League
404–401	Athens ruled by "Thirty Tyrants"
401	Expedition of Persian prince Kyros; his death in battle of Kunaxa, won by Greek mercenaries in his service
399	Death of Sokrates

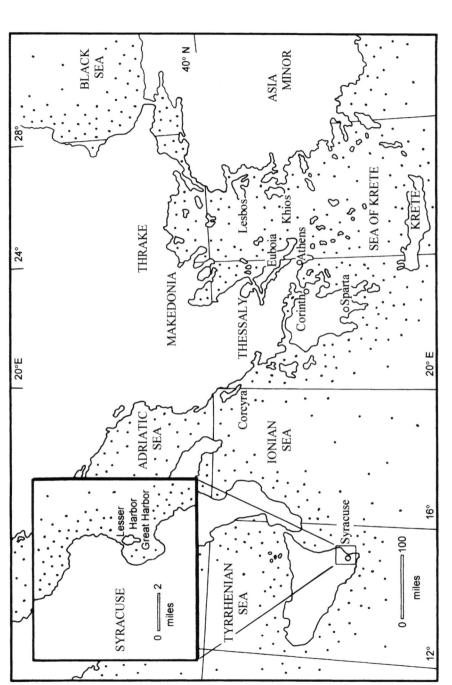

Greece and the Mediterranean World

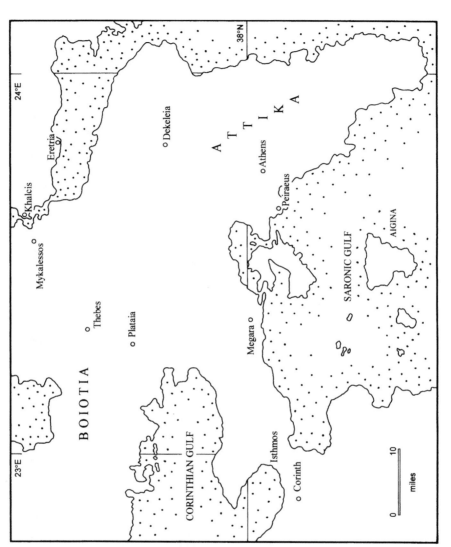

Central Greece, Attika and Boiotia

CHAPTER 1

OVERVIEW OF THE WAR

In the summer of 432, tensions in the Greek *poleis*, or city-states, were running high. Athens and Corinth had become mired in a bitter feud that proved intractable, and their quarrel slowly drew their friends and allies into the budding conflict. Months of wrangling solved nothing, and finally in exasperation the Spartans voted (in fall 432) that the Athenians had broken the 30 Years Truce, agreed upon some fourteen years before. Yet for another six months nothing happened.

BACKGROUND

In 480 Athens and Sparta had led the so-called Hellenic League in defending Greece against the massive invasion of Xerxes, Great King of Persia. The defeat of the Persians led to sharply divergent paths for the two states that had shared the burdens of command. Sparta, eager to avoid obligations far from home and traditionally not inclined to hunt down a defeated enemy, yielded to Athens the leadership of the Greeks in their fight against Persia. Moreover, many Greeks saw Spartan leadership as corrupt, which prompted their appeal to Athens. The Athenian-led campaign lasted until Greeks and Persians finally agreed to the Peace of Kallias, signed most likely in summer 449, which ended hostilities between them. During this time, Athens established the Delian League, which brought the Athenians incredible military power, enabling them to lead expeditions as far from home as Egypt (which ended in disaster). Athens also acquired great wealth, which after 450 began to be spent on building projects such as the Parthenon and other buildings on the acropolis. The wealth and power that Athens accrued empowered the democracy as well, literally making possible full political participation of all Athenians. Athenians, then, could look around their city and see the fruits of their labors and sacrifices.

Shortly after this midcentury point, a new leader, Perikles, entered the political scene, and he encouraged Athenians to stay the course and follow the paths set by their fathers. It was this attitude and policy that led the Athenians to expand into Italy and the northern Aegean. Athenians, then, were energetic, ambitious, and inclined to take chances, and this was their legacy of the Persian Wars.

As Athens grew wealthier, and more arrogant perhaps, the Spartans watched from their safe haven deep in the Peloponnesos' Eurotas River valley. Content to remain at home and keep watch over the helots, the Spartans' primary concern was to maintain their control over the Peloponnesian League. Essentially a military league forged late in the sixth century, the Spartans dominated league policy, leaving its allies free to do what Sparta allowed. But in 464 disaster struck Sparta in the form of an earthquake causing significant loss of life. Even worse, the Messenian helots rose in rebellion and the Spartans were hard-pressed to defend themselves. A thousand Athenian volunteers led by Kimon, who favored a pro-Spartan policy, came to help but were strangely sent home without even a thanks, thereby ruining Kimon's reputation. Relations between the two states hardened considerably in the following years. Athens and Corinth were soon fighting for control of nearby Megara, and the conflict spread to other parts of Greece. Sometimes called the "First" Peloponnesian War, this conflict did little but create lingering animosity for Athens, especially in Corinth. But the warring states did agree to a settlement, the 30 Years Truce of 446/5.

After this settlement there was no major conflict of Greek states, but there can be little doubt that Athenian ambitions and aggressions worried many. In the years after the truce, Athens brutally suppressed the revolt of a former ally, Samos (c. 440), and pursued various schemes in Italy, where a settlement at Thurii had been established (c. 443), and in the northern Aegean, particularly around the rich and strategic site of Amphipolis. These actions in particular concerned Sparta, but the citizen elites or Spartiates, ever anxious over a revolt of their serf-slaves, the helots, only watched quietly. Keeping things quiet and unchanged was definitely a Spartan priority. Preserving the status quo, however, was not something that appealed to Corinth. A wealthy maritime state at the isthmus of Greece, Corinth looked to expand its horizons just as Athens had and was in little mood to yield to Athens' greater power. While the two states had in olden times enjoyed some good relations, these had been strained past the breaking point in the fighting leading up to the 30 Years Truce. The occasion was the Athenian massacre of a group of Corinthian soldiers who were trapped in a field and slaughtered. Ever since, Corinth, as Thucydides says, had nursed "a bitter hatred of the Athenians." Only a match to this powder keg was missing, and a dispute between the two over Corcyra and Potidaia, two old Corinthian colonies, provided just that.

THE WAR'S ORIGINS

War came on a wintry night in early March 431. Some three hundred men from Thebes, a city allied with Sparta's Peloponnesian League, broke into the neighboring community of Plataia, an Athenian ally. This neighborly clash quickly touched off hostilities all around Greece, and soon a Spartan army was marching on Athens, while Athenian fleets were sailing and raiding around the Peloponnesos. But how had a quarrel between Corinth and Athens led to a *Theban* attack on Plataia?

Athens and Corinth

The friendship that once characterized relations between Athens and Corinth had long become by 433 a thing of the past. Corinthian trade goods had been shoved aside by Athenian goods, and Corinthian merchants were simply unable to compete with the economic and political clout of the Athenian empire. Since the mid-fifth century, however, Corinth had been developing its ties in the Greek northeast, where it had old colonial settlements in places like Leucas, Ambracia, Apollonia, and Pertum. As Corinth expanded interests in this region, conflict with Corcyra ignited. Itself an old colony of Corinth's, Corcyra hated its "mother city" and Corinth shared the sentiment for its colony. Early in 433 this rivalry and hatred boiled over into a major confrontation. Epidamnos, a city located north of Corcyra on the Adriatic, had long before been founded by both Corinth and Corcyra. Some two years earlier local peoples began attacking Epidamnos, which first appealed to nearby Corcyra for aid, which was refused. The Epidamnians then begged

Remains of ancient Corinth, with Acrocorinth ("high" Corinth) in the background. *Source: L. Tritle.*

Corinth for relief, which willingly provided emergency aid in the form of soldiers and settlers who rushed in to help. This intrusion into its sphere of influence bitterly provoked Corcyra, and with that, conflict between the two old enemies erupted.

Afraid that Corinth and its power in the region would overwhelm it, Corcyra—previously a "nonaligned state"—made appeals to Athens for relief. Athens was already expanding its power and influence westward, and an alliance with Corcyra seemed as attractive as it might prove useful. The Athenians voted to send a fleet to Corcyra, but with instructions to avoid hostilities, to fight only if Corinth attacked Corcyra. The Athenian squadrons duly arrived, and when battle, afterward called that of Sybota, between the two old enemies began, the Athenians could not help themselves and soon engaged the Corinthians and helped defeat them. As Corcyra was technically, nonaligned all this happened so as not to infringe the accords between Sparta and Athens and their respective blocs. But clearly Corinthian ambitions had been blunted, and the culprit without doubt was Athens.

The Corinthians were not happy about this Athenian intrusion into their sphere of influence. They may also have believed themselves betrayed. Only seven years before they had persuaded Sparta and other members of the Peloponnesian League not to intervene in Athens' suppression of the Samian Revolt (c. 440), arguing perhaps that it was a "local" matter (Thucydides does not explain their position). Now in 433/2 it may have been that the Corinthians thought that the Athenians "owed" them the favor of not intervening in Corcyra and, when the favor was not granted, believed themselves doubly cheated.

Corinth and Athens continued wrangling over Corcyra when a fresh issue erupted between them. In the Aegean north lay the city of Potidaia, a member of the Athenian empire but also a city that respectfully maintained its colonial ties with Corinth. After the outbreak of fighting with Corinth, Athens decided to enforce its will and ordered Potidaia to dismantle a part of its fortifications, surrender hostages, and send away its Corinthian officials. Potidaia refused, and the Athenians responded militarily, establishing a siege on the city (one Athenian soldier who fought here was Sokrates the philosopher). While the fight between Athens and Corinth over Corcyra had been a peripheral issue, Potidaia belonged in principle to the 30 Years Truce, and Athens' treatment of it was a much more serious issue, a violation of the spirit if not the law of the agreement. While Sparta might not fight over Corcyra, Potidaia was another matter.

THE ARCHIDAMIAN WAR

The Theban "sneak" attack on Plataia began what we call the Peloponnesian War, but to the Athenian Thucydides, the historian who recorded it, it was the "ten years war" (431–421). A few years after the war ended, the orator Lysias dubbed it the Archidamian War, and many scholars use that term today. Lasting ten years, the Archidamian War was witness to both horrific suffering and a hardening of attitudes.

Athens Responds

Those Thebans who entered Plataia in the dead of night found themselves quickly surrounded and trapped by a vigilant populace. Only a small number managed to save themselves by flight, but those who did escape returned with a large force that put Plataia under siege. The Plataians meanwhile had evacuated their noncombatants and with a small force of Athenian volunteers defended the city into midyear 427, finally surrendering when further resistance became impossible. By this time the Spartans and their Theban allies were in no mood to play the role of noble victor. Plataia paid a fearful price: the survivors of the siege were killed and the city was razed, its lands eventually placed into the hands of individual Thebans. As one historian has commented, "and the Athenians had not lifted a finger."[1]

Perhaps written off as expendable, little Plataia served a useful pawn's role in holding down Spartan and allied forces. And in the first years of the war, Athenian naval forces sailed around the Peloponnesos, attacking Spartan and Corinthian interests repeatedly in western Greece. As these Athenian attacks proceeded, however, other Spartan forces began what would become annual invasions of the Attic countryside—burning fields and vines, taking whatever livestock they could. They were able to do this because the Athenians had yielded the land to them and retired behind the walls of Athens. In fact, Athens was a giant fortress whose walls reached down to and included the port of the Peiraeus. Supplied by the sea, Athens was in some respects like an island and immune to Spartan attack.

But unfortunately Athens was not immune, particularly to disease. Beginning in the summer of 430 and lasting intermittently into 427, a plague struck hard on the masses of Athenians crowded behind the city walls. Perhaps a third of the population died, including thousands of men of military age and Perikles himself, the leader who had done so much to create what is still known as the golden age of Greece (see Document 1).

The Athenians, however, showed spirit and determination and continued the fight, though clearly they missed the guiding hand of Perikles in the following years, an influence never replaced. Athenian determination to stay the course is demonstrated in the response to the revolt of Mytilene, a longtime ally on the island of Lesbos. Here oligarchs had turned to Sparta for aid and, thus encouraged, rebelled. Athenian response was quick and frightening. When Mytilene fell, the Athenians initially decided to kill all the adult men and enslave everyone else. In a famous passage, Thucydides reports the tenor of a second assembly debate if not the actual speeches, which in the end prompted the Athenians to reconsider, over the objections of Kleon, a new rising figure in Athenian politics and a man much detested by both of those who tell most about him, Aristophanes and Thucydides. In the end the Athenians voted to kill *only* a thousand of those men responsible for the revolt and spared the rest (see Chapter 3).

The Peace of Nikias

As the war entered its sixth year, the fighting seemed to accomplish little for either side. Then in 425 the Athenians did what most Greeks thought impossible—they forced the surrender of nearly two hundred Spartans, who chose not to fight to the death on the small island of Sphakteria (in the bay of Pylos) where they had been cut off from support. This action—made possible by the Athenian general Demosthenes, though the politician Kleon literally cheated him of the victory—revealed two things: increasing manpower shortages in Sparta and the possibility that the Spartans could be beaten on the battlefield.

Kleon brought his Spartan captives to Athens where they were dangled before the Spartans as bait on a hook. Whenever there was a threat, whenever the Spartans tried to force concessions from the Athenians, the prisoners would be held as hostages to Spartan policy and good behavior. At this point a Spartan rarity made his way forward. Brasidas, as gifted and innovative a military commander as the Spartans ever produced, came forward with a plan to the ruling authorities in Sparta. Authorize an expedition to the northern Aegean, he claimed, and he could achieve such results that Athens would sue for peace and the hostages could be safely recovered. In 425 Brasidas marched north with a small force of mostly ex-helots, now freed and fighting (and fighting bravely!) for their former masters. Brasidas not only talked a good game, he delivered. Within a short time he captured the strategic city of Amphipolis before the Athenian general Thucydides could arrive to defend it. Thucydides' military career thus ended and rather than return to Athens a failure, he went into exile and turned to writing history—much safer than fighting! Brasidas won over many in the region with his moderate ways and thus threatened Athens' control and influence in the entire region.

The Athenians resolved, however, not to give up without a fight. Energized by the Spartan successes, they dispatched additional forces into

The island of Sphakteria in the bay of Pylos in southern Greece. Site of the important battle between Athenians and Spartans, 425. *Source: L. Tritle*.

the area in an effort to recover what they had lost. One of these forces was commanded by Kleon, whose success on Sphakteria had convinced him that he possessed talent as a soldier, when in reality he had none. In his play *Peace,* written a short time later, the comic poet Aristophanes referred to Kleon and Brasidas as the "pestles" in the "salad" bowl of war. In other words, their provocative acts stirred up the Greeks to continue fighting when there were many who wanted peace. Outside Amphipolis in 421 their armies met. Though outnumbered, Brasidas' troops fought well and won, even though he was wounded soon after the fighting began, dying upon its conclusion. The Athenians did not fare as well, as their formation broke and took to flight, including Kleon, who was overtaken and killed. In the same battle, then, the "pestles" perished and peace became a possibility (see Document 2).

Kleon's death at Amphipolis enabled his adversary, Nikias, to advance his more moderate ways and ideas. An experienced though cautious gen-

Grave stele of Demokleides, a hoplite lost in a naval battle, c. 420. National Archaeological Museum, Athens, Greece. *Source: L. Tritle.*

eral, Nikias took advantage of a prevailing war weariness in Athens to broker peace with Sparta, which had desired peace for some time and even more the return of the men captured at Sphakteria. The settlement that was reached has since been called the Peace of Nikias, and it secured a peace on the basis that everyone should keep what they had before the war, though Thebes retained Plataia and Athens kept several Corinthian territories in western Greece. In their eagerness for peace, the Spartans abandoned to the Athenians a number of communities in the north won over by Brasidas. These Athens recovered, though acknowledgment of certain freedoms guaranteed these states made the recovery incomplete. The peace agreed upon was to last fifty years, and its final clause made clear that Athens and Sparta imposed acceptance upon their allies (see Document 3).

ALL AGAINST ALL

Aside from Athens and Sparta, there was little joy in Greece over the Peace of Nikias. Corinth, Megara, and Thebes, to name the most prominent, disliked the settlement: Corinth and Megara were denied recovery of strategic sites; Thebes saw that peace meant an end to greater power. The Athenian-Spartan agreement to a separate defensive treaty was also worrisome, as the two "superpowers" appeared to be looking after their own interests as they denied the other Greek states similar arrangements. In the next year came a series of diplomatic moves that reshaped traditional alliances, which at the same time heightened tensions all around in this era of "peace."

Argos and Athens

Corinth played a key role in this diplomatic shuffle. Particularly annoyed at Sparta, Corinth made overtures to Argos for a separate alliance, basically following the example of Athens and Sparta. This could only antagonize and worry Sparta, as Argos and Sparta had a centuries-long history of bad blood, and a treaty with Argos by a member of the Peloponnesian League could only weaken Sparta's leadership of that body. Before long there were even more diplomatic overtures: Argos to Mantineia and Elis, two more Peloponnesian states, even more worries for Sparta.

While Corinth successfully concluded its defensive alliance with Argos, the Argives, still anxious and desiring a little extra security, decided to renew their "nonaggression" treaty with Sparta. As these talks went on, a new player entered the game—Alkibiades of Athens. Descended from a prominent ancient family, and one with diplomatic ties to Sparta, Alkibiades brought an Argive embassy to Athens, which, with his support, agreed to an alliance, much to the disappointment of Sparta, which attempted to block it. With Argos came Mantineia and Elis, all three possessing democratic constitutions, and all three enemies of Sparta in its own backyard. The consequences of this diplomatic shuffle were not long in coming. In the next year (summer 418), the new allies fought the Spartans at Mantineia in what Thucydides described as "the greatest battle that had taken place for a long time among Hellenic states"—a battle that Sparta won (see Document 4). The next winter, Argos abandoned its Athenian alliance, soon followed by Mantineia, which returned to the Spartan orbit. The diplomatic revolution was indeed short-lived.

Athens and Melos

The Argive experiment perhaps influenced the Athenians to look elsewhere for easier pickings. In the summer of 416 an expedition sailed for the small Aegean island state of Melos, an old colony of Sparta but nonaligned. Some ten years before Nikias had campaigned on the island but accomplished nothing. Now the Athenians returned, intent upon removing what they saw as a smudge on their power, a small community that refused to acknowledge the superior might of Athens. In the following late winter or early spring (415), Athenian reinforcements arrived, and the siege—aided by treachery within—brought victory. The punishment was severe. Men of military age (16–45) were killed, and the rest of the population was enslaved. Thucydides takes care to identify the Athenian commander, Philokrates, son of Demeas, whose name means "Lover of power, son of the people." Here Thucydides provides some none too subtle commentary on the nature of power and democracy in Athens.

Melos was a minor swirl in the vast landscape of the Peloponnesian War, but today historians look at it carefully for the "Melian Dialogue" that Thucydides provides in his history of the event. In this passage Thucydides, as in his "Debate over Mytilene," takes a probable meeting

between Athenian commanders and Melian officials and creates speeches
for them that explore the nature of raw, unadulterated power. He demonstrates that in war, it is power that dictates, above all else, who acts and
who suffers. In this instance Athens exercised the power, and the Melians
suffered its consequences (see Document 5). Thucydides also employs the
Dialogue as an introduction to the next major phase of his history and
the war, the Athenian expedition to Sicily.

Athens and Sicily

As Melos slowly died, the Athenians debated a resolution to embark
on an ambitious campaign to the Greek west—the conquest of the island of Sicily. Two speakers—Alkibiades for, Nikias against—dominated
the debate. In the end the Athenians enthusiastically endorsed Alkibiades' plan and placed in joint command the two antagonists, along with
Lamakhos, a veteran soldier. A vast expedition would sail; more than a
hundred ships and thousands of men would be employed in this vast un-
dertaking, many of them Athenian. It was an ambitious plan full of risk,
but as Thucydides had earlier told, this was the Athenian way to success
and power.

The expedition sailed in midsummer 415 but under a cloud. Only
shortly before, two incidents rocked the Athenian populace. One night
a group of young men, probably drunk after a night's carousing, mutilated
the *hermai,* or phallic charms, that stood before most homes in the city.
Revelation of worse things soon followed—the mocking of the sacred rituals of Demeter in private, again by young men drinking and partying.
Informers implicated Alkibiades in these, and while he proclaimed his
innocence, many believed the worst. Amid this turmoil, however, the expedition sailed west for Corcyra, the jumping off point for Sicily. Alkibiades sailed too (see Document 12).

Arriving in Sicily, the Athenians soon found they had been duped.
Their Sicilian allies had promised great sums of money and ready support, but all this was so much wishful thinking. The three commanders
discussed their options. Nikias, ever cautious, suggested they try to find
allies and, if that proved unsuccessful, return home. Alkibiades thought
this an admission of failure and proposed that they recruit allies among
the local Greeks and native Sicilians and then attack Syracuse, the most
powerful Greek community on the island. Lamakhos, the soldier, pro-

A herm, typical of the fertility charms outside Athenian homes. The heads and *phalloi* of these were mutilated just before the Athenian Expedition sailed to Sicily. Gregorian Profane Museum/Vatican Museum, Rome, Italy. *Source: L. Tritle.*

posed an immediate attack on a still unready Syracuse, the target of their campaign, as the likeliest way to win. Though risky, Lamakhos' strategy held the best chance for success: the Athenian force was fresh and in high spirits while the Syracusans were disorganized. The views of his colleagues prevailed, however, and with that decision, the best chance for a quick victory—and the initiative—was lost.

Athenian efforts to find local support generally failed, and except for some native Sicilians and the communities of Naxos and Katana, there was little sympathy for the Athenian cause. As Lamakhos had perhaps feared, as the Athenians dallied, the Syracusans, under the leadership of Hermokrates, prepared. Even worse, word arrived from Athens that Alkibiades was to return home to face charges for the religious vandalism of the past summer. Rather than return to a certain condemnation, he fled to Sparta where he revealed all to his hosts. Spartan aid to Syracuse was small but effective; Gylippos, a talented commander who served as a military adviser to the Syracusans, was dispatched in the coming test with Athens.

In the first serious fighting around Syracuse, Lamakhos was killed. Nikias wrote Athens for help—both for commanders to replace him, as he was ill, and for reinforcements. Nikias' plea to be relieved was ignored, but two more generals, including Demosthenes, the hero of Sphakteria, arrived with the requested reinforcements. The Athenians attempted to besiege Syracuse by building a series of walls, but in the "battle of the walls" that followed, the Syracusans won. Nikias and Demosthenes then realized that their only chance of winning was to stake all on a naval battle, which they hoped would destroy the Syracusan fleet and make possible the final defeat of their enemy. In an all or nothing gamble, the Athenian fleet challenged the Syracusans, now reinforced by a Corinthian contingent, in Syracuse's Great Harbor. In a hard-fought battle, the Athenians suffered heavily, as the Syracusans had strengthened their ships in order to ram head-on. The shoreline was lined with the armies of both sides, who, Thucydides tells, watched as though they were spectators at a game, cheering their team on. The Athenians lost.

With their fleet defeated and the survivors totally demoralized, Nikias and Demosthenes made plans to disengage and abandon the campaign. The retreat became a rout as the Syracusans harried their prey as if on a hunt. The Athenian army disintegrated and in the end was destroyed.

The Great Harbor at Syracuse in Sicily. Site of the decisive naval battle that led to the defeat of the Athenian Expedition, 413. *Source: L. Tritle.*

Nikias and Demosthenes were captured and executed, while the survivors of their armies were enslaved (see Document 6). In the words of Thucydides, "this Hellenic event turned out to be the greatest connected with this war and, at least in my opinion, of Hellenic events we have heard of, the most splendid for those who won and the most wretched for those who were ruined" (Thucydides 7.87.5).

THE IONIAN WAR

In fall 412, a sailor arrived in Athens' port, the Peiraeus, and went to the barber. As he was getting cleaned up, he remarked how tragic it was that so many Athenians had died in far-off Sicily. The barber dropped what he was doing and raced off to Athens to bring to city hall the first news of the defeat of the great Athenian armada.[2] The Athenians, however, were already reeling when this report arrived. In the summer before, the Spartans had carried out one of their usual invasions of Attika. This time, however, they established a permanent base at Dekeleia in the Athenian countryside. This enabled them to strike when and where they wanted. Word also went out that escaping slaves would find sanctuary, and more than twenty thousand Athenian slaves fled (most were handed over to the Thebans who cashed in, reselling the fugitives). But extensive damage was done to the agrarian economy, and shortages began to appear in the markets. This, combined with news of the defeat in Sicily, opened the door to further setbacks, the most notable of which was the defection of Khios, an Aegean island state and old ally. But the Athenians refused to give in. A cash reserve held on the acropolis, the "iron fund," was opened and new ships were built, and new crews recruited and paid. Clearly the Athenians would not go quietly.

The Northern War

Military action soon returned to the northern Aegean, the site of intense action in the Archidamian War. Here the Spartans began moving in on the sea lanes that fed the Athenians from the Black Sea and through the Dardanelles, site of ancient Troy and the famous World War I battle at Gallipoli. The Spartan effort was made possible by generous loans of money from neighboring Persian officials, particularly the satrap (governor) Tissaphernes, who now saw an opportunity to regain lost territories in Asia Minor. Subsidized with Persian gold, the Spartans were able to build up their own fleet and recruit sailors, often outbidding the Athenians for the same men. But Athenian ingenuity and determination paid off. The new Spartan fleet was beaten at Kynossema, and then the bad boy of Athens, Alkibiades, returned home.

Alkibiades and Athens

Sparta did not quite agree with Alkibiades, though he seems to have gotten on well enough with the wife of King Agis, who gave birth to his son, Leotychidas. But before leaving Sparta he gave his hosts some ideas about strategy, namely, to establish a base in Attika (which Agis did at Dekeleia in 413) and to carry the war against Athens into the Aegean (which came shortly afterward). Alkibiades then crossed the Aegean into Asia where he befriended the same Tissaphernes who was giving money to the Spartans. Alkibiades' personal charms and scheming ways enabled him to create a power base of his own, and with this he entered the action then taking place in northern Greece.

Alkibiades persuaded Tissaphernes that the best policy should be to weaken the warring Greeks, playing one off against the other, so as to enable the Persians to recover Asia, which King Darios II desperately wanted. Tissaphernes accepted this advice, which blunted Spartan efforts in Asia while increasing Alkibiades' influence, enabling him to make overtures to the Athenian fleet in the north and win them over. Further successes helped his cause, particularly the recovery of Kyzikos and its important naval base (411), and in 407 he returned to Athens to a hero's welcome and election as *strategos*, or general. But Alkibiades' luck soon ran out. Forces sent with him into Asia were defeated, and political enemies at home again conspired against him. When he realized that he could not reverse the situation, he retreated into exile, this time in Thrake. He never recovered from this setback, and after the war ended, agents of the Persian satrap Pharnabazos, in collusion with the Spartans, murdered him (404/3).

War's End

It was the Spartan commander Lysander who got the Persians to eliminate Alkibiades, and with the same ruthless determination Lysander now moved to the final defeat of Athens. For the previous several years, military action had centered in the northern Aegean: an Athenian victory at Arginousai (406/5) had been followed by the rejection of Spartan overtures for peace. But in that defeat, Lysander saw a way to win the war. Bringing a fleet into the Dardanelles region, he caught the Athenian fleet napping at Aigospotami and destroyed it. This was Athens' last fleet and except for its walls, the city was now defenseless. With the Spartan base at Dekeleia and their fleet blockading the city, it was only a question of time. Soon the Athenians sued for peace. The Spartans listened to the demands of the Corinthians and Thebans who wanted Athens destroyed and its people enslaved. But the Spartans refused, saying they would not deprive Greece of a city that had done such great things at a time of supreme danger.[3] Soon the walls of Athens were torn down to music provided by Spartan flutes. The great Peloponnesian War was at last over: twenty-seven years in the making, thousands dead, and many communities destroyed, if not by enemy action than by their own hand in civil war (see Document 7).[4]

NOTES

1. Donald Kagan, *The Archidamian War* (Ithaca, NY: Cornell University Press, 1974), p. 174.

2. Plutarch, *Life of Nicias* 30.

3. Xenophon, *Hellenica* 2.1.19.

4. The accounts of Thucydides and Xenophon provide the narrative for this chapter; readers should consult them for fuller details.

CHAPTER 2

THUCYDIDES EXPLAINS THE CAUSES OF WAR

How do you explain something as complicated as a major war? When Homer explained how the best known of Greek conflicts—the Trojan War—started, it was the rape and kidnapping of Helen that set armies in motion. Later when the historian Herodotus investigated the causes of the Persian Wars, he included this bit of mythmaking. The comic poet Aristophanes ridiculed all this in his play *Acharnians*, even updating these explanations of war's origins to include the Peloponnesian War, which he claimed involved the Megarian kidnapping of some prostitutes who worked for Aspasia, Perikles' mistress! (See Document 8.)

Neither Homer nor Herodotus lived at the time of the events they wrote about. But Thucydides was contemporary with the Peloponnesian War and took notes of what he saw and heard and, as we have seen, wrote them down. In fact, he tells us that from the very beginning of the conflict between the Athenians and the Peloponnesians he saw that the coming war was sure to be the biggest that the Greek world ever experienced. The approach Thucydides took to the war in many ways resembles the work of a modern war correspondent. He traveled to the places where the events took place, talked to participants in the battles, and otherwise witnessed the wartime events. The work that finally resulted from his investigation became incredibly influential for future generations as, together with his older contemporary Herodotus, he created the activity of the historian. As the nineteenth-century German historian Leopold von Ranke stated, and as historians do today, Thucydides recorded the events and attempted to explain what actually took place. Before looking more closely at the causes of the war he recorded, it is important to investigate the man who tells us what we know of these events—Thucydides of Athens.

THUCYDIDES AND WRITING ON THE WAR

Although Thucydides tells us that he realized that possibly the biggest war known to the Greeks was coming, it seems doubtful that he imagined himself its historian at the very beginning or that he suspected the war would last twenty-seven years. The son of an Athenian named Oloros, Thucydides belonged to a prominent family that included Miltiades, victor over the Persians at Marathon (490), and his son Kimon, who achieved the final victory over the Persians, defeating them at the battle of the Eurymedon in 469/8. His family enjoyed an upscale life of privilege from their economic contacts in northern Greece, and these connections enabled him to participate in the city's political life. He served as *strategos*, or general, in the year 424/3, but the records for the preceding years are incomplete, and he may have held that office (and others) in earlier years as well.[1] As we have seen, Thucydides commanded a squadron of ships in the northern Aegean in that year when the Spartan Brasidas captured Amphipolis and Thucydides arrived too late to save it. The Athenians did not take such failures lightly, and rather than return home to explain himself, he went into exile. His family's wealth and social connections enabled him to travel around the Greek world and to support himself in his new life as historian. This seems certain as various references in his account argue that he did travel, interviewing participants in the war and surveying places where the war's events occurred.

The social prominence and wealth that Thucydides enjoyed enabled him to meet and become acquainted not only with those who fought in the war, but with others known for their learning and intellectual accomplishments. For over the previous several generations (dating to the early fifth century), an intellectual revolution had been going on that today is known as the age of "Enlightenment," after the better known era of intellectual activity in eighteenth-century Europe.

INTELLECTUAL INFLUENCES

This period of intellectual growth has its roots in the Greek east in the area of Ionia, where philosophers beginning with Thales of Miletos in the seventh century and continuing with many others such as Xenophanes began to look at the world in a more rational way than ever before. Known as the pre-Sokratics, these thinkers broke with the powerful grip of Homer whose poems *Iliad* and *Odyssey* defined Greek culture and provided explanations of all things for the Greeks. Ionian rationality not only advanced ideas on the physical nature of the world, but influenced other disciplines, including medicine and what would come to be known as history.

Herodotus, the first Greek historian, wrote what he called an "inquiry" into the Persian Wars, explaining how the outnumbered and divided states of Greece combined to defeat the mighty Persian Empire. In many ways, there is a Homeric influence on Herodotus as his account unifies and interprets the Persian Wars in the image of Homer's Trojan War. But in the process of relating his story of Greeks and Persians, Herodotus composed a work very different from Homer, a "history" that included the testimony of real people and that was shaped by the ideas of the pre-Sokratics and contemporary intellectuals living in Athens as the Peloponnesian War broke out.

These later thinkers, who came to be known as the Sophists, influenced not only Herodotus but also Thucydides. They continued their experimentation with ideas as well as language, literary forms, and the meanings of words into the fifth century and beyond and stimulated the thought of such better known philosophers as Plato and Aristotle. One idea that received considerable attention at this time was freedom. Herodotus' work refers to freedom a number of times, and in the years after the Persian victory, freedom acquired important political meaning that both Athenians and Spartans manipulated throughout the course of the Peloponnesian War.[2] The influences, then, upon the history that Thucydides wrote are many and varied—Homer and his account of the "Trojan War," the philosophical and intellectual traditions of Ionia, and a desire to emulate his predecessors and at the same time to break from them.

In addition to the intellectual developments, Thucydides' work also reflects the new power of speech—rhetoric—that had become the rage among Greeks at this time. A powerful means of gaining influence, especially in the Athenian democracy, the teaching of rhetoric had arrived in Athens from Sicily through several talented intellectuals, most notably Gorgias of Leontini. Thucydides effectively used this means of expression to convey the swirl of ideas and range of attitudes current at the time.[3]

The experience with violence also figured in Thucydides' work. When the war broke out, Thucydides was about thirty, and in the seven years or so that followed, he surely witnessed all the horrors associated with war, not to mention those of the plague that ravaged Athens. It is clear that like other soldiers in other times, his use of language bears the mark of that trauma. The "horror," as it is called in Francis Ford Coppola's film *Apocalypse Now*, is brought out in his account of the death of a city, Mykalessos, whose people were "butchered" or "cut to pieces" in a paroxysm of violence that for Thucydides exemplified the conduct of the war. His battle descriptions too—for example, the last moments of the Athenian Expedition in Sicily—convey vividly the slaughter of the Athenians in the use of the verb *sphagein*, to slaughter. This dimension to his writing is one that reveals as much of him as the war he records.

Thucydides and the Writing of History

The influence of the new and rational way of thought can be seen early in Thucydides' work where he states the methods he employed in writing his history. At the beginning of this statement, he claims that his work is superior to that of poets—a reference clearly to Homer (and others)—who are more concerned with developing literary themes or ideas. He also claims that his account is superior to those of the prose chroniclers—with little doubt a criticism of Herodotus whose account of the Persian Wars had made a recent literary splash—who are not interested in the truth as much as they are in telling a good story. Instead, Thucydides intends to base his account on evidence that he has subjected to intensive scrutiny, including the reports of multiple eyewitnesses so as to avoid bias. This will enable him, he asserts, to provide the truth as to what really happened, which will allow others in the future to recognize similar events in their own time (see Document 9). This is an important aspect of Thucydides' methodological statement, as it reveals that Greek thought, and not just Thucydides', imagined that things happened in a cyclical fashion or, as some people even today think, that "history repeats itself."

Thucydides also tells his future readers that he has reported the speeches that were delivered during the war, some of which he heard himself and others that various sources reported to him. Memory of the spoken word was better in a predominantly oral society like that of the Greeks than in a modern society, which depends so much on writing. But Thucydides makes clear that it was difficult to remember the words actually spoken, both those at which he was present and those speeches that others told him about. He therefore kept to the sense of what was said—as far as he knew—and gave to the speakers those words the situation required. In reality, the speeches found in his account are his, and while the designated speaker might have said something like he reports, the actual words and ideas belong to Thucydides. The speeches, then, must be regarded carefully, for they are not the actual words of the person identified. At the same time, they remain important as a valuable source of information revealing intellectual attitudes and ideas.

THUCYDIDES EXPLAINS THE CAUSES OF WAR

When Corcyra and Corinth began squabbling and then fighting over Epidamnos, their feud entangled Athens and Sparta, each leading a powerful group of allies. As the original dispute worsened, a new one erupted over Potidaia in northern Greece between Athens and Corinth. There then seemingly began a slow but almost inevitable free fall into further conflict. Thucydides relates these events with a good deal of clarity and even with the methodology of a modern historian. In discussing the conflicts over Epidamnos and Potidaia, he identifies what historians today might refer to as "short-term causes." He recognizes, however, that there were "long-term causes" as well, particularly the growth of Athenian power. This worried the Spartans so much that in their view, there was no option but war. Thucydides identifies what could also be defined as the "necessary" cause, that is, the type of cause without which a conflict could not begin—the Theban "sneak" attack on Plataia. Like the assassination of the Austrian Arch-Duke Franz Ferdinand in 1914, this event initiated the mobilization of the armies after which war could not be stopped. Thucydides makes clear that after the failed Theban attack on Plataia—followed by the Plataian execution of 180 Theban prisoners—nothing could stop the mobilization of the armies of Greece, and the war that so many feared imminent became a reality.[4]

Yet Thucydides states that in going to war, both Athens and Sparta broke the 30 Years Peace that had been in place since 446/5, when the

Greeks negotiated a settlement ending a decade-long period of unde-clared war. When Thucydides' account of the outbreak of war in 431 is probed, several factors emerge that shed light on the origins of this great war. First, and perhaps most critically, is the issue of arbitration. He ad-vanced this issue first in the Athenian speech at Sparta at the beginning of the dispute between Corcyra and Corinth. He returned to it in Perik-les' final speech to the Athenians, urging them to vote for war with Sparta in the late fall of 432. Perikles stated plainly that the Spartans had refused, and at the very least had failed to act upon, Athenian of-fers to arbitrate their differences as called for by the 30 Years Peace.

This Spartan refusal to arbitrate would suggest that the Spartans were indeed looking to provoke war. Yet if this were true, they followed a most unusual diplomatic strategy, our second factor to investigate. For on four different occasions Spartan embassies or ambassadors approached the Athenians, attempting, evidently, to find some way to stop the escala-tion to violence. What did the Spartans hope to accomplish with these negotiations? Why did the Athenians refuse to negotiate? And finally, the failed efforts to preserve the 30 Years Peace are of some importance as they tell us something about how the Greeks, while recognizing that war was an unpleasant fact of life, also attempted through formal means to avoid war and keep peace. Sadly, the efforts made in 433–431 were unsuccessful, and the result was a conflict that proved as terrible as it was long.[5]

Arbitration and Peace

In late fall of 432, the Athenians again took up the issue of war with Sparta, which, as we have seen, had been brewing for a year now. Al-ready two embassies from Sparta had come to Athens with various diplo-matic initiatives, which the Athenians had rebuffed. Upon the third embassy, Perikles, whom Thucydides (1.127.3) described as "the leading man of his time among the Athenians and the most powerful both in ac-tion and in debate," responded with a speech intended not only to bring about a rejection of the Spartan overture, but to incite a vote for war with Sparta. It was in this speech that Perikles claimed the Spartans were plotting against Athens and had refused any offer of arbitration. He re-ferred specifically to a treaty clause stipulating the grant of arbitration upon the offer of one party in a dispute and that until a decision was reached, "each side should keep what it has" (1.140.2). This statement by Perikles would appear to put the Spartans in the wrong in causing a war that Athens scrupulously tried to avoid. The Spartans, however, as Thucydides makes clear, knew of this arbitration clause, as the Spartan king Archidamos in an earlier speech at Sparta refers to it, as well as the idea that one requesting arbitration should not be presumed to be in the wrong for requesting it (Thucydides 1.85.2). Why was there no arbitration?

In the end there is no clear answer to this question. It would seem that there was a flaw in the process in terms of identifying an arbitrator that would satisfy each disputant. By this time, the Greek city-states had fallen into one of two armed camps now preparing for war, so it would be difficult to choose one from these. The only major nonaligned state in Greece proper was Argos, a community that hated the Spartans (and whom the Spartans hated in turn), who would never consent to Argive mediation. In western Greece, as we have seen, Corcyra was the major nonaligned state, but Corcyra was now party to the dispute and could not possibly act as an arbiter. There were several other nonaligned communities in western Greece, but these—Aitolia and Achaia—lacked the necessary political organization and sophistication to arbitrate the complex issues involving the two Greek superpowers and could offer no real assistance.

These difficulties may have played into the hands of the Athenians. In those speeches Thucydides gives to the Athenians, and seen as well in the words of the Corinthians and Spartans, the Athenians come across as intellectually gifted, quick on their feet to think, and able to solve most any problem. The Athenians seem to have seized upon a diplomatic technicality that they used to bewilder and confuse the less sophisticated Spartans. They realized the difficulty in finding and then agreeing on an arbiter, and this suited them just fine. It allowed them to assume the role of the injured party in their negotiations with the Spartans, as they could always claim that they were prepared to submit their quarrel to a third party, when in fact they knew it would be difficult, if not impossible, to find one. With such delaying tactics, they could put off negotiations and at the same time continue their provocative policies, which were at the root of Spartan fears and anxieties all along. It was a perfect strategy, yet in the end it backfired and brought a war that the Athenians believed was winnable.

The Spartan Embassies

In a final effort to avoid war, a Spartan embassy of three leading men, Ramphias, Melesippos, and Agesander, came to Athens in late winter 431 and announced, "Sparta wants peace. Peace is still possible if you will give the Hellenes their autonomy" (Thucydides 1.139.3).[6] Perikles' speech in response was uncompromising and influenced the Athenians to reject the Spartan bid, which led to a vote for war and an end to any negotiations. Before this embassy, however, the Spartans had approached Athens at least twice, attempting to find some way to head off war.[7]

The first Spartan embassy arrived in Athens not long after the second debate in Sparta (perhaps August 432), at which Sparta's allies had voted that Athens had broken the treaty and that war should be declared. This embassy is a strange affair of demands and counterdemands to acknowledge old religious-political misdeeds of both Athenians and Spartans. Thucydides' intent is not clear. It appears that he creates an occasion to recount old instances of Athenian-Spartan conflict. He also reveals to the modern reader the role played by religion and religious pollution in political affairs.[8]

The second embassy, coming later in the fall of 432 perhaps, was much more pointed and much more of a diplomatic effort. The Spartans told the Athenians that war could be avoided if they abandoned the siege of Potidaia and restored autonomy to Aigina, a defeated island community hated by the Athenians. The issue of freedom, as noted above, had emerged after the Persian Wars and was a powerful intellectual idea in Herodotus' *Histories*. Now it took on new and greater meaning as a political slogan that both Athens and Sparta would use in order to win influence with the other Greeks. Another issue with which the Spartans confronted Athens was revocation of the Megarian Decree, a measure enacted by the Athenians several years before. This punitive measure severely damaged Megara's economic vitality and created a slump that put its citizens out of work, reducing many to near starvation (see Documents 8 and 10).

The Athenian response was pointed. Encouraged by Perikles, they refused to lift the siege of Potidaia. Furthermore, the ban on Megara was justified by accusations that the Megarians were cultivating sacred land and providing shelter to fugitive slaves, measures unsubstantiated and most likely pretexts created for the occasion. In a speech during these negotiations, Perikles stated that the Megarians and their goods would be admitted to Athenian ports and markets, but only when the Spartans agreed not to expel Athenians and their allies from their lands (Thucydides 1.144.2).

Sources preserved in the later Greek writer Plutarch add that Perikles told the Spartans that a law had been enacted that prevented repeal of the Megarian Decree. Puzzled by this, Polyalkes, one of the Spartan envoys, said, "Well, turn it to the wall. There's no law against that, is there?" The simplicity of Polyalkes' reasoning ensures its authenticity—who else but a Spartan, a people famous for their brevity of speech, could say something so plain and direct? Aristophanes, living through these events, also tells in his play *Acharnians* (line 538) how the Spartans asked "many times" about the Megarians, but the Athenians would not yield. This, too, supports the authenticity of Polyalkes' comment.

Perikles' reference to the expulsion of Athenians and other Greeks from Sparta may be another Athenian diplomatic stratagem. The reference points to an old Spartan custom whereby "foreigners" were periodically expelled from the country. What its connection might be to the Megarians Thucydides does not explain. If he has reported this charge accurately, the argument might be nothing more than a rhetorical argument raised by the Athenians to confuse things further.

The final Spartan effort to avert war came shortly after the Theban sneak attack on Plataia in March 431. Archidamos, not eager for war, sent back to Athens Melesippos, who had been in Athens only a short time before on a similar mission (Thucydides 2.12.1). Archidamos hoped that the Athenians might now finally talk as they could see that the Peloponnesian allies had not only mobilized for war but were moving. The Athenians, however, would not budge. This was largely the work of Perikles, who had persuaded the Athenians to enact a decree that upon Peloponnesian mobilization and movement, further negotiations would be barred. Melisippos was refused entry to the city and escorted to the borders of Attika, where he was sent on his way. As he departed, he said to those present, "This day will be the beginning of great misfortunes for Greece" (Thucydides 2.12.3). He was right.

One final embassy deserves mention here, though it is not Spartan. In the months preceding the outbreak of war, the oligarchic rulers of Mytilene—the strongest *polis* on Lesbos and an old Athenian ally—sent an embassy to Sparta, attempting to win Spartan aid. Even before war erupted, the Mytilenian rulers were hoping to enlist Spartan support for a takeover of the island and to break away from Athenian control (Thucydides 3.2). The Spartans refused even to hear this delegation's offer, which also argues that the Spartans were not eager for war, for if they were, the Mytilenian embassy would surely have been given a hearing.

Fighting for Peace

Was this war preventable? Or was it, as Thucydides relates, inevitable?[9] Thucydides is too good a thinker, too good a historian, to be satisfied with arguments of inevitability in explaining what happened in Greece between 433 and 431. His reference to the notion of inevitability may be no more than a reflection of popular opinion. This finds support in his explanation of the war's short- and long-term causes (as well as the "necessary" cause in the Theban attack on Plataia), and his own interpretation that Athens' provocative actions led Sparta to think that there was no recourse but to fight when diplomatic overtures failed.

This sophisticated account of the war's outbreak bears an eerie resemblance to Europe in August 1914 and the outbreak of World War I.[10] In both instances, there was the combination of complex causes to the war—short term, long term, and necessary. In addition, there were several related factors that also evoke similarity: the apparent enthusiasm of young men who were inexperienced in war and thereby drawn to it; the willingness of many to imagine that a war would follow a predictable course (an idea that remains strong even in the early twenty-first century); the hard "no negotiations" line taken by Athens in negotiating with the Spartans. These all suggest that Thucydides had thought long and hard on what happened in 433–431 and did not see war as "inevitable," but rather the result of decisions made by those caught up in the events. These factors require further examination.

In discussing the aftermath of the Theban attack on Plataia, Thucydides adds to his analysis of the events the observation that there was widespread enthusiasm for the war. He relates how many Peloponnesian and Athenian young men had never been to war and, not unlike the youth of Europe in 1914, were thrilled at the prospect (Thucydides 2.8.1, 6.24). These young men feared that unless they became personally involved, the whole effort itself would be handicapped. Thucydides also notes that many in Greece supported the Spartans. The Athenians had created such bitterness as a result of their suppression of Naxos in 466/5 and Samos in 440/39 that other communities worried they might be next. Thucydides' analysis of the "enthusiasm" for war then is twofold: it refers to youthful exuberance for the unknown and to a wider belief that Athens was indeed the "tyrant city" as the Corinthians said, that those upholding the "freedom" of the Greeks were the Spartans, as they increasingly proclaimed. This enthusiasm for war also supports the more general view of the war's outbreak that Thucydides takes—that it was the expansion of Athenian power that evoked such fear in Sparta and, as just noted, a willingness to fight.

Enthusiasm for war was matched by the popular belief that war was predictable. In his speech after the Theban attack on Plataia, Archidamos reminded the allies that war is uncertainty and that too often attacks are made in a sudden impulse. At the beginning of his *History*, Thucydides had stressed this idea of war's unpredictability. His reference to it again in Archidamos' speech underlines the idea of popular enthusiasm for war—that people thought they could anticipate the sequence of events once war began—just as others did on the outbreak of World War I.[11]

Although the war may have seemed inevitable to many in Athens and perhaps others elsewhere, the Spartans, as noted above, sent at least four embassies to Athens in an attempt to head off the conflict. Certainly Corinth saw a war as inevitable, aggressively pushing it as the only way to rescue frustrated ambitions in western Greece, and other states shared the Corinthian position even if for other reasons. One Athenian who suffered no illusions about what was at stake was Perikles. He realized that war brought with it the opportunity to increase Athenian power and wealth, and so he took advantage of a legalistic interpretation of the arbitration clause of the 30 Years Peace to disguise an Athenian bid for domination.

This pursuit of war may also be explained by cultural attitudes that saw war simply as a way of life. Such a value emerged from the Homeric heroic-epic idea, which saw success in war as the clearest expression of manly excellence. The epitaph of the playwright Aeschylus, for example, tells not of his many contributions to drama, but rather of his fighting at Marathon. Herodotus' work on the Persian Wars enlarged this ethos by making it that of the larger community, the *polis*, as demonstrated in Athens' heroic stature in leading the Greeks to victory over the Persians. War, then, was not only glorious and noble; it also brought power and wealth.[12]

Since the Persian Wars, Athens and Sparta had taken divergent paths. Sparta remained the old-fashioned, even primitive community of old (where decisions in the assembly were decided by the loudest voices), whose outlook was still that of preserving the status quo—maintaining control over the Peloponnesians to ensure control over the helots. Athens, however, was becoming increasingly a "modern" state, where democracy had reshaped its citizens into lovers of the *polis*. Democratic institutions established at the end of the sixth century continued to be expanded and refined throughout the fifth century—magistrates with defined tenures of office, a functioning assembly that wielded real authority, law courts and juries that expressed the will of the people. To maintain this development, and the wealth of empire that came with it, Athens had to remain aggressive and exercise power and authority wherever possible.[13]

Influenced by the new and "enlightened" thinking of the Sophists, Thucydides recognized that it was this quest for power that drove the "modern" state that Athens had now become. Power brought security; power brought the good things in life that the Athenians had fought so hard to win since defeating the Persians. Thucydides saw that states flourish or decay as they are militarily effective and that the successful wielding of such power allows them to rule others as an empire—an experience altogether preferable to being ruled—and to achieve that greatest of political values—freedom. In a sense, then, Thucydides updates both Homer and Herodotus. These two authors wrote so that the deeds of brave men might not be forgotten. Thucydides wrote not only to do this, but also to show how men's exploits in war enabled states to become strong and successful. In the same way he relates the fate of those states, like Melos, which, lacking in power, will be overcome by their more powerful opponents and will have no choice but to accept whatever the strong impose upon them.

War as a "Modern" Experience

What happened, then, in 433–431? Athens, Corinth, and Sparta, as well as the lesser states of Greece, became locked into a way of looking at life that saw conflict as natural, even manly, and the solving of disputes by recourse to war as being in the nature of both men and states. This explains why Athens hid behind the demand for arbitration and denied the Spartan embassies: war would bring out the best in the Athenians, and they would prevail in their adversities as their history demonstrated. In some ways, war was seen as almost a good thing; it would protect the power and position already possessed and might even bring more. To carry this argument a step further, for the Athenians to negotiate would be to show weakness, to retreat from the prospects of winning even greater power. Athens had to stand up to Sparta (and Corinth) because not to do so would be to deny the opportunity for greater gain and to surrender the power they possessed. Such an admission of weakness might well lead to further conflicts and problems that could deprive the Athenians of their empire. In the debate over Mytilene (see Chapter 3), Thucydides attributes this very idea to the Athenian politician Kleon as justification for imposing a reign of terror over the subjects of the Empire. Driven by such perceptions, Athens, then, in one sense had no choice but to frustrate and deny Spartan overtures and go to war in 431.[14]

NOTES

1. See Simon Hornblower, *Thucydides* (Baltimore, MD: Johns Hopkins University Press, 1987), pp. 1–4, or John H. Finley, Jr., *Thucydides* (Cambridge, MA: Harvard University Press, 1942), pp. 3–35.

2. See, for example, Herodotos 3.82.5, 7.147.1, 8.143.1, 9.41.3, 9.98.3, and Donald Lateiner, *The Historical Method of Herodotus* (Toronto: University of Toronto Press, 1989), p. 182.

3. On intellectual influences, see, for example, W.K.C. Guthrie, *The Sophists* (Cambridge: Cambridge University Press, 1969/71), or Finley, *Thucydides*, pp. 36–73.

4. Thucydides 2.1–6 (attack on Plataia), 2.7 (outbreak of general war).

5. Donald Kagan, *The Outbreak of the Peloponnesian War* (Ithaca, NY: Cornell University Press, 1969), pp. 353–54.

6. This is perhaps the third (known) embassy, coming after the "curse" embassy, the "Megarian" embassy of Polyalkes; Melisippos' abortive mission after the Theban attack on Plataia would be the fourth.

7. E. Badian, *From Plataea to Potidaea: Studies in the History and Historiography of the Pentecontaetia* (Baltimore, MD: Johns Hopkins University Press, 1993),

p. 155, notes (on Thucydides 1.139.1) that there were "many" such embassies, though Thucydides comments only on those discussed here.

8. Thucydides 1.126.2–12, 128–34. The first passage deals with Perikles and his family, while the second recounts Spartan problems with Pausanias, victor over the Persians at the battle of Plataia (479). Thucydides perhaps uses these to illustrate Spartan religiosity as well as the apparent reality of such charges among the Greeks.

9. Thucydides 1.23.6, usually translated as "inevitable" (see, e.g., the translations of S. Lattimore and R. Warner), but the Greek is rather more complicated, meaning something like "forced into something necessary." For purposes of this discussion inevitability will be used.

10. N. M. Heyman, *World War I* (Westport, CT: Greenwood Press, 1997).

11. Kagan, *Outbreak*, pp. 365–66, discusses the idea of inevitability. Thucydides' remarks on the *unpredictability* of war (2.11.4, 1.78.1) argue against the idea that he saw war as inevitable—how can that which is changeable be predicted?

12. Discussion in E. A. Havelock, "War as a Way of Life in Classical Culture," in *Classical Values and the Modern World*, ed. by E. Gareau (Ottawa: University of Ottawa Press, 1972), p. 75.

13. Discussion in Kurt A. Raaflaub, "Democracy, Power, and Imperialism in Fifth-Century Athens," in *Athenian Political Thought and the Reconstruction of American Democracy*, ed. by J. P. Euben, J. R. Wallach, and J. Ober (Ithaca, NY: Cornell University Press, 1994), pp. 113–18, 130–31.

14. On democracies and war, see Michael W. Doyle, *Ways of War and Peace: Realism, Liberalism, and Socialism* (New York: W. W. Norton, 1997), pp. 76–80.

CHAPTER 3

DEMOCRACY AND IMPERIALISM

Democratic Athens provided the leadership that made possible the Greek victory over Persia in 480/79. Refusing to negotiate, the Athenians allowed their city to be burned not once but twice and fled wherever they might to escape Persian forces. Themistokles, the Athenian general and statesman, devised a strategy that destroyed a Persian fleet half as large as the combined Greek fleet at Salamis (480), which set up the final victories over the Persians at Plataia and Mykale (479). In 478/7, the Athenians took advantage of island communities unhappy with Spartan leadership to assume the burdens of command, and what followed was the organization of the Delian League, which swept the seas of the Persian menace, making the Aegean a Greek sea. Some thirty years later, probably in 454, the Athenians took advantage of their power to move the league treasury from Apollo's island home of Delos to Athens, a move that most historians today see as the beginnings of the Athenian Empire.

Athenian democracy, then, created empire. But in the act of creation, this democratic community was to find that the power and wealth of empire posed fundamental questions that the crisis of war only made greater. After the first Spartan devastation of Attika during which the Athenians saw extensive loss, the Athenians turned on Perikles as the cause of their misfortunes. In defending himself, Perikles told the Athenians that what they held they held as tyranny, and while it might have been unjust to take it in the first place, letting it go was dangerous—"for you are hated by those you have ruled" (Thucydides 2.63.2). Two great debates provide direct testimony to the presence of these issues in wartime democratic and imperial Athens. The first of these debates was the one held in 427 to deliberate the fate of the people of Mytilene, a community that had for long followed Athens loyally, but succumbing to wartime pressures had turned rebellious. The lives of thousands literally hung in the balance. Eleven years later another great debate occurred that would, in the end, approve the plan of Alkibiades to invade Sicily with the object of expanding Athenian influence and power. That expedition ended in an Athenian catastrophe. Both debates reveal much about Athenian attitudes on the meaning of democracy and imperialism.

THE REVOLT OF MYTILENE

Famous for its wine and poets Alkaios and Sappho, Lesbos, a large island lying in the eastern Aegean, supported a number of communities of which Mytilene was the most important. Since the founding of the Delian League, all the communities of Lesbos had played a valuable role in supplying ships and crews to the Athenian-led operations that had swept the Persians from the Aegean, but Mytilene's was most significant. As the conflict between Athens and Corinth mushroomed into a major confrontation between Athens and Sparta, the ruling faction in Mytilene grew uneasy.

At least this is the view of Thucydides. He observes that Mytilenean authorities were worried over Athenian power and feared that they might share the fates of Samos and other island states that had supported the Athenians, only to be beaten down when they attempted to break away from Athenian control (Thucydides 3.9–14). There were other motives, however. Mytilene was not democratic, but rather a community ruled by its oligarchs, that is, the few and the rich. Three of the other communities on the island, Antissa, Eresos, and Pyrrha, were ruled in the same fashion, while Methymna, a city that though smaller rivaled Mytilene, was a democracy. The ruling faction on Mytilene was ambitious to unite all of Lesbos under its rule, and the ruling oligarchs in the three smaller cities were apparently willing to help. But the Mytilenean oligarchs knew that Athens would not allow a potential rival in its own backyard to emerge and would deny their ambitions. Overtures to Sparta for support were made before war broke out, but the Spartans rejected their request, evidently without even a hearing. The outbreak of war played into the hands of the Mytilenean oligarchs and provided them with the opportunity to make their move. All they had to do was wait for the right moment.

That moment came in 428 with the plague. The plague had struck Athens hard, killing thousands, including Perikles, architect of Athenian power. Athenian resources were strained as the effort to maintain the war effort continued, and this was the moment the Mytileneans chose to revolt. As Spartan forces under Archidamos invaded Attika for the third time, the Lesbians—except for Methymna—sprang into action, gathering provisions and otherwise preparing for war. Report of all this, when it reached Athens, was discouraging, and Thucydides even notes that the Athenians did not want to believe it: "at first [they] did not credit the accusations, giving priority to wishing them untrue" (Thucydides 3.3.1). Though hard-pressed and discouraged, the Athenians gathered a forty-ship squadron and dispatched it, hoping to take advantage of a festival of Apollo and catch the population of Mytilene off guard. But the Mytileneans were forewarned of the approaching Athenian force and were able to blunt an initial attack on the harbor. An armistice was arranged, and the Mytileneans sent a representative to Athens in an effort to persuade the Athenians that they really were not doing anything provocative. This measure, however, was probably designed to buy time, as another representative traveled to Sparta to negotiate for support against the Athenians. The overture to Athens failed, as perhaps anticipated, while aid and encouragement arrived from the Spartans. Soon the Athenians were engaged in an all-out campaign to besiege Mytilene and take it.

As fall began, an Athenian relief force of one thousand hoplites commanded by the general Paches arrived in Lesbos. Along with those Athenians and allies already present, Paches surrounded Mytilene with a wall and supporting strong points, effectively cutting the city off from the sea. The Spartans and their allies had promised to send a relief force, but Alkidas, the Spartan commander, proved inept and Mytilene remained surrounded with food stocks steadily decreasing. One Spartan officer, Salaithos, had been able to slip into Mytilene and proposed an emergency solution to the Mytilenean rulers—arm the common people and with their help attack the Athenians and break the siege. His suggestion was taken and the people were armed. At this point, Salaithos' plan broke down. Once armed, the common people demanded a fair sharing of the food the rich had been hoarding; otherwise, they threatened surrender of the city to the Athenians. The oligarchs realized that they were in no position to stop what they threatened. They opened the city to Paches, on the condition that he would take no action against them until an embassy to Athens had brokered a settlement. Paches accepted the surrender, and Athenian forces entered Mytilene, shortly afterward taking Antissa and the other small rebellious cities as well (Thucydides 3.27–35).[1]

Paches sent to Athens the Mytilenean ringleaders and the Spartan Salaithos, who had also fallen captive. The Athenians executed Salaithos immediately, evidently without a trial, and then debated what to do with the Mytileneans. Emotions ran high as the Athenians believed that they had been betrayed by those whom they had treated well, by whose actions the Spartans had attacked Athenian interests in Aegean waters. The decree approved by the Athenians was harsh. The adult men of Mytilene, including those who had forced surrender of the city, were to be killed and everyone else enslaved. A ship was dispatched to Paches to carry out the order, literally a death sentence for Mytilene. The next day some Athenians thought the previous day's decision too harsh, and a few Mytileneans living in Athens pleaded with these to reopen the debate and reconsider the fate of the Mytileneans (Thucydides 3.36).

The Debate over Mytilene

Thucydides reports this debate, but it is unlikely that it went exactly as he describes it. While he relates that various opinions were given on what to do with the Mytileneans, he gives the purported speeches of only two men, Kleon and Diodotos. He depicts Kleon, now emerging as the prime successor to the dead Perikles, as a man of outspoken, blunt opinions, for whom radical measures—like the death of a city—were of little concern when the safety and well-being of Athens were at stake. Thucydides also did not like him. In now introducing Kleon to his *History*, he characterized Kleon as "the most violent" of the Athenians, a remark that should be considered when discussing Thucydides' famed objectivity. Diodotos, Kleon's opponent in the debate, is otherwise unknown, which Thucydides might intend as delicious irony—an unknown challenging the violent and obnoxious Kleon (see Document 11).

Thucydides constructed this debate and while it is impossible to know what the two speakers actually said, he probably does represent accurately the contrasting positions: Kleon upheld the decision to kill all the adult males of Mytilene, while Diodotos proposed killing only those most responsible for starting the revolt. Doubtless, the words and the ideas in the two speeches are those of Thucydides, as the two speeches feature opposing positions on the same points in a staged debate, something unlikely to have really happened in a forum where speakers engaged in sometimes vicious rhetorical give and take.

Kleon's speech began literally with an attack on the Athenian democracy, particularly the assembly and the politicians who catered to it. He claims that democracy is incapable of ruling others—that the present Athenian empire is in fact a dictatorship presiding over subjects. In such a relationship, leadership depends on superior strength, and if that superiority is not exercised with an iron will and hand, control of the empire will be lost. Kleon goes on to rebuke those who would lead the people in their debates, claiming that they must have great confidence in their speaking abilities or be prompted by prospects of personal gain. He attacks those speakers who give dazzling speeches that impress the crowd but that are empty in meaning. Much better is the advice of the less gifted who give plain and direct advice unmotivated by concerns of personal gain. All this amounts to an attack on the assembly as a group of "theater-goers" coming to see a spectacle and accepting the advice of the one who makes the greatest display of fine and flattering words. This last point may well constitute a critique by Thucydides of the democracy, which among other excesses perhaps agreed to a decree that led to his exile.

Diodotos also took up this issue of the "fickleness" of the Athenian assembly but responded in a rather more favorable tone. While admitting that the crowd in the assembly either fell for the flattery of speakers who catered to it or disapproved honest but blunt (or painful) advice, Diodotos concentrated on the obstacles to good counsel. He argued that haste in making a decision was made worse by anger, the mark of a primitive and narrow mind (and here he may have targeted Kleon as an example). These obstacles to good advice were made worse by Kleon's assertion that anyone standing before the assembly was dishonest or self-seeking. Such accusations, Diodotos claimed, undermined honest but unpopular advice, as also the assembly's way of blaming a failure of policy on a particular speaker when in fact the assembly had voted in its support.

The opening parts of the speeches by Kleon and Diodotos are different in tone and perspective, yet each complements the other in giving a "powerful indictment of all [the assembly's] deplorable habits."[2] Haste and anger, and the failure to recognize good advice, Diodotos would have argued, had gotten the Athenians into the situation they now faced regarding the Mytileneans. How were they to understand what had caused their former allies to act the way they had?

Kleon's portrait of the Mytileneans is typically harsh and suspicious in outlook. The Mytileneans, he argues, are motivated by prosperity, a prosperity brought by the successes of the Athenian Empire, which has bred arrogance in them. The only just response that the Athenians can make, he argues, is to kill the Mytileneans for their wrong doing, something that will instruct others as well. This will at the same time be in Athens' self-interest, as it will allow for greater control over the empire. Here Kleon asserts that punishment deters further crime, that people can learn from others' mistakes—an idea held even today, for example, in supporting the death penalty. What Kleon has argued amounts to an endorsement of a policy of fear and terror to maintain order and control over the empire.

The policy of terror proposed by Kleon finds a devastating critique in Diodotos. Although he accepts Kleon's assertion that self-interest must be considered, he asserts that it is the self-interest of Athens that holds priority. How is it in Athens' interest to destroy cities that might revolt, when indemnities and tribute will be lost in the destruction? Should those states that rebel know that an unforgiving policy of annihilation awaits them, they will only fight harder, again to Athens' further loss. But it is in Diodotos' explanation of human nature that he finds the strongest justification for his argument. Punishment and the threat of punishment are no deterrent to crime or wrong doing. No law will prevent someone from committing a wrong—all one need do is look at the long list of punishments prescribed for every crime to see that this is clearly the case.

Diodotos argues persuasively that poverty forces men to take risks—that affluence creates a wish to have more. Hope and desire are the source of ambition and crime, Diodotos (or rather Thucydides) states, the "one leading, the other following, one conceiving the enterprise, and the other suggesting that it will be successful" (Thucydides 3.45.5). In this fashion, Diodotos rejects Kleon's statement that justice and self-interest are combined in this case and that it is Athens' self-interest that is of paramount importance. That his view prevailed in the debate suggests that the majority of Athenians thought as he did.

Mytilene and the Popularity of the Athenian Empire

The revolt organized by the Mytilenean oligarchs gives some indica-
tion of the popularity of Athenian rule in the later fifth century. What
happened in Mytilene had occurred before (Naxos and Samos), and it is
clear that these communities, or rather their leadership, resented the
Athenians, perhaps for the reason that Athens so dominated them that
they regarded themselves as not being free. Yet it is just as true that other
communities supported the Athenians. This includes the democratic
regime in Mythymna, which actively supported the Athenians against
their own neighbors, and other island communities that also provided assistance. Thucydides identifies these as Imbros and Lemnos, both nearby
islands that stood to benefit from Mytilene's fall. Defeated, Mytilene lost
its fleet and the city walls were dismantled, a measure that would make
a future revolt difficult, if not impossible. In addition, the Athenians sent
out 2,700 cleruchs, that is, Athenian citizens, who were assigned grants
of Lesbian land and who would receive cash payments from the Lesbians
who actually worked it. The income of another three hundred grants of
land was assigned to the goddess Athena, a means of providing the
Athenian treasury with an infusion of capital, compensation for the ex-
penditure of funds used to capture Mytilene. The Athenian citizens
would receive incomes and at the same time provide a garrison to protect Athenian interests. In other words, the Athenians occupied Lesbos,
except for Methymna, directly.

This was not the first time that Athenian cleruchs had been dispatched
to a defeated community, and this may have influenced the policies of
Imbros and Lemnos. It was simply better to work with the Athenians
than to challenge them because the consequences of opposition were severe. The islanders who supported Athens perhaps did so too as fellow
democrats. Democratic societies are open societies, and they share the
same values regarding political rights and equality, which encourages
their alliance.[3] But war also makes for good business, and those who stood
by the Athenians may have done so simply because it paid well.

THE SICILIAN EXPEDITION

As events in Mytilene were taking shape, the Athenians found themselves drawn in to affairs in Sicily, an island now in the late fifth century

as Hellenic in culture and spirit as the "old" Greece that had founded the islands' *poleis* hundreds of years before. Syracuse, the island's most powerful city, was at war with Leontini, a community that maintained ties with Athens. A modest-sized squadron was dispatched with orders to help the Leontinians break a Syracusan siege, but also, as Thucydides relates, to look for an opening that would allow the Athenians to expand their dominion over the island. Over the next several years the Athenians did this, making shows of force and friends wherever possible (Thucydides 3.90, 103, 4.2.2, 24–25). But in 424 the Sicilian Greeks convened a congress at Gela where they settled their disputes, which sent the Athenians home, though they kept their ties of alliance with several of the Sicilian communities (Thucydides 4.58–65.2). Thucydides, again writing after the destruction of the later expedition in 412, takes pains to show the Athenians greedily looking for more empire, and some modern authors have criticized him for this. But it is difficult to explain away the Athenian incursion so far from home, or to see it as other than what it was—an opportunistic grab for greater power.

It was not long before the settlement brokered at Gela began to break down. Syracuse again began to threaten Leontini, while in the western part of the island the people of Egesta, a non-Greek native Sicilian community, became involved in a dispute with their neighbor Selinos (a Greek *polis*), which called in Syracuse for assistance. The embattled Egestaians asked their distant Athenian allies for help, arguing that otherwise Syracuse would control all of Sicily. It would only then be a matter of time, they told the Athenians, before Syracuse would cross over to Greece and aid Athens' Peloponnesian enemies and bring war to Athens' doorstep again (Thucydides 6.1.1, 6.1–26).

The Athenians saw another opportunity, but they wanted some assurance that Egesta could help pay the bills for a military campaign, as they promised. Athenian envoys duly arrived in Egesta and fell for one of the shrewdest of tricks, rather unexpected for the usually so clever Athenians. The Egestaians borrowed from everywhere all the silver plate and luxury goods they could find and passed these from home to home that entertained the visiting Athenians. The envoys were completely taken in by this charade.[4] On returning home they reported the immense wealth that the Egestaians had dazzled before them and were able to show as well enough cash to support a fleet of sixty ships for one month.[5] The Athenians greedily fell for the Egestaian trick.

Discussions continued between the Egestaians, now joined by the Leontinians, and the Athenians into the late spring and summer of 415. After much wrangling and debate, a vastly increased fleet and ground force—more than one hundred warships and no fewer than five thousand Athenian and allied hoplites plus a large number of mercenaries—sailed to Sicily under the joint command of Alkibiades, Lamakhos, and Nikias. As recounted above, this great armada struggled with Syracuse and its allies—with great displays of skill and courage on both sides—before it was at last totally destroyed in the summer of 413. As Thucydides pathetically comments, "few out of many returned home" (Thucydides 7.87.6).[6]

The Debate over Sicily

The debate that Thucydides relates was fiercely contested and shows just how heated the exchanges of words and ideas could be in the Athenian assembly. Although his account alludes to the participation of various speakers in the debate (including one unnamed Athenian who challenged Nikias to take action), the debate that Thucydides gives us revolved around Alkibiades and Nikias, the two leading figures of the day. Nikias, known for his luck (and caution), had negotiated the Peace that took his name and was plainly unenthusiastic about the planned invasion of Sicily. In the debate he did everything he could to derail it as well as give the Athenians an opportunity to replace him as one of its commanders. On the other side was Alkibiades, heir to the family of Perikles and known about town for his extravagant ways but also for the recently concluded alliance with Argos, an agreement that, if Thucydides is read carefully, failed to deliver all that Alkibiades either hoped for or bragged about. Thucydides adds to the contrast between the two, noting not only an age difference (which embodies an idea of old versus new as well) but also a sense of caution and foreboding versus a spirit of adventure bordering on recklessness.

In his first speech on the proposed expedition (Thucydides 6.8.4–14), Nikias argued that the Athenians were entering into a conflict that did not concern them, that they were being swayed by foreigners begging for help, who would say anything to let the Athenians do their fighting. Dispatch of even the moderate-sized force to Sicily then being debated also struck him as shortsighted in view of the precarious situation closer to home. The recent Peace was hardly stable. Sparta had accepted it only to achieve the release of those men captured at Sphakteria and now surely planned ways to trip up the Athenians. Corinth, though not named by Nikias but surely implied, had not even accepted the Peace and remained as hostile as ever, as were also a number of other rebellious peoples. Nikias pointed out to the Athenians that in all these struggles, if they prevailed, they might be able to maintain their rule. But Sicily, so far away, was a different situation, and maintaining rule over such a faraway place would be much more difficult.

Nikias also made the interesting argument that sometimes a power was all the greater because it remained at a distance, allowing its reputation to intimidate would-be enemies. A failed attack, even a partially successful one where reinforcements had to be brought in, could have severe repercussions as enemies would imagine the feared power to be a paper tiger and would join others in attacking it (Thucydides 6.11.4). It was far better, Nikias suggested, to let people think you were powerful and so remain fearful and awed, than to show them other. What Nikias argued to the Athenians then was a policy of restraint, to keep what they possessed and not to exceed their grasp.

The restraint and caution proposed by Nikias found its opposite in Alkibiades (see Document 12). Proud, almost arrogantly so of his athletic successes, and bold, Alkibiades told the Athenians in his counter speech (Thucydides 6.16–18) that they had nothing to fear in Sicily, that the many cities there were disorganized from extensive internal unrest and lacking in military strength (Thucydides 6.17.2–3). Syracuse, the island's great power, was so hated that once the Athenians showed up, it would face a rising of the island's native population who would rally to the Athenian cause (Thucydides 6.17.6). With even fewer resources than what they now possessed, their fathers, Alkibiades claims, had achieved even greater success against the Persians, and so now they should not hesitate to act. Empire over all of the Greeks—from those in Sicily to those at home—was the prospect, and the very least that they would achieve was the elimination of the power and arrogance of Syracuse.

In making this bold and extravagant claim, which was so much in keeping with his personality, Alkibiades also talked about empire. He makes the point that the Athenians had an obligation to aid the Egestaians, whom the Athenians had made allies in order to defend themselves against attack closer to home. Alliances such as these contributed to the empire the Athenians now ruled, but more to the point, an energetic response to an ally in need was crucial to keeping that empire. Empires survive, he said, because when they see danger coming, they strike rather than wait for it to arrive. A moderate-sized empire, or "just enough" empire, is not a reality. Instead, empires must grow and expand if they are to survive. For this reason, he told the Athenians, an aggressive policy was needed not only toward Sicily but also in suppressing any and all defections and challenges to Athenian imperial power. And here Alkibiades spoke his mind. At about the same time as this debate was going on in Athens, Athenian military forces were reducing Melos, the small island community whose only offense was not to yield to—or recognize—the superior power of Athens. Among those Athenians responsible for this policy was Alkibiades. Unless you change your ways, he claimed, others will rule you if you do not rule them (Thucydides 6.18.3).

Alkibiades' speech was electric. The pleas of the Egestaians and Leontinians only reinforced what he had said and fixed the resolve of the Athenians to embark on the expedition. Nikias made one final effort to stop what he clearly regarded as folly (Thucydides 6.20–23). He spoke again to the Athenians and attempted to scare them with report of the great military forces that awaited them in Sicily and how they must increase their own. On this an unnamed Athenian challenged him to state what was needed then and there so that the Athenians might approve of whatever resources he thought necessary (Thucydides 6.25.1). At this Nikias yielded to popular demand and said that he would consult with Alkibiades and Lamakhos, the other commanders of the expedition, as he had also failed in having himself removed from the command.

Thucydides paints a scene of general satisfaction in Athens at what had been decided. Older Athenians thought with some satisfaction on the places that would now be added to the empire. Younger men looked forward to traveling to a far-off place and the exciting experiences they would have—an enthusiasm that finds counterparts in all eras of history, in virtually every army that has ever been assembled. Poorer Athenians, the men who would row the fleet of ships now assembling, looked at the expedition as a means of making a living wage, both now and later as a result of the empire that would be made greater (Thucydides 6.24.3–4).

Thucydides on the Sicilian Debate

Since he was exiled and not present for the debate over Sicily that he records, how accurate are the speeches that Thucydides provides? Witnesses would have provided some information that he used to construct the debate.[7] Other known facts such as Alkibiades' negotiation of the Argive alliance (Thucydides 5.43–46) and his unpopularity with the masses, who then supported his enemies (Thucydides 6.15.4, which proved disastrous to Athenian policies), would have provided additional background material. Interest in psychology and how people performed in critical situations also gave Thucydides certain perspectives that he added to the speeches (including his characterization of the age divisions among the Athenians and the idea that a distant power inspires greater awe than one near). But it is also clear that Thucydides writes from a position of superior knowledge, namely, that the Sicilian expedition ended in disaster for the Athenians, which gives the speeches a certain irony. This can be seen best in Alkibiades' speech, which makes little of the resources of Sicily or the power of Syracuse and exaggerates the Athenians' might and destiny.

Although this might seem to rob these speeches of meaning for the historian, the opposite is in fact the case. For what Thucydides has given us is a diverse look into the past. He tells us about people living in a democracy making critical decisions for themselves and others. He reveals, too, the tensions that these people faced as they attempted to resolve what were troubling issues to them, and no less to us today—namely, questions of the use of power and how that is reconciled by a democratic society.

BALANCE SHEET: DEMOCRACY AND EMPIRE

Perikles told the Athenians that the empire they held was a tyranny—a statement echoed certainly by the Corinthians and probably other Greeks as well—but that once held it was too dangerous to surrender (Thucydides 1.122.3, 2.63.3). Alkibiades echoed his uncle's words in the debate over Sicily, arguing to the Athenians that they had to invade Sicily or else change their ways and prepare to be ruled instead of ruling. Although it is possible that Perikles was rather more democratically inclined than his nephew, both spoke as committed members of a democracy. Their comments reveal, however, a conflict in how a democratic community deals with others and how and to what end it wields superior power. This issue remains very much alive in the modern world, where democracies decide on what occasions and to what ends they will use military power. This is one reason why Thucydides' history remains so fascinating even today.

Democracy arose in Athens not even twenty years before the Persians invaded the first time in 490. In this baptism of fire, democracy not only survived, but provided the critical leadership that brought victory. In the years following the Persian defeat, the democracy grew in both confidence and power as it led the Delian League in driving the Persians out of the Aegean and destroying Persian authority over the Greeks of the east. But as this occurred, the Athenians became accustomed to wielding power, especially military power, and to their allies doing as they were told.

Perhaps this is what Sophocles had in mind when he said that pride bred tyranny. The Athenians were proud of their accomplishments and their city, as Alkibiades remarked, encouraging them to emulate their fathers and invade Sicily. As this happened, however, the allies, now casually regarded as subjects as Aristophanes shows in his plays, chafed as they saw their freedom, their ability to rule even themselves, disappear. This drove the Mytileneans, for example, to attempt to throw off Athenian rule, to inspire little Melos to refuse the Athenian "offer" to join the empire. Rule not to be ruled, strike first not to be struck. Power, as Thucydides relates through the personalities of war and the structures of Athenian democracy alike, is an alluring and corrupting force, beguiling individuals and states alike. This remains a valuable lesson today.

NOTES

1. See Donald Kagan, *The Archidamian War* (Ithaca, NY: Cornell University Press, 1974), pp. 124–46, who discusses the evidence.

2. F. Solmsen, *Intellectual Experiments of the Greek Enlightenment* (Princeton, NJ: Princeton University Press, 1975), p. 39.

3. For further discussion on democracies and war, see Doyle, *Ways of War and Peace*, pp. 76–80, and John Mearsheimer, *The Tragedy of Great Power Politics* (New York: W. W. Norton, 2001), pp. 367, 406.

4. Reported by both Thucydides 6.46.3–5 and the later historian Diodoros 12.83.3.

5. Thucydides 6.8.1–2.

6. See Donald Kagan, *The Peace of Nicias and the Sicilian Expedition* (Ithaca, NY: Cornell University Press, 1981), pp. 157–353, who again discusses the evidence for this great event.

7. Both Thucydides and Alkibiades were exiles from Athens. At 5.26.4 Thucydides mentions how his exile enabled him to interview people on the Peloponnesian side about the war. Such circumstances suggest that he could have just as easily met Alkibiades, who gave him valuable information that he included in his account of these and other events.

CHAPTER 4

ART AND CULTURE IN A TIME OF WAR

Around 425 the Athenians dedicated a small temple on the southwestern corner of the acropolis. It was built to Athena and was called "Nike," or victory; perhaps it did double duty celebrating the recent Athenian victory over the Spartans (at Sphakteria?) and the traditional enemy of old, the Persians. Although the object of the dedication is uncertain, it remains clear that the temple had some unusual features. A parapet below carried a scene of bulls being led to slaughter, a scene actually depicted, while the frieze reliefs on the temple showed Greeks fighting Greeks, not the more customary Greek versus barbarian theme. Such realism captures the classical idea itself: realism to the point of perfection.

THE CLASSICAL IDEA

By the time the temple of Athena Nike was built, "Classical" Greek art had been slowly taking form, emerging from the "Archaic" style that preceded it. It reached a kind of perfection, what is sometimes called "High" classical, with the building of the Parthenon (447–432), though not all scholars would agree with this view. John Boardman, a leading scholar of Greek art, places the origins of the Classical ideal in the growing rationalization in the Greek world—a view that applied to gods, ideas, and behavior—that gave an impulse to generalization and idealization of the human form. As Boardman notes, "this is Classicism in its narrower sense, attempting to perceive patterns, to set standards."[1] There is a tendency to imagine that Athens took the lead in the creation of this Classical ideal, but evidence suggests that Greeks outside of Athens also played a part. One such artist was Polykleitos of Argos, who is as "classic" a sculptor as can be found, as shown in his famous statue the *Doryphoros* ("spear-bearer"), with its ideal proportions of the male body (which he explained in a lost book, the *Kanon*) and balanced pose. The realism of the Classical ideal is reflected as well in the famous contest of the artists Zeuxis and Parrhasios told by the Roman writer and scientist Pliny the Elder. These two artists entered into a competition and

> Zeuxis exhibited at the theater grapes painted with such success that birds flew down to the stage. Parrhasios exhibited a curtain painted to represent truth so well that Zeuxis, glorying in the judgment of the birds, demanded that the curtain be drawn back and the picture shown. When he realized his error Zeuxis conceded the prize with honest shame, saying that he had tricked birds but Parrhasios had tricked him. It is held that later Zeuxis painted a boy carrying grapes, and when the birds flew down to the grapes Zeuxis walked up to the work with the same frankness and said "I have painted the grapes better than the boy, since if I had perfected the boy the birds should have been afraid of him."[2]

War's Impact on Art and Culture

Thucydides wrote that "war is a violent teacher" (Thucydides 3.82.2), and his account shows this in many ways: the violent outbreak of civil war in the island state of Corcyra, the execution of prisoners of war in Plataia, and the plague in Athens. The occasion of the plague in Athens prompted lawlessness and cynicism and, over time, escapism, which became another feature of life, certainly in Athens but elsewhere in Greece as well. The appearance of new religious cults in Athens among other places supports this view. In 420 the healer god Asklepios was brought to Athens, as it was believed that his presence would heal the sick and calm the worried. Bendis, a Thracian deity celebrated with noisy nighttime rituals, also entered Athens at this time, and the rituals of Dionysos, depicted so vividly by Euripides in his *Bacchae* (406), point again to the psychic stress present not only in Athens but throughout the Greek world.

The pressure exerted on Greek culture and society by war has led some art historians to argue that there occurred in art a wartime expression that reflected this era of stress. Art historian J. J. Pollitt has likened de-

velopments in art at the end of the fifth century to the kind of entertainment Americans watched during the era of the Great Depression in
the 1930s—movies with heroes and heroines tap-dancing "their way with
unfailing elegance through a series of soothing, inconsequential episodes
to an inevitable happy, if never very believable conclusion."[3]

Not all art historians agree with Pollitt's views, but classicist Steven
Lattimore adds that the sculpture of this so-called Rich Style becomes
at once pretty and softer, and tends to be viewed from one angle, a technique he sees as rhetorical, something that again reflects the intellectual climate of the era and Greek fondness for oratory.[4] That Greek
artists and intellectuals could perceive such ideas and attitudes and bring
them to their work seems evident in a conversation between Sokrates
and Parrhasios, the painter mentioned above. In this discussion Parrhasios assured Sokrates that he could imitate nature, right down to the
hostile expressions of a man, as well as happiness or displeasure (see Document 13). This valuable passage argues that Greek artists and sculptors
recognized the wide range of human emotions and expressions and could
bring these to life in their work. Euripides dramatically confirms this. In
relating the heroic death of the Trojan princess Polyxena, he tells how
she defiantly tore her dress, "exposing her naked breasts, bare and lovely
like a sculptured goddess" (*Hecuba* lines 559–60). It seems certain then
that in a time of great stress and anxiety caused by war and violence,
artists would not only pick up on these but bring them to life as well.
Some examples from this period of stress and worry show that these anxieties did manifest themselves in the art and buildings, and also in literature.

ART AND ARCHITECTURE IN A TIME OF TROUBLE

In a remote corner of Greece even today stands one of the great buildings of classical antiquity, the temple of Apollo Epikourios—"the
Helper"—at Bassai. Virtually forgotten until the eighteenth century
when foreign travelers discovered it, construction of this temple lasted
throughout the Peloponnesian War (c. 429–400). Once thought dedicated to a "friendly," helpful Apollo, it is now argued that the cult epi-
thet *epikourios* actually refers to mercenary soldiers who were the
principal export of this otherwise poor area of Greece known as Arkadia. Excavations have revealed a number of votive offerings of armor,

which argues that mercenary soldiers were the probable donors of the funds that built the temple.

The frieze reliefs at Bassai are marked by extensive violence: centaurs attacking women and Amazons attacking men. Such scenes had been depicted before, as on the Parthenon frieze whose craftsmen perhaps worked here too: the chief architect at Bassai was Iktinos who had also worked on the Parthenon. But at Bassai the violence is more shocking. In one scene a woman clings to a clothed cult statue while a centaur tears off her clothing; the artist's goal of creating a contrast could not be plainer. In most temples frieze reliefs are usually difficult to see. At Bassai the frieze was closer to the viewer (though still not easy to make out), and its effect, in addition to the orientation of the figures, was to engage the observer. The Parthenon frieze invites the spectator to feel at one with those on the frieze. The Bassai frieze does not. Its orientation seems almost helter-skelter—Greek soldiers fighting and struggling, their opponents seemingly looking to the spectator for relief—and offers not unity but a strong sense of individualism. But this makes sense. The warriors depicted on the Parthenon frieze are citizens fighting for Athens and the community; the warriors on the Bassai frieze fight for themselves and for money.[5]

At about the same time that the Arkadian mercenaries were funding the building of their temple at Bassai, the Athenians erected the small temple to Athena Nike on the acropolis (sometime in the 420s). The frieze on the temple depicted a series of combat scenes, some involving the Athenians and Persians at Marathon (the south panel), but other scenes clearly show Athenians fighting other Greeks. The subject of these fights, though not certain, could well be contemporary battles of the Peloponnesian War (north and west panels; the east panel featured an assembly of gods, perhaps honoring Athena). The temple stood on a parapet below which was a balustrade or stairway designed to protect visitors from falling off the temple site. This frieze features a series of Nikai, or winged victories, leading animals to sacrifice and, in one place, slaughtering a bull. This is significant, for as Robin Osborne observes, "the sex of the victim [makes] this a sacrifice in a military context and not to Athena (goddesses receive female victims). What we see is the sacrifice before battle juxtaposed to the raising of trophies that happened when battle was won."[6]

The Nikai presented on the balustrade convey a strong aura of sexiness and desirability and military victory and violence. One Nike in particular shows this clearly. As she reaches down to adjust a loose sandal, her clothes slip off her shoulder bearing it and outlining her breast clearly (perhaps the figure Euripides had in mind in his *Hecuba*). Men viewing this Nike would likely imagine Victory sexually—desirable yet fleeting—but certainly something to be possessed and worth fighting for. As Steven Lattimore observes, the Nikai are unreal in their beauty and sensuousness and stand in sharp contrast with the subject matter—war and violence. But they show as well the emotional and sexual appeal of the Rich Style and its escapist message.[7]

Victory in battle and victory in sexual pursuits were goals that drove the Greeks as they waged the Peloponnesian War. But Victory could provide another statement—propaganda. This is seen in the famous Nike of Paionios, which was set up in Olympia circa 420. An accompanying inscription records that Messenian allies of the Athenians commissioned Paionios, an Ionian Greek sculptor, to create a Victory to commemorate their role in defeating the Spartans at Sphakteria in 425. The sculpture was set up at Olympia, site of the famous Games, and was a place frequented by all Greeks who could see this Messenian celebration of their victory over the hated Spartans who had oppressed them for hundreds of years. In this way, the Nike of Paionios assumes the role of political propaganda.

But like her sister Nikai in Athens, Paionios' Nike is also alluring in her sexuality. Designed to stand atop a column and so seen from below, this Nike appeared in the act of landing on her pillar. Paionios' intent was to depict Victory as sensuous and desirable: as the wind blows her garments up and back, creating a large sail from her billowing clothes, the sensuous contours of her body beneath are revealed.

If Victory could be represented in sexual terms—fleeting yet desirable, beautiful to behold—so too could death and defeat, the tragedy of war. This is seen in the earliest large female nude in Greek art, the Dying Niobid, designed for a temple pediment (once thought to be Bassai, now disproved) circa 430. Niobe, proud of her childrens' beauty, boasted that they were more beautiful than those of Leto, Apollo, and Artemis. Enraged, the gods killed all seven sons and seven daughters. The Niobid is shown being cut down by a divine arrow; she reaches back to pull it

Nike tying her sandal. Balustrade of the temple of Athena Nike, Athens, c. 424. Acropolis Museum, Athens, Greece. *Source: Scala / Art Resource, New York.*

Nike of Paionios, c. 420. Archaeological Museum, Olympia, Greece. *Source: Scala / Art Resource, New York.*

from her back, and as she does, her dress slips from her body to reveal the beautiful body underneath. As in the case of the Nikai, a sexual allure to the throes of defeat—the opposite of victory—is created in a pathetic scene that must have been familiar to the Greeks of this war-torn time.

The allure and escapism of the Rich Style, its appeal to violence, reflects the stress and strain of wartime Greece that took artistic forms in a new direction. The same sort of thing appears to have happened with pictorial art, especially that seen on *lekythoi*, or the oil flasks that were left at tombs as offerings to the dead. From the end of the sixth century, the *lekythos* (plural form, *lekythoi*) dominates all others as the offering of choice to the deceased. In the mid–fifth century the white-ground technique overcame the older black-figure *lekythoi* and pushed its way forward as the preferred form. This success seems the result of the form itself— more could be painted on it—and the growing desire to show real people—the heroic dead, ladies with their maids, visits to tombs—then mythical scenes of adventure, satyrs, and maenads.

Commemoration of the dead in Athens may also have played a part in this development. Beginning in the mid–fifth century, those who died in war were remembered annually and received public notice in the form of inscriptions listing their names (much like the Vietnam Veterans Memorial in Washington, DC). But the dead were grouped by tribe and without reference to their "hometown" or their father's name, so it was quite possible that men of the same name in the same tribe could appear one after the other but without separate identity. Such inscriptions began to appear about the time the white-ground *lekythoi* gained popularity. This suggests that the democratic but anonymous commemoration of the dead may have encouraged the new and more personal and individualized *lekythoi*.

Many examples of the white-ground *lekythoi* survive, but a work of the Group R Painters, circa 425–400, provides a good illustration of the new depiction of the dead. On this vessel a young man sits before a grave, another young man to his right, a young woman holding a helmet on his left. The surviving colors on the vessel are rich, especially the dark brown hair of the two young men, and the eyes are treated in rich detail, giving some idea of what the original colors would have been like. What we have here is the memorialization of a dead young soldier, but the scene conveyed evokes the sorrow of war, not the glory. The dead soldier gazes somberly ahead, seemingly deep in thought, as the young man on his right gazes on him with an outstretched hand, at once directing the viewer to the dead but also in a gesture suggesting sorrowful loss. Both the expressions and gestures call to mind Parrhasios' assurances to Sokrates that feelings, features, and emotions could be depicted in paint-

Niobid, from the Sallustian Gardens, Rome. Graeco-Roman after Greek original, c. 430. Museo Nazionale Romano delle Terme, Rome, Italy. *Source: Scala / Art Resource, New York.*

ing (see Document 13). The overall effect of the scene is one of "moody contemplation."[8]

The *lekythoi,* then, with their domestic scenes of matrons and maids, mothers and children, and departing soldiers, break with the earlier archaic painting that depicted death as something terrible, an event reflected in the presence of monsters of all kinds. In the *lekythoi* death becomes natural, something like a family event, and this in some way is escapist—death is not something to be feared but is instead an event that all share.

The painters of the *lekythoi* and the sculptors and craftsmen who created the art and buildings of Greece during this era of war did not keep their ideas and visions of war and peace to themselves. At the end of the war, the Spartan commander Lysander sponsored a large commemorative monument at Delphi to his victory over the Athenians. Created by Peloponnesian artists affiliated with the famous sculptor Polykleitos, this monument was elaborate and awe-inspiring. The travel-writer Pausanias, who saw it in the second century c.e., listed those honored with some details of the overall arrangement (Pausanias 10.9.4).

After the war, times were hard in Athens and elsewhere in the Greek world, and it appears that some artists may have traveled abroad looking for work and new patrons for whom they could express their ideas and display their talents. One such example seems to be the Nereid monument in Lykia on the southern coast of modern Turkey built around 400. This tomb to a prince features the same sort of wind-blown drapery seen in the Nike of Paionios. This suggests that just as Greek mercenaries went off in search of employment abroad, so too did artists in what J. J. Pollitt calls "an age of bewilderment and destruction."[9]

LITERATURE IN A TIME OF TROUBLE

Literature, like art, expresses the temper of the times and reveals what people are thinking about. Art historian John Boardman suggests that the "poets of Athens brought to the public stage plays which were based on Greece's myth-history, but which they used to explore such eternal human problems as loyalty, the conflict of civil and moral law, sin and retribution, in a manner which laid the foundations of western civilization."[10] Most scholars would agree with these remarks, but dramas presented on the stage also explored real-life situations and reflected recent

Soldier at his tomb. Attic white-ground *lekythos* from grave in Eretria, late fifth century, attributed to artists of "Group R." National Archaeological Museum, Athens, Greece. *Source: Scala / Art Resource, New York.*

events. In 494 the playwright Phrynichos staged *The Sack of Miletus*, which took as its theme the devastation of that city by the Persians in 499; the Athenians fined Phrynichos a large sum of money for reminding them of this great disaster. Little more than twenty years later, Aeschylus put before the Athenians *The Persians* (472), a play that is both contemporaneous and pointed, which suggests that playwrights did take a bit of literary license and explore issues that reflected current events.

The contemporaneity of the Athenian stage is best seen in the comedies of Aristophanes. References to contemporary generals and politicians as well as events abound in his plays, and as most of these date to the era of the Peloponnesian War, they provide rich commentary on the personalities and happenings of war. His play *Birds* is clearly "escapist," a description that applies as well though in a different light to *Acharnians* and *Lysistrata*. More subtle in its commentary on the current events of war are the plays of Euripides, particularly his "war plays" *Andromache*, *Hecuba*, *Heracles*, and *Trojan Women*, to which can be added those plays that are, like Aristophanes' *Birds*, "escapist": *Helen* and *Iphigenia in Tauris*.

Argument for contemporary events spilling over into literature finds support in the conversations that have been reported as in Plato's *Symposium* (set in the year 416). Though written after Sokrates' death and perhaps ahistorical, the reported conversations are important in that they reveal intellectuals—a physician, comic and tragic poets, philosophers, and a statesman—debating issues (in this instance the idea of Love) and exchanging ideas. War touched the Greeks directly and immediately, and that there would be no discussion among intellectuals of its impact on society and culture seems unlikely.

Aristophanes and the Peloponnesian War

Aristophanes' *Acharnians*, presented in the sixth year of the Peloponnesian War (425), takes as its principal theme the idea of war weariness, which prompts the play's hero, Dikaiopolis (meaning "Just city"), to seek a private truce with the Spartans. This brings him into conflict with a group of old Athenian men, the Acharnians, whose land and homes had been particularly hard hit by the annual Spartan invasions. Through his main character, Aristophanes ridicules the causes of war (and his references to the Megarian Decree, which Thucydides had virtually ignored, says much of what most Athenians thought had caused the war) and also takes aim on one of the contemporary war heroes, Lamakhos. In the end Dikaiopolis prevails in a drinking party contest, which provides the play with a comic and happy ending but which may also suggest that the best way to end a war is with a drinking contest— rather like the suggestion in the 1970 film M*A*S*H* that the Korean War ought to be ended through a giant cocktail party, victory going to the last man standing.

If *Acharnians* is nearly escapist, *Birds* is without question. Performed in 414 as the Athenian Expedition to Sicily was coming to grief, *Birds*, with its brilliant and probably comical costumes, must have been a dazzling spectacle that brings to mind the 1930s films that J. J. Pollitt refers to as the escapist fare of the Great Depression. The play's heroes, Euelpides ("Hopefulson") and Peisetairos ("Persuading friend"), decide to abandon Athens, Greece, and the war by leaving it all behind to fly off into space, where they establish a new city, "Cloudcuckooland," or *Nephelokokkygia* (a compound word for cloud and cuckoo, the latter being a type of bird's call, as in cuckoo clock). What follows shows that it is a city that the two dissident Athenians create.[11] Once established, the heroes rid their community of obnoxious types of people—oracle sellers and sycophants in particular—and set about to enjoy themselves with feasting and other pleasurable pursuits. This action and other allusions to wartime conditions (references to war orphans, internal disorder that would lead to oligarchic revolution) supports the idea of a prevailing war weariness in Athens that Aristophanes attempted to ease with comic relief.

Within three years the war's course had taken a critical turn for Athens. The Sicilian Expedition had come to ruin, and many former allies had joined the Spartans. It was in this context that Aristophanes staged *Lysistrata* (411). Perhaps the best known of all his plays, *Lysistrata* is similar to *Acharnians* and *Birds* in that it takes as its theme the impact of war with an escapist twist. Lysistrata ("Dissolving armies") leads the women of Greece in a sex strike by which they hope to force their husbands to stop the bloody war among them—a conflict that will only empower the Persians and weaken the Greeks. Aristophanes takes aim at the violent consequences of the war, perhaps seen best in the exchange

between Lysistrata and the Athenian commissioner who has come to negotiate with her and the striking women occupying the acropolis (where
among other things the Athenians stored their money reserves). Lysistrata explains how the women of Greece will bring peace to the Greeks
by comparing it to the untangling of thread and wool, something the
commissioner rejects with derision:

> How terrible is it to stand here and watch them
> carding and winding at will with our fate,
> witless in war as they are.

To this Lysistrata responds,

> What of us then,
> who ever in vain for our children must weep
> Borne but to perish afar and in vain?

The commissioner responds to this with "not that, O let that one
memory sleep!" (Aristophanes, *Lysistrata* lines 587–90). While not explicit, the lines almost certainly refer to the Sicilian Expedition and its
great loss of life, something that the mothers of Athens would have felt
especially keenly. *Lysistrata* then refers to the stress and trauma of war,
but Aristophanes disguises this by placing women in charge of the administration of the community, something that most Athenian men
would have thought preposterous and hugely funny. In this sense, then,
Lysistrata is escapist, while at the same time revealing the impact of war
on society, especially its women (on this drama, see also Chapter 6).

To say that Aristophanes is a comic genius is an understatement. He
writes so as to amuse all—the bathroom jokes for those in the audience
who think that sort of thing is funny, the political barbs for the more as-
tute and thinking members of the audience, and the philosophical and
rhetorical allusions that surely delighted the likes of Sokrates, whom
Aristophanes perhaps found at once interesting as also the most dangerous citizen in Athens. Mixed in with all this was the background of war.
War permeated Athenian and Greek society, and its violence and trau-
mas echoed everywhere. Aristophanes attempted to ease the fear and
anxiety, the war weariness and suffering, and while he found success and
fame in this, he could never remove these altogether.

Euripides and the Peloponnesian War

A little older than Aristophanes, Euripides is the youngest of the three great tragic playwrights, and more of his work survives than that of Aeschylus and Sophocles. As he lived through the Peloponnesian War, it is only natural that his dramas reflect the stress and strain of those events. A number of his surviving plays have been regarded as "war" plays, while others are clearly war related with their escapist themes (see p. 58).

Andromache (c. 430–424), *Hecuba* (425/4), and *Trojan Women* (416/5) are dramas whose protagonists are women. This must be seen as at least a bit curious, if not important, in a society as dominated by men as Athens and Greece were. This is not to say that men do not play roles in these plays—they do—only that it is women who figure prominently. All three plays also share a "Trojan" identity—Andromakhe and Hekuba, respectively Hektor's and Priam's widows, and finally the Trojan women, widows and survivors of all the Trojans slain by the Greeks in the taking of Troy. This "otherness" allows Euripides considerable freedom in stating his views on the horror of war, something that he sees striking women and children with particular cruelty.

Euripides' *Andromache* may reflect his attitudes early in the Peloponnesian War when feelings ran high against the Spartans for provoking war with Athens. In one place he refers to the Spartans as "devious schemers, masters of falsehood, specialists in evil," whose ambitions ruined the prosperity of Greece (*Andromache* lines 445–49). But it is already clear in this drama, written early in the course of war, that Euripides saw some ominous things—the rape and abuse of women, the killing of children. These would be themes he would return to in *Hecuba* and *Trojan Women* with bitter insight.

Hecuba is a play of retribution. Hekuba, the widowed ex-queen of Troy, has seen her whole family killed, first her sons in war and then the last, Polydoros, killed for money by his greedy guardian, King Polymestor of Thrace; of her daughters only Kassandra, the crazed voice of Apollo, and Polyxena remain alive. Kassandra, fated to die with her captor Agamemnon, is momentarily safe, but Polyxena, the Greeks decide, must die to appease the departed spirit of Achilles. In a chilling scene, Hekuba and the other women of Troy kill the sons of Polymestor before him and then gouge out his eyes. Revenge, or payback, carried out by women delivers a double lesson of violence, and Euripides' point that violence begets violence seems clear. He also shows that women can be as courageous as men. Standing before the whole Greek army, Polyxena bravely meets death, telling her guards to stand aside as she embraces the sword of Neoptolemaios, Achilles' son (see Document 14).

In *Trojan Women* Euripides presents similar themes. The captive Trojan women, assigned to their captors, wait departure to Greece to begin their slaves' existence. Euripides paints a bleak picture of a destroyed city, a picture made emphatic by his statement, delivered by the god Poseidon, "That mortal who sacks fallen cities is a fool, who gives the temples and the tombs, the hallowed places of the dead to desolation. His own turn must come" (*Trojan Women* lines 95–98). War's cruelties are made even more explicit in the rational debate of the Greeks to kill Astyanax, the surviving young son of Hektor. That such a discussion could take place reveals the depths to which the war's violence can take a community. Euripides sees this as so much foolishness, something he expresses through the voice of Kassandra, who delivers a stunning indictment on the waste that is war (see Document 15).

That Euripides sees war as wasteful is brought home all the more in two plays that develop an escapist theme, *Helen* (412) and *Iphigenia in Tauris* (c. 414–411). In *Helen* Euripides spins a fantastic romantic comedy in which Helen of Sparta, supposedly kidnapped by the Trojan prince Paris, is found never to have been in Troy, but rather in Egypt where the gods had spirited her away. Euripides' point could not be clearer. War and the deaths of thousands followed by the destruction of an old and venerable city, Troy, was for nothing. He conveys this same message in the *Iphigenia*. Here the daughter of Agamemnon, believed sacrificed by her father to win the favor of the gods, is found not to have been killed but rather whisked away to safety by the gods. Since she is found living among non-Greeks, Euripides brings out a sense of "otherness" for the Greeks, who come to realize that they belong together wherever that might be. In this sense, then, he explores the theme of Greek killing Greek and leads the audience to imagine that if Greeks see themselves as belonging together, why do they continually fight and kill each other?

War, Violence, and Culture in Fifth-Century Greece

War brings out the best of the human intellect, just as it reveals the worst examples of cruelty and inhumanity. For Thucydides, war was a violent teacher, and the surviving art and literature of ancient Greece shows that other intellectuals, artists and craftsmen, playwrights and thinkers, saw this too. Whether reacting to war visually and exploring its impact or offering an escape from it, these intellectuals attempted to understand what was happening to their culture and society in an era of great stress and anxiety. Different views on what this all meant are to be expected of them, as well as us interpreting what we find in the way of evidence today.[12]

NOTES

1. J. Boardman, "The Classical Period," in *The Oxford History of Classical Art* (Oxford: Oxford University Press, 1993), pp. 83–84.

2. Pliny the Elder, *Natural Histories* 35.65, cited in R. Osborne, *Archaic and Classical Greek Art* (Oxford: Oxford University Press, 1998), p. 209.

3. J. J. Pollitt, *Art and Experience in Classical Greece* (Cambridge: Cambridge University Press, 1972), p. 125.

4. S. Lattimore, "Classical Art," in *The Blackwell Companion to the Classical Greek World* (forthcoming).

5. See Osborne, *Archaic and Classical Greek Art*, pp. 205–10.

6. Ibid., p. 184. See also J. Hurwit, *The Athenian Acropolis* (Cambridge: Cambridge University Press, 1999), pp. 209–15.

7. See discussions in Osborne, *Archaic and Classical Greek Art*, pp. 184–87, and Lattimore, "Classical Art."

8. Osborne, pp. 194–95.

9. Pollitt, *Art and Experience*, pp. 134–35.

10. Boardman, "The Classical Period," p. 83.

11. D. M. MacDowell, *Aristophanes and Athens* (Oxford: Oxford University Press, 1995), pp. 201, 209.

12. For a different view on the plays of Euripides discussed here, see P. Green, "War and Morality in Fifth-Century Athens: The Case of Euripides' *Trojan Women*," *Ancient History Bulletin* 13 (1999): 97–110.

WAR, PHILOSOPHY, AND SOKRATES

Located in a corner of the Athenian *agora*, or town center, the small building that serves as the public jail is filled this day in 399, not with prisoners—there is only one—but with his friends saying goodbye. Soon this evidently popular man will be compelled to drink the deadly hemlock, a poisonous drug that will bring slow and painful death as it makes its way up his body beginning with the feet. The prisoner is of course Sokrates, and the scene about to unfold ranks among the most famous of Western civilization—probably only the death of Jesus of Nazareth holds greater significance for generations to come.

Although Sokrates' death comes some five years after the end of the Peloponnesian War, there can be little question that it is linked to that great conflict. As the war dragged on, Sokrates became a lightning rod for controversial issues of wartime politics—democrat versus oligarch ideology—and the birth pains of a new philosophy—literally the clash of new ideas with the old, as Aristophanes shows clearly in his play *Clouds*. In the end these hotly debated issues would take Sokrates as a sacrificial victim, though few in Athens really wanted events to go the way they did. But as Thucydides might have reminded his countrymen, events often take an unpredictable course.

SOKRATES OF ATHENS

Who was this man who so radicalized opinion in Athens? Sokrates was born in about 469 (we know that because Plato tells us he was seventy when he died) to Sophroniskos, a stonemason and sculptor, and Phainarete, who was known for her ability as a midwife. This Athenian family possessed some social status as Sokrates served in several campaigns early in the Peloponnesian War as a hoplite, a clear indicator of something like "middle-class" wealth. During the so-called Archidamian War, he served in the campaigns at Potidaia (c. 430), and in the battles of Delion (424) and Amphipolis (422), where he distinguished himself by his bravery. Plato in his dialogue *Symposium* provides what is likely the eyewitness testimony of the famous general Alkibiades as to Sokrates' courage and hardiness as a soldier (see Document 16).

Because of his age, Sokrates saw little active duty in the years that followed the Peace of Nikias, but he served the community in other ways. In 406 he was a member of the Council of 500, a body that prepared legislation for the assembly and in a sense was responsible for the daily administration of the city. This service would catapult him into the public eye. In July Athens won a great naval battle at Arginousai over the Spartans, but in the aftermath a number of ships were disabled, and a fast-moving storm destroyed them along with their crews. Loss of life was great. The failure as well to recover the bodies of the dead set off a public fury that fixed responsibility on the generals commanding the fleet. When they returned to Athens, the Athenians demanded "justice"—vengeance really—and the generals were charged en bloc, contrary to the law. As a member of the presiding committee of the 500 (i.e., the *prytaneis*, consisting of fifty men from each of ten tribes in Athens), Sokrates argued with the mob demanding blood that what they wanted was illegal—not right or just—and that he would oppose it. As Xenophon, a witness to all this, wrote:

> When some of the *prytaneis* asserted they would not propose a vote that was contrary to the law, Kallixenos in turn rose to speak and denounced them with the same charges. The crowd shouted out that those *prytaneis* thinking this should be summoned to court. With this all the *prytaneis* were terrified except Sokrates, the son of Sophroniskos, and agreed to propose the motion. Sokrates said that he would act only in accordance with the law.[1]

Imagine standing up against an angry crowd, refusing to give an inch to their demands! This is what Sokrates did, and the courage he showed this day matches that of his soldier's life when he refused to run and play the coward's part. In spite of his efforts, however, the public's anger could not be appeased, and the generals were found guilty of dereliction of duty, condemned, and executed.

Soon after the war ended, a group of Athenian oligarchs, propped up by the Spartan general Lysander, ruled over Athens. They abolished the hateful (in their eyes) democracy and set about establishing a new regime based on their oligarchic ideas. The reforms, however, did not go very far, and the Thirty Tyrants, as they came to be called, ruled Athens themselves and did so with a program of terror. Weapons were taken away from individual Athenians, a thousand and more were killed and their wealth confiscated. Among the Thirty were Kritias and Kharmides, relatives of the philosopher Plato, and all three had connections to Sokrates. At one point Kritias and Kharmides attempted to widen the circle of evil by ordering Sokrates to join some others in arresting a wealthy resident alien, Leon of Salamis, the idea being really to kill him and take over his property. Sokrates, when "asked" but really ordered, refused to go along with this plan and simply went home. Others less conscience-stricken complied and arrested the unfortunate Leon, who was later killed. Clearly, Sokrates refused to recognize the authority of the Thirty, friends or not.

In the eyes of many Athenians, however, Sokrates was an accomplice and, perhaps even worse, a teacher who inspired Kritias and Kharmides (and others like Alkibiades) with their evil ideas. This association lies at the root of the charges that Anytos and Meletos would bring against Sokrates in 399, after the restoration of the democracy, for "corrupting the youth" of Athens, to which they added the charge of "worshiping false gods."

Sokrates and His "Mission"

His battlefield exploits show that Sokrates possessed physical courage. He was also morally courageous and would refuse to budge from his belief in doing what was right and just. What motivated this courageous behavior? In his *Apology*, an account defending Sokrates' memory and describing his trial, Plato writes that Sokrates said that the Athenians should look inward and care for their souls.[2] This remark seems to make the best sense when placed in a context of wartime stress and strain. The Athenians had suffered greatly not only from battlefield deaths but also from the ravages of the plague. Thucydides reports how during the great epidemic so many people died that bodies were left unburied on the streets, while others were disposed of cruelly and without care, simply being dumped wherever a funeral fire was already lit. He notes too that the great loss of life caused people to take a "live today because there is no tomorrow" attitude, while others paid little regard to the law, thinking they would die before ever being brought to trial.[3] In such a breakdown of social mores and values, Sokrates' admonition to the Athenians to think about their actions and take care of their psyches makes great sense.

This mission that drove Sokrates to urge the Athenians to examine their lives also seems driven by a genuine spirituality. One of his friends, Khairephon, went once to the Delphic oracle and asked the question, "Is Sokrates the wisest man in Greece?" The oracle responded yes, and Khairephon returned to Athens to tell Sokrates of the god's pronouncement. This report, in addition to his own observations on current conditions in Athens, led Sokrates to question the Athenians on their actions and how they justified them. This took him into all areas of thought as well as politics, both of which were hotly debated, all in a context of war and uncertainty.

In this Sokrates saw himself as a facilitator or, as he put it, a "midwife" to the thought of others, a description he probably borrowed from the work of his mother, Phainarete, a noted midwife. Although Sokrates was famous for going around Athens and asking people why they thought what they did, he also frequented what many would have seen as elite circles. This was perhaps the result of what is surely (at least) a second marriage, that to Xanthippe. That this is a second marriage seems certain from the fact that on his death, Sokrates had young sons, something unlikely for a man his age (seventy) unless from a second marriage. Xanthippe's name suggests an elite, if not aristocratic, family, and it may have been through this connection that Sokrates came into contact with other elites. This included not only the extended family of Plato, his relatives the later oligarchs Kritias and Kharmides, but also Alkibiades of the family of Perikles, and Xenophon, another Athenian of birth and wealth. These contacts in turn brought Sokrates into contact with a number of other prominent intellectuals, Sophists such as Protagoras and Gorgias, men who were bringing new ideas of thought and rhetoric to the Athenians as well as other Greeks.

Associations such as these provided the scenes that Plato would later use for his famous dialogues. An example is the scene depicted in the

Symposium, Plato's great discussion of the meaning of Love. Besides Sokrates, those attending this dinner-drinking party were two playwrights, the comic poet Aristophanes and the tragic poet Agathon, as well as a physician, Eryximachos, and several friends of Sokrates; later, Alkibiades crashes the party and joins in. Whereas the discussion early in the evening focused on Love, later Sokrates engaged the poets in the nature of their craft. Plato writes that Sokrates pressed them to agree that someone who could write tragedy should also be able to write comedy (Plato, *Symposium* 223D). This passage is of particular interest, for it attests to the interaction of intellectuals debating issues of literature and thought, and suggests how ideas from one discipline could influence developments in another.

THE NEW THOUGHT

Greek authors such as the historian Thucydides writing in the era of the Peloponnesian War brought to their work the ideas and techniques of what today is called the "Greek Enlightenment" (see Chapter 2). This movement had been ongoing since the early fifth century, but increasingly during the Peloponnesian War the focus of thinkers and especially Sokrates was man. Aristotle wrote that Sokrates left behind the study of nature, which had been the major emphasis in Greek philosophy, to explore questions of ethics and definitions. Later philosophers in the Greek Hellenistic era (c. 323–31) such as Panaetius would conclude that "Sokrates brought philosophy down from the skies" and turned it to man, a view that the Roman Cicero would later repeat.[4] Although it is surely right to credit Sokrates with a key role in this development, others also played a part in this birth of thought, namely the Sophists. Sometimes the Sophists are seen only as teachers of rhetoric (something that Sokrates seems not to have paid much attention to), but the evidence suggests that their interests were broad and wide ranging.

Sokrates and the Sophists are interconnected in many ways. They freely associated in democratic Athens, which itself provided the environment in which they could debate their ideas and make them known. Plato immortalized several of them by naming some of his dialogues after them—for example, the *Protagoras* and *Gorgias* named for Protagoras of Abdera and Gorgias of Leontini—but this does not imply his approval, usually the opposite! But the dialogues provide settings for debates that probably occurred between them and Sokrates, which Plato develops further with his own ideas.

The Sophists (after the Greek *sophistes*, or teacher) were a loose collection of intellectuals and thinkers who provoked and led discussions in the new ways of thinking that were becoming popular in the fifth-century Greek world. This new thought itself was something that followed from the Greek exploration of the world and the resulting explosion of learning that came with finding new lands and peoples and different ways of doing things. The Sophists advertised their ideas and techniques, which ranged from new approaches to understanding cultural values to teaching the new rhetoric originating in Greek Sicily, and offered to teach them to others but for a price. In doing so they broke with the traditional manner of learning in the Greek world, which had taken place in the home and in the institutions of the *polis*. Such a change was perhaps bound to create conflict as the old ways were challenged by the new. Add to this the stress and strain of war, and what you have are all the ingredients for the brilliant comedy, and intellectual satire, of Aristophanes.

Aristophanes, the Sophists, and Sokrates

While appreciated and admired on the one hand, some teachers also provide their students with a certain amount of amusement with their sometimes eccentric ideas and ways, their sometimes strange manners and dress. That this was true in Athens during Aristophanes' time is borne out by his bitterly funny comedy *Clouds*, which he staged in spring 423 at the festival of Dionysos (see Document 17). In *Clouds* Aristophanes tells the story of Strepsiades, an Athenian farmer, whose son Pheidippides pushes him deeper into debt in pursuit of expensive aristocratic activities. In order to cheat his creditors, Strepsiades decides to enroll his son in Sokrates' school. After a false start, Pheidippides finally learns what Sokrates has to teach, but Strepsiades finds it was not what he had in mind. Pheidippides rips the old-fashioned poetry of Aeschylus in praise of Euripides, and then beats his father and threatens his mother! Strepsiades now realizes his error and returns to Sokrates' school, which he burns down, driving Sokrates away.

Aristophanes' portrait of Sokrates is hardly flattering, but then the portrait is intended to ridicule him and all the other Sophists whom Aristophanes sees as just like him. Sokrates splits hairs in argument, appears

lost in thought and out of touch with the realities of life, and indulges
in stargazing. (Aristophanes at one point has Sokrates hanging in a bas-
ket over the stage so he can think better!) These were typical Sophist
ways in Aristophanes' view. Aristophanes also makes fun of Sokrates'
barefoot ways and simple dress, actual details that Plato confirms in the
Symposium as part of the lifestyle Sokrates adopted. It may well be that
in all this Aristophanes simply finds in Sokrates the best known example of a Sophist, which suits his comic purposes perfectly. Yet there is a
serious edge to this drama found in the critique of rhetoric and moral
values, something that Aristophanes clearly sees in the Sophists—with
Sokrates as the best example of these—as a threat to the old Athenian
values and ways.

Strepsiades had sent Pheidippides to learn the new rhetoric that some
of the Sophists but not Sokrates were teaching in Athens. Public speaking played an important role in the Athenian democracy, influencing and
shaping opinion, and several of the Sophists, especially Protagoras and
Gorgias, advertised that they could teach how to argue both sides of a
question with equal success. Such rhetorical techniques were seen as useful in a political career, and young Athenians and would-be politicians
were eager to acquire such learning. Aristophanes, however, saw this as
so much hot air, as seen in the gods he identifies as Sokrates'—Empti-
ness, Clouds, and Tongue. A debate that he stages between Superior
Logic and Inferior Logic, or Right and Wrong as they are sometimes
translated, drives this point home emphatically. In their debate, Superior
Logic or Right praises the culture and morality of earlier Athenian generations, those who had beaten the Persians at Marathon, for example.
Inferior Logic or Wrong traps Superior Logic in a cross-examination of
these, paints a lively picture of the pleasures, success, and security of the
young who will follow his ways, and so defeats Superior Logic. Aristophanes' point could not be clearer—the old ways of Athens are being destroyed by the new intellectual ways brought by the Sophists, which as
we have seen, include Sokrates in their ranks.

Aristophanes finds other ways to drive home his view that the Sophists
and Sokrates are undermining Athens' moral values. When Pheidippides
returns from his "education" with Sokrates, he ridicules the poetry of Si-
monides and Aeschylus—literature his father viewed as positive and
moralistic—as not only old-fashioned but the sort of stuff the simple-
minded enjoy. When Strepsiades protests this and his son's praise for Eu-

ripides, Pheidippides responds by beating his father and threatening to beat his mother too. The average Athenian would have viewed such actions with horror, and it is clear that Aristophanes links such behavior with the new values and literature of writers like Euripides who draw their ideas from thinkers like the Sophists and Sokrates.

Aristophanes' critique of the intellectual scene in Athens during the Peloponnesian War shows that he regarded Sokrates as a model Sophist, though this seems unfair as Sokrates did not accept money as did the Sophists. But in other ways Sokrates did sophistic-like things, for example, debating issues (what seemed like splitting hairs to most), challenging the traditional way of doing things. As far as the average Athenian could see, Sokrates was little different from the likes of Protagoras and Gorgias. His eccentricities and his disregard for what most Athenians would have regarded as "normal" would later get him into trouble when the crisis of wartime conditions took their course and threatened the democratic structures of Athenian society.

THE POLITICS OF WAR

Thucydides saw war as a violent teacher, as his *History* clearly relates: the breakdown of social mores in plague-ravaged Athens, the destruction of little Melos whose population is destroyed by the Athenian commander, Philokrates Demeas, "Lover of power, son of the people." As the stress and strain of war continued, Athenian elites found themselves pressed financially as they bore responsibility for providing the military resources of Athens, both in subsidizing the great fleet that went to sea annually (literally hundreds of ships) and a wartime tax, the *eisphora*, which fell on them as well. Numbers of elite Athenians then saw their wealth disappearing along with their political influence. Increasingly, these elites saw their voice in public debate drowned out by the "average" Athenians who had been empowered by a series of reforms reaching back decades. That these conditions and attitudes existed and rankled wealthy Athenians is confirmed by a political tract attributed to an author called simply the "Old Oligarch." Young oligarchs, however, embittered at the loss of authority and wealth, moved to challenge the democracy and briefly overthrew it in 411/10. Their attempts to change the political structures collapsed when the Spartans defeated a naval force of theirs and prominent members, especially Theramenes, broke ranks. This enabled the democratic opposition to overthrow the radical oligarchic faction and reestablish the democracy. With the Spartan victory five years later, radical oligarchs, now organized as the Thirty Tyrants, returned to Athens with a vengeance, carrying out a reign of terror that left hundreds dead and the community in turmoil. Though not party to any of these activities, a number of Athenians saw Sokrates as a sort of political guru to these reactionaries.

Sokrates, Politics, and Philosophy

In part, this was clearly the result of association. Sokrates knew Alkibiades (who had encouraged the oligarchs to act in 411/10) as well as Kritias and Kharmides among the Thirty. But he was also a critic of the democracy; for example, he challenged the idea that anyone could offer an opinion in the assembly, when in fact if someone wanted something done, an expert would be consulted. In the *Protagoras* (319B), for example, Sokrates said that if the assembly wanted an expert opinion on shipbuilding, they would bring in a shipwright. But in the conduct of public affairs the Athenians generally believed that one man's view was as good as another's, which Sokrates saw as wrong. This contradicted prevailing Athenian opinion. Sokrates' popularity would not have been enhanced by such views or by his assessment of the Athenian assembly as consisting of "a group of dunces and weaklings, fullers, cobblers, joiners, smiths, farmers, merchants, traffickers in the market whose minds are on buying cheap and selling dear . . . men who have never given a thought to public affairs."[5] That Sokrates made no secret of his views seems confirmed not only by Aristophanes but also by Euripides. In his play the *Suppliants*, a herald sent by the tyrant Kreon states that "a poor laborer even though he is no fool, is by his work made incapable of giving heed to the common good" (line 420). Cambridge scholar W.K.C. Guthrie sees this as "pure Socratic doctrine [put] into the mouth of a tyrant's lackey, to be refuted by Theseos as the champion of popular power."[6]

Sokrates' intent, to argue that which seems self-evident, seems to be critical: that the use of a lottery to appoint officials was not the best way to do things, or that the popular election of the key office of general (*strategos*) seemed equally foolish. In Sokrates' view, if you were sick you went to a doctor because he had training in what he did; if you wanted to train a horse, you would seek an expert in such matters for advice.

Sokrates thought and argued that it should be the same way for "government" (the Greeks did not have such a word, but for sake of discussion it will be used here). Politics, he maintained, was like any other craft in that it required natural gifts—the ability to stand up before a crowd and speak to them comfortably, for example (something not everyone can do), and study and application of the skills and knowledge that go into political life.[7]

Many of Sokrates' fellow Athenians probably thought that he had aristocrats in mind for the role of political leadership and decision making, but this does not appear to be the case. In his work *Memorabilia*, Xenophon reproduces a conversation between Sokrates and Glaukon, Plato's half-brother, in which Sokrates demolishes Glaukon's political ambitions by asking him a few questions. Glaukon's ignorance of such things as the nature of the city's finances, its spending and income, military strength, and so on reveals that his ambitions lack a basis in knowledge and skills.[8] How can someone so ill equipped expect to take up a political career?

Sokrates' criticisms of Glaukon's ignorance as well as that of the crowd of Athenians suggests that he had no "class" bias in his observations and criticisms of either. He probably believed that the average citizen, pressed down by the necessity to make a living, would not be able to find the time to acquire the necessary political skills and knowledge that someone of Glaukon's status (or Alkibiades, Kritias, and Kharmides for that matter) could. Some might find in that opinion contempt for the average citizen, but it might also be a simple recognition of realities.[9] It is clear, however, that at least one of Sokrates' accusers at his trial believed him to be an "enemy" of the people, and no doubt a number of Athenians felt this way about him. But his rebuke to Glaukon argues that such a view was an unjust and false perception of his ideas.

In his defense, Sokrates spoke to the laws of the city and how these were binding on the members of the community. No one could pick and choose which of the laws he approved of and would follow, and which he would ignore as unjust or wrong. Such conduct would undermine the city altogether. As far as Sokrates could see, "the choice before the individual was either to obey the laws, or to get them changed by peaceful persuasion, or else to emigrate."[10] Guthrie, who follows Plato here, attributes this to Sokrates' sense of justice and doing the right thing, an attitude of personal conduct that appears repeatedly in his life. But what explains this tenacious will not just to do the right thing but to do it with such discipline that he would die for it?

Part of the answer may lie in Sokrates' military service. Sokrates' courageous conduct in several key battles in the early phase of the Peloponnesian War has been already noted, but the implications of this conduct have not been fully explored. This service would have begun around 450, which would have exposed him to some of the struggles in the so-called First Peloponnesian War that ended with the 30 Years Peace of 446/5. Altogether then Sokrates spent many years as a soldier, standing in the ranks of the hoplite phalanx where discipline and keeping one's place was not simply important but literally a matter of life and death, as each man depended on those around him for defense, as he defended them. Were the ranks of the phalanx to break and the formation as a whole to lose its cohesion, then the whole formation would simply disintegrate, exposing every man not only to attack but to slaughter. Soldiers like Sokrates knew that discipline and obedience to the "law of the phalanx" was of utmost importance. This may also explain why he refused to abandon his post in the jail where he awaited death when he could have easily fled Athens after his condemnation. Such flight was not only cowardly, it was not the way of an Athenian citizen soldier, something contemporary accounts suggest he valued highly.

While all soldiers knew this, not all could keep their place in the line like Sokrates. His adherence to doing the right thing, while influenced by military discipline, must also have been the result of his own intellectual convictions. These he seemingly formed in the midst of the Peloponnesian War when so many Athenians clearly lost their moral compasses, as Thucydides tells in the aftermath of the plague (2.53).

Sokrates' Trial as Intellectual and Political Conflict

The reign of terror conducted by the Thirty Tyrants was a painful memory for the Athenians and also an embarrassment, particularly for those members of the community who either passively or actively supported the acts of the oligarchs. An amnesty that accompanied the restoration of the democracy in 403 provided blanket protection to any who might have supported the Thirty, who themselves and a few others remained liable for prosecution for their crimes. When Sokrates' accusers, Anytos, Meletos and Polykrates, then moved against him, they could not legally charge him for anything he might have done at this time (e.g., his brief involvement in the arrest of Leon of Salamis) or his associations with Kritias and Kharmides. Other charges, however, could be made up that would accomplish the same thing. What the prosecutors came up with then were the charges of "worshiping strange gods" and "corrupting the youth."

The first of these charges reflects the intellectual debate in Athens like that mirrored in Aristophanes' *Clouds*. Here Aristophanes claims that Sokrates rejected the commonplace view that Zeus, father of all the gods, either existed or brought rain (line 367); Plato's *Apology* (31C-D) ascribes to Sokrates belief in a personal *daimonion*, or personal sign or spiritual god, something that Sokrates' prosecutor Meletos misrepresented as "worshiping strange gods" in the charges brought against him. These charges reflect an underlying animosity (perhaps even hostility) of the Athenians toward "intellectuals," or those who simply thought differently than the rest of the community. Years before, Perikles' friend and teacher Anaxagoras of Clazomenai, had been prosecuted for impiety and forced to leave Athens. Politics may also have colored this prosecution as Anaxagoras was attacked in order to embarrass Perikles.[11] In addition to Anaxagoras, the philosophers Protagoras and Diagoras suffered similar attacks, which suggest that the ideas Aristophanes and Meletos ascribe to Sokrates would have opened him to attack as well.

"Worshiping strange gods" would have given Sokrates problems enough, but the added charge of "corrupting the youth" was more damaging still. Xenophon makes clear that Socrates' accusers argued to the jury hearing the charges against him that Sokrates had incited young men to despise the established political order and turned them into violent revolutionaries.[12] In the defense that Plato (see Document 18) gives to Sokrates, he rejected this accusation categorically (*Apology* 33A). He argued that he had never gone along with any action that was contrary to the law on the part of anyone, including those that were widely believed to be his "students." In making this statement, Sokrates notes that he had never set himself up as a teacher, never taken money, and was willing to talk to anyone who would listen to him. How then can he be responsible for what others do (*Apology* 33A)? In his defense, Sokrates also refers to the efforts of the Thirty to implicate him in their activities by ordering him to arrest Leon of Salamis. Sokrates states clearly that he refused their order, not only because he saw it as wicked, but also because he would not do anything wrong or bad (*Apology* 32D). This is a point that he returned to in the sentencing part of his speech after he had been condemned, where he repeats his assertion that he had never wronged anyone intentionally (*Apology* 37A). After listening to his defense, the jurors voted; just over half, 280 of 501 jurors, found him guilty. In the penalty phase of the trial, Sokrates argued that he had done nothing but good for the community, so he thought that free food at city hall for life was an appropriate penalty. This approach antagonized the jurors, for another eighty then voted the death penalty. In both cases, it is clear that a substantial number of Athenians found that Sokrates had done nothing especially wrong or outrageous.

Sokrates of Athens, Martyr

The impact of Sokrates on later generations is immense. He was a soldier of Athens whose discipline and devotion to duty, along with the horrific experiences of the Peloponnesian War, led him to see a different standard of personal conduct—that one must always do right whatever pressures were brought to bear. It is difficult to know what constitutes "Sokratic" thought, for Sokrates did not write and his ideas come down to us through the medium of his student Plato. But it is clear that moral conduct was of great importance to him as he argued that the Athenians should look inward and care for their souls. Such an admonition was clearly in keeping with the violence of the war, which provides the background to Sokrates and his thought. In the same vein, his statement that he would rather suffer the wrong than commit it seemingly reflects, too, the experience with violence and the reaction of one who had seen too much suffering. It would be Plato's accomplishment to elaborate these and other of Sokrates' teachings and ideas and in doing so establish the idea of philosophy in the Western world that remains part of our lives today.

NOTES

1. Xenophon, *Hellenica* 1.7.14–15.
2. Plato, *Apology* 29D.
3. Thucydides, 2.52–53.

4. W.K.C. Guthrie, *Socrates* (Cambridge: Cambridge University Press, 1971), pp. 97–99.

5. Xenophon, *Memorabilia* 3.7.6.

6. Guthrie, *Socrates*, p. 89.

7. Ibid., p. 90.

8. Xenophon, *Memorabilia* 3.6.

9. Guthrie, *Socrates*, p. 91, sees Sokrates' attitude as one of contempt, and many others would too.

10. Guthrie, ibid., p. 92, citing Plato's *Crito*.

11. R. Meiggs, *The Athenian Empire* (Oxford: Clarendon Press, 1972), pp. 304, 435–36.

12. Xenophon, *Memorabilia* 1.2.9.

CHAPTER 6

WOMEN AND WAR

War has always been hard on women. They are married to the husbands, and bear the sons, who die, and when a city falls, their fates are such that the living truly envy the dead. In the Greek world, this was well known from Homeric times. The Peloponnesian War experience was no different. Dramatists such as Euripides told of the suffering of women in plays like *Andromache, Hecuba,* and *Trojan Women,* and what was told was not only brutal but real. When Plataia fell in 427 to the Thebans and Spartans, some one hundred women who had remained to cook for the garrison were enslaved (Thucydides 3.68.2). The same fate befell the women of Melos when that city surrendered to the Athenians in 416. Older women would live out their lives as servants and cooks, while younger women would become the concubines, literally the sex slaves, of men like Alkibiades, who bought a young Melian woman who bore him a son and lived with him in Athens (Plutarch, *Life of Alcibiades* 16.5). While her name is unrecorded, it could have been Andromakhe.

None of the Plataian or Melian women are known individually, and only a few such as Aspasia, Perikles' lover, emerges from the sources in her own light. We learn the reasons for this anonymity, especially in Athens but for the Greeks generally, from Perikles himself. In the winter of 431/0, the Athenians conducted the first of what would be many funeral rituals conducted for the war dead. As the city's leader and most talented orator, Perikles was chosen to deliver a speech to commemorate the dead and encourage the living. As he drew near the end of his speech, Perikles turned his attention to the widows now mourning their lost husbands and told them that their virtue would be known by the degree to which their reputations were known, whether for good or bad.[1] Women then are a "muted group," as historian Sarah Pomeroy termed them, but yet a group whose influence in society is often underestimated.[2]

Perikles' brief comment speaks volumes for the problem of studying Greek women in classical antiquity. As he makes clear, the best thing that could be said of a woman was that she was not even known, and the surviving sources bear this out. Seldom are the names of women given. Revealing their roles in war, or what they might have thought about the events that drew the attention of their fathers, husbands, and sons, is an investigation handicapped from the outset.

Yet women living through the terrible years of the Peloponnesian War are known, as are their thoughts and fears of the events around them. The picture that emerges, however, is one slightly out of focus, the result of male-dominated sources, which give us their view on what they imagine women thought and the issues that concerned them. Much of this source material, such as the plays of Aristophanes, particularly his *Lysistrata* and *Thesmophoriazousae* (or "Ladies' Day"), is overlaid with male fantasy, comedy, and satire and so must be doubly considered in order to arrive at a reliable portrait of women in war. Plutarch provides information from non-Athenian traditions, especially that which sheds light on the women of Sparta and their roles in the military state in which they lived. Finally, additional useful information comes from surviving art and artifacts—particularly funeral reliefs of women and their depiction on *lekythoi*, the vases left as offerings to the dead. These are silent, however, and must be prodded to reveal their secrets. It is to this body of information that we now turn.

ARISTOPHANES AND WOMEN IN WAR

One of the best-known comedies from the ancient Greek world, one that even figured in the worldwide effort to avert war with Iraq in the spring of 2003, was Aristophanes' *Lysistrata*. Produced in the spring of 411 at the Athenian spring festival of the Lenaia, *Lysistrata* is regarded by many, including classical scholars, to be Aristophanes' third "peace" play, the first two being *Acharnians* and *Peace*, produced in 425 and 421, respectively. The action in this play is dominated by women—in fact, the women of all Greece who have come together to demand that their men end the war and establish peace. To accomplish their goal, the women unite and swear to abstain from sex with their husbands until they agree to stop the violence and bring about what they desire, namely peace. This comic vehicle creates some hilarious scenes that were surely as amusing to Aristophanes' audience as to modern readers and viewers of the play. But what does the play say about women and war?

Women Dissolve the Armies of Greece

Lysistrata's name means "Dissolving armies," and the contemporary priestess of Athena Polias, Lysimakhe ("Dissolving battles"), may have inspired Aristophanes in the choice of his heroine's name. More than simple wordplay may be at work here. The cult of Athena Polias was an ancient one, and its priestess always came from an equally ancient family, the Eteobutadai, who claimed to be present at the beginnings of Athenian history.[3] Moreover, the priestess of Athena Polias performed important ritual functions in Athens, particularly the Panathenaic festival, the rituals of which were depicted on the Parthenon frieze. The real-life Lysimakhe, then, not only occupied a high-profile position in Athenian society, but also one in which she performed ancient rituals that she surely helped organize. So when the Athenian audience saw Lysistrata appear on stage, they would have seen not only a fictional equivalent of a real-life person, but also one who was an organizer of the most important ritual celebrated in Athens. Organizing a sex strike to end the war was only a little more complicated than organizing the great celebration in honor of Athena.

These organizational talents first appear as the different women from around Greece come to Athens in response to the summons sent out by Lysistrata. This, too, would have supplied great comic relief to the audience, especially when the Spartan representative Lampito ("Shining one") walked on to the stage. Lampito is tanned and muscular, so much so that even Lysistrata comments that she could strangle a bull! Spartan women, the rest of the Greeks knew, spent a good deal of time outdoors exercising nude and competing in various athletic contests, activities unknown to the rest of the women of Greece. He adds additional appropriate comments on the Boiotian and Corinthian women who have accompanied Lampito. The Boiotian and Corinthian women are unnamed and only referred to by the stage characters, but they accompany

Lampito as real-life Spartan armies were accompanied in military campaigns by their Boiotian and Corinthian allies.

Under Lysistrata's leadership (another source of humor as it shows her acting assertively like Athenian men, convinced they have a right to lead any group), the united women of Greece seize the Athenian acropolis, which leads to a confrontation between Lysistrata and authorities (see Document 19). A commissioner sent to find out what the women are doing there (which suggests it was normally a place they only frequented at festival times) is aghast at learning they intend to stop the war by blocking access to the money that fuels it. Lysistrata and the commissioner debate the issue of money, budgets, and war, which enables Lysistrata to make the point that women know something about all this as they control their household budgets. She refers to women's long suffering at the foolish decisions made by their husbands in assembly, noting that if a wife said something, she would likely hear the words of Homer's Hektor to his wife Andromakhe, "War's a man's affair!" accompanied with a threat of a beating.[4]

Lysistrata then asserts that war could be a "woman's affair" too, and proceeds to debate the issue with the commissioner (*Lysistrata* lines 506–614). Jokes about arrogant generals parading around, handsome young cavalrymen, and wild Thracian mercenaries terrifying civilians provide humorous distraction, but then Lysistrata gets serious (lines 557–64). She tells the commissioner that her plan to end the war is no more complicated than weaving, a household occupation of Greek women as old as Homer's Penelope. That Lysistrata could reduce the complexities of war and planning for war to the simple chore of weaving amazes the commissioner, who tells Lysistrata to explain (lines 564–65). She first explains that the yarn or wool has to be washed to get the dirt out. So too in Athens, she explains, the plague of corrupt officials must be purged, and then those Athenians living in distant colonies should be brought home and made part of the whole (lines 567–86). The commissioner reacts to this foolish plan with the remark that only a woman could reduce war and military planning to something as simple as weaving (lines 587–88). Lysistrata responds harshly, reminding him that the women of Greece were also the mothers of those young men who sailed off to war, many never to return home (lines 588–89). This muted reminder of the losses of the Sicilian Expedition silences the commissioner, who begs Lysistrata not to mention the matter further (lines 589–90).

The commissioner's appeal to Lysistrata to silence these painful memories conforms with other evidence on the Athenian reaction to the Sicilian disaster. One of these sources, from the late author Athenaios, tells that a report of the disaster arrived in Athens the day the comic poet Hegemon was staging his play, *The Battle of the Giants*. The audience found the play so entertaining, the story goes, that no one left the theater to mourn, even though nearly all had lost relatives.[5] Athenaios' story only makes sense if the Athenians ought to have left the theater and gone home to conduct proper observances for the dead. Of course, this was impossible as the men lost died in far away Sicily, which meant that there would be no bodies to wash and attend to, a departure from the usual pattern of grieving.[6]

The importance of Athenaios' report and the deviation from the rituals of mourning rituals has been little discussed by those who have noted this passage.[7] The Greeks followed fixed and clear rituals of mourning, and the suggestion in Athenaios that these were not followed argues that the reports of the disaster in Sicily not only stunned the Athenians into disbelief, but left them so emotionally drained that proper rituals could not be observed. Coming after so many other losses, the commissioner's breakdown on hearing Lysistrata merely alluding to the Sicilian disaster suggests that the Athenians as a whole were suffering from a kind of psychic numbing.

Lysistrata concludes her argument for the authority of women to pronounce on war and its effects by noting that the time lost when men are away fighting is hardest on women. Not only do they suffer in the absence of their husbands, but they also grow older and grayer and so less attractive with each passing day. The commissioner attempts to argue back that men age too, but Lysistrata will not hear it. She tells him that even an old man bald and toothless can find a pretty young girl easily, while the women left home become old with the first gray hair (lines 591–97). Aristophanes' comments are timeless and have been the reactions of many women enduring other wars and long periods of separation.

In the scenes that follow this sequence, Aristophanes creates the vividly (and wildly) funny situations for which this play is famous: the returning Athenian soldier Kinesias Paionides (whose names are actually slang words for sexual intercourse) attempts to bed his wife Myrrhine, who frustrates his every move; the arrival in Athens of the Spartans who have been similarly put off by their women and who conceal their enormous erections under their famous purple cloaks. In the end, Lysistrata and her allies force a settlement on their men, and in doing so Aristophanes makes the point that while the Greeks have been so busy fighting each other they have scarcely noticed that the Persians—the ancient enemy—have been watching and waiting to take advantage of the warring Greeks (lines 1133–35). The drama ends amid great celebration and Spartans dancing before the temple of Athena of the Bronze House, the cult temple at Sparta. Aristophanes' point could not appear clearer—Athenians and Spartans are one and should stand against the barbarian menace.

Lysistrata, a Peace Play?

As noted earlier, Lysistrata is possibly the best known of any Greek drama, comedy, or tragedy. But is it a drama that takes peace as its theme? British scholar K. J. Dover argues that "as in the case of Acharnians and Peace, reservations and complications beset any statement to the effect that Lysistrata positively advocates peace by showing us war through women's eyes."[8] More recently, another British scholar, D. M. MacDowell, has argued the opposite, claiming that "the main theme of the play, then, is not women, and not citizenship. It is peace—once again."[9] MacDowell adds that most critics take Lysistrata (the character) seriously, and this judgment seems right. But does this play speak to the subject of women and war as Dover denies?

Aristophanes builds into Lysistrata all kinds of jokes and situations to entertain and make the audience laugh; he is, after all, writing comedy and hoping to win the prize. So there are jokes about how women love to drink and how sex-crazed they are, views that the men in the audience pretty much shared. Early in the play, for example, Lysistrata raises the idea of a sex strike to stop the war, and one of her Athenian friends responds, "I couldn't. No. Let the war go on," a sentiment echoed quickly by another (Lysistrata lines 129–30). Lampito's support for Lysistrata's plan, however, overcomes initial resistance, and Lysistrata leads the women on.

In doing all this, however, Aristophanes also mentions the long absences of the men off fighting in various places and throws in jokes about how women responded to this with sex toys and drink (lines 102–10). It should not be thought that masturbation is a modern invention, and in fact scenes on Greek pottery earlier in the fifth century depict women using the dildoes that Aristophanes jokes about. But the women shown on pottery are prostitutes, not citizen wives, and so the Aristophanic humor appears again to reflect male fantasies and ideas. While the use of sex toys cannot be entirely discounted, most Greek women endured the long periods of separation doing whatever they could to pass the time. Unknowingly, Hektor summed it up best when he said that war was man's affair. Mesmerized by the glory, he overlooked the fact that war was woman's affair too, and countless other men have made the same mistake too. But Aristophanes was not one of them.

There is more than enough serious matter in this play to support the view that *Lysistrata* is a "peace" play and that Aristophanes realizes and conveys in the play the hardships of war that women endure. This is seen most clearly in those passages discussed above when Lysistrata and the commissioner are arguing back and forth: clearly she is the level-headed one who makes sense, while the commissioner is full of male arrogance and bluster. What Lysistrata says about cleaning house on corruption— that women knew too well the sorrow of war—were all sentiments that would have struck a resonant chord in the more thinking members of the audience, which was as much Aristophanes' goal as to make them (and the dullards in the audience) laugh. Aristophanes surely knew the difficulties of making peace with the Spartans but saw that however hard that might be, it was not only important in itself but necessary in order to defend Greece as a whole against the growing menace of Persia, waiting in the wings to move against Greek states weakened by unending war.[10]

Ladies' Day: Aristophanes, Euripides, and Women

Aristophanes' drama *Thesmophoriazousae* does not have quite the same political punch of *Lysistrata*. It is rich in detail, however, about the lives of women and what Aristophanes (among others) imagined as Euripidean bias, even hate, toward women. The play takes its name from a women's festival, the Thesmophoria, an annual celebration of Demeter and her daughter Persephone in thanks for the laws they gave to humankind.[11] It is not clear where this celebration was held (possibly in Athens or in Eleusis, the cult home of Demeter and where her ceremonies, the Mysteries, were observed), but the rituals observed were off-limits to men. Aristophanes used both elements for comic effect. The opening of the play mimics that of the Athenian assembly (of men), right down to such formulaic elements as the opening prayers and the herald's call, "Who wishes to speak?" that initiated business. Part of the play's humor also comes from the character, a male relative of Euripides, who attempts to sneak into the rituals to gather intelligence on the doings of women for Euripides. As might be imagined, this creates a number of humorous scenes.

Although *Thesmophoriazousae* is rich in detail for reconstructing the lives of Athenian women and in Euripidean literary criticism, it does comment on the contemporary political situation. This comes up primarily in a choral song in which the women respond to typical male criticisms of the day: if women are a plague, why do men seek wives? Why do men rave if their wives are not at home when they return there? More importantly, Aristophanes concludes that women are best because they do not steal from the state—like so many politicians—and they run their homes efficiently, a restatement of a similar assessment found in *Lysistrata*.

Women of Sparta

Lampito's entrance onto the stage in *Lysistrata* must have delighted the largely male audience in attendance, both with the caricature of Spartan women that Aristophanes created and also with more than a bit of male voyeurism. Spartan women were known for their nude athletic practices and scanty dress, practices foreign to the rest of the women of Greece.[12] They were also part of a military society as even their names reveal: Megalostrata ("Great army"), Agido ("Leader"), and Klesimbrota ("Renown to man"). But Spartan women, particularly Spartan mothers, appear to have also played a key role in promoting the values of that society through their sons.

A series of "sayings" of both Spartan men and women were preserved in antiquity by the Greek writer Plutarch. Those sayings of the men, mostly kings and famous generals, refer to battles and military situations, as do those of the women but with the added twist that sons and mothers are the focus. These sayings reveal first what was widely perceived and believed of the Spartans by other Greeks, both in the classical era and

later. The origins of these remarks are obscure and not helped by the fact
that the Spartans did not write things down. But memory was stronger
in the ancient world than in the modern, and people could remember
better what was said and pass it on (this is what scholars refer to as "oral
tradition"). Already in the fourth century knowledge of these "laconic"
sayings was emerging, as Aristotle refers to them in his study of oratory,
Rhetoric. This suggests that they came to the attention of others (for instance, the Athenian writer Xenophon who lived in Sparta) who could
have easily written them down. The sayings that Aristotle and others
heard grew with invention as time passed, and the Greeks looked back
on the classical era as one of freedom and heroism compared with life
under Roman rule.[13] Though of uncertain maternity then, the sayings of
Spartan women remain of value for what they reveal of women's contri-
butions to war.

The first contribution that Spartan women made was in giving birth
to men. Gorgo, the daughter and wife of kings (Kleomenes and Leonidas,
respectively), was asked once by an Athenian woman, "Why are you
Spartan women the only ones who can rule men?" Gorgo responded, "because we are the only ones who give birth to men."[14] This reveals at once
the influence of Spartan women over men, an influence that came in part
from their wealth. Unlike most Greek women, Spartan women could own
property and later in the classical period they would own such extensive
tracts of land that Aristotle concluded that Sparta was female dominated.[15] But as the Athenian woman's question reveals, there was also a
perception among Greeks outside Sparta that the women possessed an
unusual authority.

This authority extended to war. The Spartan mother giving her son
his shield and saying "With this or on this" has passed proverbially from
antiquity to the modern world, but the sentiment has many parallels. One
Spartan mother, on hearing that her sons had fled from battle, reproached
them with the taunt, " 'In making your escape, vile slaves, where is it
you've come to? Or do you plan to creep back in here where you emerged
from?' At this she pulled up her clothes and exposed her belly to them."[16]
This accusation of cowardice and suggestion that her sons wanted to
crawl back into their mother's womb has its modern-day counterparts.
Historian Sarah Pomeroy relates cases from the American South during
the Civil War when women left bonnets and hoopskirts at the homes of

young men who had not volunteered for military service. Another woman wrote her local Virginia newspaper telling how she had but one young son of seventeen to offer up to the cause, but thanked God she had a son to do so.[17] This latter sentiment has its counterpart in the response of a Spartan describing his brother's death to their mother. She replied, "Isn't it a disgrace, then, not to have gone on such a fine journey with him?"[18]

Spartan women, from the fictitious Lampito of Aristophanes' *Lysistrata* to the anonymous mothers of Plutarch, were strong, both physically and morally. Their strength emerged from social values that gave them freedoms unknown to most Greek women, and these they asserted by enforcing an equally strong code of courage among their sons.

PORTRAITURE IN DEATH: THE ATHENIAN MODEL

Spartan women left their memorials to themselves and to war in their admonitions and words to their sons. In Sparta, only women who had died in childbirth (and men who had died in war) could have any kind of (semi-)permanent memorial erected to their memory, and this conforms to the societal value that placed the group first. But in Athens, where a somewhat different set of values and attitudes reigned and where displays of wealth came to be accepted as normal, individual monuments to the departed became commonplace by the mid–fifth century. Not only that, but into the latter part of the century and into the fourth, women dominate the classical Athenian tombstone.[19]

This may seem surprising in view of the male-oriented society that was ancient Athens. The explanation, however, is to be found in politics. In 451/0, Perikles had carried a new law that based Athenian citizenship on descent from an Athenian father *and* mother. Previously, Athenian men had sometimes married outside Attica, and even some famous Athenians were the product of these unions; men like Themistokles, the hero of the Persian Wars, and Thucydides the historian were descended from families whose women came from outside Athens. With Perikles' new law, such unions would cease, and whereas before one's choice in a wife was personal, it now became political. This brought women out of the private sphere and into the public. As British scholar Robin Osborne concludes, the increased appearance of sculpted reliefs shows that "women matter."[20]

Two Women: Hegeso and Ampharete

In the Athenian cemetery of the Kerameikos today are to be found grave monuments of two women, Hegeso and Ampharete, who died during the Peloponnesian War. That of Hegeso depicts her with her maid who holds her jewelry box out to her so that she may inspect its contents. As Robin Osborne notes, Hegeso's stylish chair and the maid overlap the frame of the *stele* so that both figures seem to step forward from a doorway toward the viewer. Above the scene only her name is given along with that of her husband (Proxenos). This seems to conform with the idea noted at the start of this chapter—Perikles' observation that the less said of a woman the better. The scene depicting Hegeso is reserved and undemonstrative. Although this may seem to reflect women's lack of political status and active role in the community apart from being a good wife and mother, the depiction may also point to the esteem in which women are held, that again women are important.

Of interest too is the style in which Hegeso is carved. The character conveyed by the relief sculpture is reserved and modest, not that of a sensuous Nike whose flowing clothes hang seductively over the body for the viewer to gaze upon. Hegeso, as Osborne notes, appears to have stepped right off the Parthenon frieze.[21]

The grave monument of Ampharete is presented in very much the same way as Hegeso's. Her chair, right arm (in which she holds a bird, an offering to the dead), and left foot are outside and on the frame of the *stele* on which she is depicted, as she gazes down on her infant granddaughter also dead. Ampharete appears younger than a grandmother, and it has been suggested that this monument was adapted for this joint memorial.[22] The scene is a somber one, made even more so by a relatively long inscription that tells the story: "My daughter's beloved child is the one I hold here, the one whom I held on my lap while we looked at the light of the sun when we were alive and still hold now that we are both dead."

The grave monuments of Hegeso and Ampharete, carved with respect and even love perhaps, suggest that the flourishing of Athenian democracy amid the circumstances of the war in the late fifth century has indeed been accompanied by a greater respect and esteem of the status of women. While a hundred years before, marriage had been a private matter, it was now of vital importance to the state at large. The importance

Grave stele of Ampharete and her granddaughter. Athens, c. 410. Kerameikos Museum, Athens, Greece. *Source: L. Tritle.*

of this also sheds some light on the issues of sex, marriage, and war comically addressed by Aristophanes in *Lysistrata*.

Women in White: Faces from Athenian Lekythoi

The grave monuments dedicated to the elite women of Athens reflected societal views and even laws defining the status of women in the state. But in private or family graveside gifts to the dead, opportunities were presented in which more personal feelings might be expressed. Such expressions are to be found on the *lekythoi*, the oil flasks used to make offerings to the dead at their tombs (see also Chapter 4). These date from the sixth century, but beginning after about 460, a new style, using a white background, begins to appear in Athens. The older black-figure *lekythos* had favored scenes from mythology—adventures, satyrs, and other wild figures—but the new style is intensely personal. It shows departing warriors, ladies and their maids, and visits to tombs. From these it is possible to visualize not only the pathos of death but also wartime emotions.

An example of this personal touch comes from the Achilles Painter (c. 450–425). In a well-known example, the artist shows a farewell scene in which a seated woman gazes upon her husband, who stands prepared for battle—holding helmet and shield—and about to depart for war—a scene universal and timeless. The young woman sits with one arm drawn over the chair as her right foot nestles that of her husband—an expression of affection without doubt. Presented in three-quarter view, the scenes on the *lekythos* allow the viewer to focus on one of those depicted. As they gaze upon one another, one can almost imagine that this might have been the last private moment they shared before death intervened, taking one, whether in battle or in illness, it was all the same. Interestingly, the shape of the *lekythos* provides a view of only one figure at a time, which makes the scene at once individualized and yet dependent for understanding on the unified relationship of man and wife. As Robin Osborne comments, the scene encourages empathy on the part of the viewer, but without identifying with either figure.[23]

WOMEN AND THE SORROW OF WAR

The Plataian women enslaved by their Theban neighbors, Lysistrata, Hegeso, and the anonymous "women in white" each reveal dimensions

Warrior taking leave of his wife. Attic white-ground *lekythos*, from Eretria, c. 425. Attributed to the Achilles Painter, Athens. National Archaeological Museum, Athens, Greece. *Source: Scala / Art Resource, New York.*

of the role and suffering of women in war. While often overlooked by historians and classicists, these are the women who bring to life the stories told of Andromakhe, Hekuba, Polyxena, and countless others.

NOTES

1. Thucydides 2.45.2.

2. Sarah Pomeroy, *Women in Hellenistic Egypt* (New York: Schocken, 1984), pp. 18–19. While speaking of a later place and era, Pomeroy's comment remains valuable in understanding women in classical Athens.

3. See H. W. Parke, *Festivals of the Athenians* (Ithaca, NY: Cornell University Press, 1977), p. 17.

4. Homer, *Iliad* 6.492.

5. Athenaios 9.406E–407B. See also A. Bowie, "Myth and Ritual in the Rivals of Aristophanes," in *The Rivals of Aristophanes*, ed. by D. Harvey and J. Wilkins (London and Swansea: Duckworth and the University Press of Wales, 2000), p. 333 n. 37.

6. For further discussion, see R. Garland, *The Greek Way of Death* (Ithaca, NY: Cornell University Press, 1985), p. 13, who notes that the Greeks saw death as a process "requiring strenuous action on the part of the survivors in order to be successfully terminated." For washing the dead, see pp. 24, 92.

7. E.g., D. Kagan, *The Fall of the Athenian Empire* (Ithaca, NY: Cornell University Press, 1987), p. 1.

8. K. J. Dover, *Aristophanic Comedy* (Berkeley: University of California Press, 1972), pp. 158–59.

9. D. M. McDowell, *Aristophanes and Athens: An Introduction to the Plays* (Oxford: Oxford University Press, 1995), p. 248.

10. A point not addressed by Dover, *Aristophanic Comedy*, pp. 150–61.

11. Noted by MacDowell, *Aristophanes and Athens*, p. 259.

12. Sarah Pomeroy, *Spartan Women* (Oxford: Oxford University Press, 2002), pp. 25–27.

13. Richard J. A. Talbert, in his edition of Plutarch, *On Sparta* (London: Penguin Books, 1988), pp. 106–8.

14. Gorgo, no. 5, in Talbert, ibid., p. 158.

15. Aristotle, *Politics* 1270A24, claimed two-fifths of the land was in the hands of women. See also Pomeroy, *Spartan Women*, pp. 77–82.

16. Unnamed Spartan women, no. 4, in Talbert, *On Sparta*, pp. 159–60.

17. Pomeroy, *Spartan Women*, p. 62, citing P. G. Faust, *Mothers of Invention* (Chapel Hill: University of North Carolina Press, 1996), pp. 14–17.

18. Unnamed Spartan women, no. 6, in Talbert, *On Sparta*, p. 160.

19. Osborne, *Archaic and Classical Greek Art*, p. 195.

20. Ibid., p. 199.

21. Ibid., pp. 196–97.

22. John Boardman, *Greek Sculpture: The Classical Period, a Handbook* (London: Thames & Hudson, 1985), plate 150.

23. Ibid., pp. 189–94.

CHAPTER 7

CONCLUSIONS

War is a violent teacher.

Thucydides

The modern world is a violent place. Since 1900, hardly a year has passed in which a war somewhere has not been known, while in today's American society, street violence and family violence are commonplaces of another kind. Contemporary society understands that those who experience the horrors of war, the violence of the street and family, will always be marked by what they see and the experiences they endure, though these may not always be readily apparent. Such experiences were not substantially different in the ancient Greek world. Cases of hysterical blindness occurred on the battlefields of both World Wars (and other places), but they are known, too, from ancient Greece, as are the shocks of horrific violence visited on communities like that suffered by Mykalessos by Athenian-paid Thrakian mercenaries in 413.[1]

Yet modern scholarship seems unwilling to recognize the impact of such events on the Greeks as they suffered through more than twenty years of violence during the Peloponnesian War. The most recent study of the war by Donald Kagan, a scholar who has written four volumes recounting the war's events, relates the Athenian-Thrakian slaughter at Mykalessos and repeats Thucydides' graphic description of the destruction of Nikias' army in Sicily, as well as the horrific bloodshed in Corcyra where fathers killed sons and sons fathers.[2] Beyond a statement of such violent happenings, however, no analysis of the impact of these events and the countless other examples that occurred during the war is made. Yet such an effort seems not only important but necessary for the events of the Peloponnesian War to be meaningful to us twenty-five hundred years after.

VIOLENCE—A UNIVERSAL EXPERIENCE

Such an assertion might seem to force upon the past a contemporary-oriented interpretation of events, a view British scholar F. M. Cornford once called the "Modernist Fallacy."[3] Modern scholars, Cornford thought, treated Greek authors and intellectuals as if they too were moderns and ignored the poetical and mythical worlds that shaped their work. But as Greek literature as early as Homer's *Iliad* shows, violence was a constant force in Greek culture. A recent study by Oxford scholar Terry Eagleton on the place of violence in literature observes that societies around the world and throughout time have the same concerns for the nature of the human experience. Eagleton refers to the Italian philosopher Sebastiano Timpanaro, "who points out that phenomena such as love, ageing, disease, fear of one's own death and sorrow for the death of others, the brevity and frailty of human existence, the contrast between the weakness of humanity and the apparent infinity of the cosmos: these are recurrent features of human cultures, however variously they may be represented."[4] Violence—whether in war or in such private acts as murder—is another dimension in the continuum of this human experience, and a reality all the more terrifying when it is remembered that, as Timpanaro (and others) have noted, "man as a biological being has remained essentially unchanged from the beginnings of civilization to the present."[5]

Thucydides' reference to the power of violence, cited at the beginning of this conclusion, calls attention to his awareness not only of its presence in his time, but also of its power. Others among his contemporaries, the poet Euripides and the Spartan king Archidamos to name but two, also recognized what war and violence could do. In closing this study of the Peloponnesian War, we will review how the Greeks might have seen war and violence converging before them.

THE GREEKS AND THE VIOLENCE OF WAR

The experience of war and the lessons of violence were well known to the Greeks through Homer's *Iliad* and *Odyssey*. Homer's stories (espe-

cially those of the *Iliad*) were depicted in sculpture in several temple ped-
iments (such as that on the island of Aigina, c. 480) and in drama (as
early as Aeschylus' *Oresteia*, c. 458). Other heroic sagas, such as the story
of the Seven against Thebes (part of the Theban legend of Oidipos),
would only have added to the whole picture of war. Some scholars—for
example, Edith Hall—have argued that the Greeks of the fifth century
would have been hard-pressed to determine the differences between these
stories of legend and their own time.[6] Other scholars have noted that the
Athenian dead of Marathon were regarded as possessing near demigod or
heroic stature by later generations, though the point may be exaggerated,
as Aristophanes' mocking of the "Marathon-fighters" in several plays suggests.[7]

Yet the line between heroic past and unheroic present may have been
more discrete than scholars like Hall allow. One reason for thinking this
is the role played by artifacts, that is, battlefield trophies and the like,
which would have allowed the Greeks in the later fifth century to make
the events of their own time concrete.[8] For this reason it can be argued
that the Greeks of the Peloponnesian War era understood the grim realities of the conflict around them. They would have seen these as real,
not as a simple extension of the heroic and mythic past, and would have
attempted to explain their reactions to it to themselves and others as best
they could.

The Soldiers

Early in his account of the war's outbreak, Thucydides introduces the
Spartan king Archidamos. As the Spartans debated a possible war with
Athens, Archidamos spoke against it, and in doing so he referred to his
own wartime experiences, which left him clearly unenthusiastic about
the prospects of yet another conflict. Archidamos contrasted his own re-
luctance for war with those who were inexperienced in it and somehow
imagined that it could be good or safe (Thucydides 1.80.1). In advising
the Spartans, Archidamos went on to counsel negotiations with the
Athenians in the hope that these might prove successful, while at the
same time preparing for war. Archidamos' position on war—that it is neither good nor safe and that diplomacy was preferable—is like that of
many other veterans of battle, including living veterans today, who have
experienced its horrors and would prefer peace. In Archidamos' speech

we find no glory or heroism, only a grim and somber analysis of war's realities. Archidamos' realism certainly contrasts with any picture of war as glorious and proper.

To what extent Thucydides accurately presents Archidamos' position may be debatable, though it seems likely that Thucydides was in a position to learn of what the Spartan king said. It also stands to reason that Thucydides agreed with him. When the war began, Thucydides was in the early stages of a career of political influence and military command in Athens. But failure ended this career as he arrived too late to save the key northern city of Amphipolis from the Spartan commander Brasidas. It is important to note, however, that this wartime service would have exposed him to the same kind of experiences to which Archidamos alludes in the speech noted above. That his views on war and violence were little different from those of Archidamos finds support in what he wrote of the war and its events.

In Thucydides' view, war was a violent teacher. His history shows this perspective in numerous ways: as group suicide illustrated in Corcyra as that community turned upon itself in civil war; as butchery related in the annihilation of another community, Mykalessos, where Thucydides notes the slaughter of children twice, and how what happened there was only the worst example of its kind; as bringing moral and social collapse as shown in plague-ravaged Athens and the violation of ancient rituals surrounding the burial of the dead. War brought all this and more, and relating this notion seems to be Thucydides' goal as much as relating a war that he lived through and saw as greater than any other. The position itself challenges the idea that the Greeks could not imagine that the "real" present was different from the "heroic" past.

The Poets

Although the history that Thucydides wrote (and that of his predecessor Herodotus) drew its inspiration from Homer's poetry, it remains that Thucydides broke from Homer's grip and took a different approach to conveying the world's reality. But poets remained, and in the Peloponnesian War era there were two—Euripides and Aristophanes—who in different ways conveyed the reality of the war around them.

Euripides was probably too old for active wartime service in the Peloponnesian War (at most he would have stood guard on the city walls), but he likely participated in military actions in the 460s and 450s against both the Persians and Athens' Greek enemies. This is important to keep in mind, for his experiences here surely gave him an understanding of war's realities that transcended anything in Homer and tales from mythology. Early in the war, in his drama *Andromache*, Euripides expresses hostility toward the Spartans, accusing them of treachery and duplicity in bringing the present war to the Greeks. Yet the drama also conveys a sympathetic portrayal of the plight of women in war, a theme he returns to in later work.

It is in his "war plays"—*Hecuba*, *Heracles*, and *Trojan Women*, in particular—that Euripides explores realistically the consequences of violence: Hekuba, who mutilates a defenseless enemy after killing his sons before his eyes; Herakles, who mistakenly kills his own children in a rage, a reflection perhaps on the warrior's inability to keep war's violence on the battlefield; and finally, the Trojan women, without husbands and grown children, about to be led away into lives of slavery. Presented to Athenian audiences filled with active-duty soldiers, these dramas suggest that Euripides is meditating on the violence of the war around him and is asking his fellow citizens to take stock of where they were and what they were doing. As the "instruction of the Athenians," Euripides' drama in particular attempted to confront his neighbors with those universal issues that Italian philosopher Timpanaro sees as occupying all cultures in some way—what do we make of suffering? What do we make of the horrors of war?

Whereas Euripides attempted to pose "deep" questions with his dramas, Aristophanes wanted his audience to laugh. Much younger than Euripides, Aristophanes is sure to have seen active duty in the war, and the biting humor made of politicians and generals may owe its inspiration to the reactions of a young man serving under commanders regarded as incompetent clowns—a not uncommon experience. In *Knights* Aristophanes does just this with Demosthenes and Nikias, not to mention Kleon (and Lamakhos in *Acharnians* and *Peace*), while in *Acharnians*, *Peace*, and *Lysistrata* the theme of peace that he explores reflects at once popular opinion and the opinion of a serving soldier who would prefer the comforts of home to the hardships of military campaigning (as noted in *Peace*).

But the comedy of Aristophanes, as we have discussed, is a complex comedy, one that allows him to present much deeper issues to his audience, including the hardships of war that women endured. This, the subject of *Lysistrata*, must be seen as a serious treatment despite its comedic appearance. Elsewhere in his plays, for example in *Acharnians*, Aristophanes anticipates this portrayal of women, referring to brides wanting to keep their new husbands with them at home and win for them exemptions from active military service (*Acharnians*). Although Aristophanes builds into his comedy enough laughs to engage the duller members of the audience, his treatment of the suffering of women especially in *Lysistrata* offers striking commentary on what the women and people of Athens (and Greece) endured during the long years of war. In much the same way, Aristophanes has equally poignant remarks about war orphans in Athens, of whom there must have been a good number (*Birds*). Again Aristophanes presents to the audience one of war's bitter legacies, again couched in humor.

Although Greek tragedy addressed issues of heady intellectual import, there can be little doubt that Euripides and his older contemporary Sophocles (in his *Ajax* and *Philoctetes*) brought to their dramas the suffering of contemporary times including the Peloponnesian War. That Aristophanes did so there can be no doubt, and although his humor conceals the deeper issues of war and violence, these can be detected, lurking not far below the surface of his plays.

The Artists

Euripides' reference in his play *Hecuba* to Polyxena defiantly tearing her dress, and so exposing her naked breasts like a sculptured goddess (lines 559–560), points to the influence of art on literature. Written in 424, *Hecuba* tells us that the artists at work in the era of the Peloponnesian War saw the same horrors of war as the poets and depicted this in their work. Examples abound. In the statue of the Dying Niobid, the first known female nude statue in Greek art (c. 430), we find perhaps the model for Euripides' Polyxena. In the years following, as experienced Athenian artists and craftsmen created the temple of Apollo at Bassai, similar scenes are repeated. The combination of seminude women being attacked amid scenes of violence argues strongly that the artists, both those of the Niobid and those at Bassai, are drawing inspiration from the many acts of violence occurring in the world around them.

This reality of life's experiences in a war-torn world also appears in the

Athenian white-ground *lekythoi*. These oil flasks, which appear only in Athens (only two examples have been found outside Attica, both probably taken abroad by travelers)[9] and which were brought to gravesides by women, convey real scenes of wartime sorrow—the parting of husband and wife, the dead soldier surrounded by family and friends (see Figures 10 and 11). We know from Parrhasios' conversation with Sokrates that artists were aware of all these emotions and knew how to depict them. Why, then, should it be doubted that it was not the war and wartime emotions and conditions that were influencing artists in painting these scenes? The question answers itself, and we should see the horrific violence of the Peloponnesian War as the root cause of this development in art that has been coined both Rich and Escapist, occurring in what J. J. Pollitt calls "an age of bewilderment and destruction."[10]

VIOLENCE AND CULTURE IN AN ERA OF WAR

At the beginning of the fifth century, the philosopher Herakleitos observed that "war is the father of all things." He was right then, and in many ways the world today is as influenced by the acts and violence of war as was the Greek world in the later years of the fifth century.

Thucydides probably knew of Herakleitos' statement and added his own soldier's perspective when he noted that war is a violent teacher. When it is seen that the history that Thucydides wrote grew out of Homer's *Iliad*—itself a poem of war and force[11]—and was itself a story of war, the truth of both observations may be seen. As in the case of his near contemporary Herodotus, Thucydides' achievement in writing an account of the war between Athens and Sparta can hardly be underestimated. Though influenced to some extent by Herodotus as well as Homer, in many ways what Thucydides composed represents a new kind of historical writing. Although his style of writing was not influential with later generations, his methodology and his efforts to get at what really happened and to write a possession for all time did gain for him adherents, especially in the Italian Renaissance. Historians such as Guiccardini and Machiavelli established Thucydides as the model, and this endorsement defined the technique and art of the historian that would remain strong into the modern era. Moreover, Thucydides' definitions of what constitutes power and what defines a state, namely the ability to use or inflict power, remained constants into the twentieth century as demonstrated in the attitudes and behaviors of European statesmen on the eve of World War I.

But the impact of war does not stop with the development of historical writing. Literature and art also carry the influences of war, as seen in not just the works that have been discussed in this volume but in so many other examples. This is not to claim that only the violence of war gives birth to literature and art—far from it. But too often historians and intellectuals discount the stories of war as simple(minded) military history, a study often dismissed as "drum and bugle history," when in fact war has brought out the best of the human intellect, along with the worst examples of cruelty and inhumanity. Above all else the role of the historian is to understand. It is my hope here that the readers of this volume understand that the Peloponnesian War was a conflict like so many others, but also one that led artists, poets, and others to see their world differently and to interpret the human experience in new and often revolutionary ways.

NOTES

1. See L. A. Tritle, *From Melos to My Lai: War and Survival* (London: Routledge, 2000), pp. 63–64, for the case of Epizelos the Athenian at Marathon in 490; another example is Antikrates of Knidos, cited in the Epidaurian miracle inscriptions (see E. J. Edelstein and L. Edelstein, with Intro. by G. B. Ferngren, *Asclepius. Collection and Interpretation of the Testimonies* (Baltimore, MD: Johns Hopkins University Press, 1945/98), p. 235). For the destruction of Mykalessos, see Thuc. 7.29–30.

2. Donald Kagan, *The Peloponnesian War* (New York: Viking Press, 2003), pp. 117, 300, 320. With regard to the civil war in Corcyra, Thucydides says that "every form" of violence occurred, and then he mentions in particular fathers killing sons. This suggests that sons killing fathers would have occurred too, based on his remark that "every form" of violence took place.

3. F. M. Cornford, *Thucydides Mythistoricus* (London: Edward Arnold, 1907), p. xi, though how Cornford's ideas might have changed after the colossal slaughter of World War I is an interesting speculation.

4. T. Eagleton, *Sweet Violence: The Idea of the Tragic* (Oxford: Blackwell, 2003), p. xiii, citing S. Timpanaro, *On Materialism*, trans. by L. Garner (Atlantic Highlands, NJ: Humanities Press, 1975), ch. 1. Additional support for Timpanaro's argument is even found in the grave offerings of the earliest peoples of the Stone Age.

5. Timpanaro, ibid., p. 52, cited in Eagleton, ibid.

6. An argument made by E. Hall in Aeschylus, *Persians*, ed. with introduction, translation, and commentary by E. Hall (Warminster: Aris & Phillips, 1996), p. 9; see also J. Hurwit, *The Athenian Acropolis: History, Mythology and Archaeology from the Neolithic Era to the Present* (Cambridge: Cambridge University Press, 1999), p. 212.

7. John Boardman, "The Parthenon Frieze—Another View," in *Festschrift für Frank Brommer*, ed. U. Höckmann and A. Krug (Mainz: von Zabern, 1977), pp. 39–49, argues that the famous Parthenon frieze depicts the glorious dead of Marathon. Against this see Jenifer Neils, *The Parthenon Frieze* (Cambridge: Cambridge University Press, 2001), pp. 18–81; see also Aristophanes, *Acharnians* 181, *Clouds* 986, *Lysistrata* 317–18, which poke fun at the (self) importance of the "Marathon-fighters."

8. See Marita Sturken, *Tangled Memories: The Vietnam War, the AIDS Epidemic, and the Politics of Remembering* (Berkeley: University of California Press, 1997), p. 19. Note also the opening words of Thucydides' *History*, which clearly suggests that he knew his war was bigger and also more real than Homer's Trojan War. See also Finley, *Thucydides*, pp. 83–87.

9. Noted to me by my colleague Professor C. Mihalopoulos.

10. Pollitt, *Art and Experience*, pp. 134–35.

11. A phrase borrowed from Simone Weil, "The *Iliad*, or the Poem of Force," in *The Simone Weil Reader*, ed. by G. A. Panichas (New York: McKay, 1977), pp. 153–83, whose essay, written in Nazi-occupied France in 1940/41 (Weil later died in an English sanatorium), perhaps best conveys the spirit of the *Iliad*.

BIOGRAPHIES: THE PERSONALITIES OF THE WAR

Agis II (c. 450–400)

Son of the Spartan king Archidamos II, Agis succeeded his father in 427 but seems not to have accomplished anything remarkable before 418 when he commanded the Spartan army that defeated the Athenian and Argive coalition at the battle of Mantineia. In 413 he took up command of the permanent fort established in Athenian territory at Dekeleia, a suggestion possibly of the renegade Alkibiades who remained as Agis' houseguest in Sparta, where he may have seduced Agis' wife. The Peloponnesian War, however, was won not by Agis in Attika but by Lysander in the Aegean. After the war, Agis attempted to prosecute his royal colleague Pausanias on charges of treason but failed. Spartan authorities entrusted him with a war against Elis, a sometime Spartan ally, and this he did energetically. His death in 400 created a royal scandal as the questionable paternity of his son Leotychides emerged and resulted in the election of the younger (and crippled) half-brother Agesilaos, thanks to the manipulation of Lysander, Agesilaos' former lover.

Alkibiades (451/0–404/3)

Alkibiades, son of Kleinias, belonged through his mother to the influential Alkmeonidai family. Upon his father's death (killed in the battle of Koroneia, 447/6), Alkibiades grew up in the house of his guardian Perikles, which brought him into contact with many prominent Athenians, including Sokrates.

Alkibiades first gained prominence with the treaty he negotiated for

Athens in 419 with Argos, bitter enemy of Sparta. This alliance did not achieve its hoped-for success, largely because of the defeat the Athenians and their new allies suffered the next year at Mantineia. Alkibiades then conceived the ambitious plan to invade Sicily, a venture in which he was opposed by the elder statesman Nikias. In a debate before the Athenians, Alkibiades was able to prevail over Nikias' objections, though the Athenians confused things considerably by appointing the two of them to the expedition's command (with the veteran general Lamakhos). Shortly before the Sicilian Expedition sailed (summer 415), religious controversy shocked Athens. Occurring together within a short time, domestic fertility symbols, the *hermai*, were mutilated and a scurrilous skit mocking the holy Mysteries of Eleusis became known. Alkibiades was implicated in both. Though he sailed with the expedition to Sicily, he was soon recalled to stand trial for his alleged role in the religious mischief. Alkibiades feared he would be condemned whatever he said in his own defense, and so he defected to Sparta, where he revealed all regarding the recently arrived Athenian force in Sicily.

Alkibiades' intelligence enabled the Spartans to aid the Greek city of Syracuse, the principal target of the Athenian attack. Alkibiades suggested to the Spartans that they establish a permanent fortified post in Attika in order to prosecute the war against Athens year-round. This the Spartans did in 413 with the building of their base at Dekeleia. These suggestions argue that Alkibiades possessed an understanding of strategy and tactics that might have made a difference had he remained with the expedition in Sicily. Alkibiades subsequently fled Sparta, possibly after his affair with the wife of Agis became known, and it is possible that she did bear his child (see Agis II, p. 105).

As an exile, Alkibiades attempted to win over Persian authorities in Asia, particularly the satrap Tissaphernes, as much for personal gain as to win favor in returning to Athens. Alkibiades negotiated with the Athenian fleet stationed at Samos, which elected him general and won a victory for him at Kyzikos (411). He then returned to Athens with great celebration, and the old charges for impiety still hanging over his head were dropped. He was again elected general, but his efforts in Asia did not succeed and he again abandoned the Athenian cause. He first withdrew to Thrace where he attempted to warn the Athenian fleet at Aigospotami that it was in danger (405), but his overtures were ignored. After the defeat of Athens, he fled to Asia where he was murdered at the instigation of his enemies in Athens, the Thirty Tyrants, and the Spartan commander Lysander. Alkibiades was flamboyant and self-centered, brilliant and unscrupulous.

Archidamos II (c. 489–427)

Spartan king whose name means "leader of the people," Archidamos reigned for more than forty years (c. 469–427). He first gained prominence by his skillful handling of affairs in Sparta after the great earthquake of 464, which ignited rebellions of the helots and other allied communities in Sparta. In the events leading up to the outbreak of the Peloponnesian War, Archidamos failed in his efforts to dampen Spartan enthusiasm for war. Once war broke out, he led military forces in invasions of Attika on three occasions (431, 430, 428) and ordered the siege of Plataia in 429. Archidamos exemplifies the veteran soldier who knows what the business of war is all about and enters it only with great deliberation.

Aristophanes (c. 460/50–386)

The greatest poet of Old Attic comedy, perhaps the greatest comic genius ever, Aristophanes wrote over forty plays that are themselves a rich source of information regarding virtually every aspect of life in classical Greece, as well as events in the Peloponnesian War. Aristophanes' plays are carefully structured around the entry of the chorus and the chorus' address to the audience, though in later plays Aristophanes broke with this sequence. The language that he uses is rich and imaginative, and the lyric poetry found in his plays is equally adept. He is a great satirist and his keen eye missed nothing; he attacked and satirized politicians (*Knights*, 424—Kleon), generals (*Peace*, 421—Kleon, Brasidas, Lamakhos), poets (*Frogs*, 405—Euripides), and intellectuals (*Clouds*, 423—Sokrates) with equal enthusiasm and zeal, just as he did the common citizen. His political sympathies are difficult to disentangle from his comedy, but he did not appear to favor the cause of the oligarchs who gained prominence late in the Peloponnesian War. Yet he was critical of the Athenian *demos* who fell over themselves embracing one popular leader after another, only to discard each in turn. Aristophanes became embroiled with Kleon, who prosecuted him for defaming city officials before foreigners but failed to win a conviction. While Aristophanes omitted no trick, joke, or slander in ridiculing Kleon in *Knights*, the *demos* elected him general all the same. Essentially, Aristophanes made fun of politicians in much the same way that comedians on *Saturday Night Live!* do today.

Aristophanes' plays also reveal much about the intellectual attitudes of the day. His *Clouds* famously attacked Sokrates and the intellectuals of the day known as Sophists, the itinerant teachers of classical Greece, who taught for pay. Some argue that this play was all good clean fun enjoyed by Sokrates himself. Yet against this view the burning down of Sokrates' "thinkery," or school, at the end of the play argues for a much more serious theme, one that viewed "thinkers" like Sokrates as indeed dangerous to the mores of the community. This is seen nowhere more clearly than in the choral debate between two groups named "Right Thinking" and "Wrong Thinking"; in the battle, "Wrong Thinking" prevails, which demonstrates that Aristophanes saw the new logic and new education taught by the Sophists as harmful to Athenian society (see Document 17). Elsewhere Aristophanes shows deft familiarity with the rhetorical tools of intellectuals and with literary criticism (as in *Frogs* and *Thesmophoriazousae*).

Aspasia (c. 465–?)

Born in Miletos in Asia Minor, the daughter of a prosperous businessman, Aspasia practiced the world's oldest profession, what in classical Greece were called *hetairai* (cf. "high-class call girls" in modern American society). These women were literate and accomplished in the arts and provided companionship to men of the leisure class in Athens, such as Perikles. Aspasia became Perikles' companion around 445, and he divorced his wife to live with her. Their relationship provided much material for gossip and humor as well as political attack. Aristophanes in his play *Acharnians* blamed her for starting the Peloponnesian War, and others joked that she held great influence over Perikles. Aspasia reportedly held discussions with Sokrates, and in Plato's dialogue *Menexenos*, Aspasia recites a funeral oration that she had composed for Perikles (a report not generally accepted). Aspasia gave birth to Perikles' son, also named Perikles, who was afterward made legitimate by a special vote, as Perikles' own law barred his son from citizenship (see entry on Perikles). This son, usually known as Perikles the Younger, was one of the generals commanding at the battle of Arginusai and was later executed by the Athenians for failing to rescue the survivors of damaged warships. Perikles' death in the plague circa 429 left Aspasia unattached only temporarily. A short time later she became the companion to another politician, Lysikles, who died not long after.

Brasidas (c. 455–422)

Energetic and, for a Spartan, atypically innovative, Brasidas won a number of successes in the Archidamian War. He gained prominence with a vigorous defense of Methone against Athenian forces soon after war began, and this won for him further commands. In 424 he was sent into northern Greece with a small force composed of freed helots and mercenaries and singlehandedly disrupted Athenian fortunes in the area. He won the strategic city of Amphipolis (and thus caused the exile of the Athenian general Thucydides, who turned to writing history as a result), among others, and prompted the revolts of other cities in the region. In 422 an Athenian army commanded by Kleon forced him into set battle outside of Amphipolis. Here his troops won a decisive victory, but he was killed as was Kleon, an event marked by Aristophanes in his play *Peace* where the two commanders are called the "pestles" who stirred up the war in Greece. Thucydides depicts Brasidas as a brave and noble soldier, in contrast with the weak and incompetent Kleon. Although Brasidas had caused Thucydides' exile, it was still possible for Thucydides to view him as a noble and worthy adversary. But Kleon was perhaps responsible for making Thucydides' exile legal, which would have given him more than adequate reason to extol Brasidas and condemn Kleon. Later in the war the Spartans created similar independent commands (termed *harmostai* or harmosts) as those held by Brasidas, and again freed helots (*neodamodeis*, or "new men") participated (among others) as the fighting force.

Demosthenes (d. 413)

One of the more innovative Athenian military commanders during the war, Demosthenes first gained a reputation in fighting in western Greece, where in 426 he won several spectacular victories, in one instance effectively knocking Ambracia out of the war with devastating loss (see Thucydides 3.105–113). The next year Demosthenes won even greater fame with his stunning victory over the Spartan garrison on Sphakteria Island in the bay of Pylos, a victory that Aristophanes would have us believe Kleon stole (see *Knights* lines 54–58). The 292 Spartan prisoners that were brought to Athens played a key part in bringing about the negotiations that led to the Peace of Nikias that ended the so-called Archidamian War (421). Demosthenes does not appear to have commanded a major force again until the Athenians sent him to Sicily (413) with a relief force to assist Nikias in the attack on Syracuse. After the failure of a night attack on the Syracusan strong point at Epipolai, Demosthenes urged Nikias to retreat but could not persuade him to do so. The fateful withdrawal began only after the Syracusans defeated the Athenian fleet in the battle of the Great Harbor, and ended in total disaster. Demosthenes surrendered that portion of the Athenian army that fell to his command and attempted suicide, failing. Subsequently, the Syracusans executed him along with Nikias, over the objections of Gylippos, who wanted to take Demosthenes to Sparta to parade the "conqueror" of Sphakteria at home.

Euripides (c. 480s–406)

The youngest of the three great writers of tragic drama, Euripides wrote ninety-two plays of which nineteen survive in a career stretching from 455 to 406. The target of Aristophanic comedy in the *Thesmophoriazousae* (411) and *Frogs* (405), Aristophanes leaves Euripides in Hades bringing Aeschylus back to Athens, which suggests what Aristophanes thought of him. Influenced by such humor, popular opinion in Athens seems to have associated Euripides with the intellectual theories and views of the Sophists. His lack of popularity also seems confirmed by a story that he wrote his plays in a cave in Salamis. Even if untrue, the story points to his aloofness and lack of interest in politics. Toward 408 and perhaps repelled by the war and political turmoil in Athens, Euripides retreated to Makedonia at the invitation of its king Archelaos. Here he wrote his last play, *Bacchae*, and died.

Later Aristotle discussed Euripides and his contemporary and rival Sophocles. In his view Sophocles depicted men as they ought to be, whereas Euripides showed them as they are (*Poetics* 1460B 33–34). Aristotle also thought that Euripides was "the most tragic of poets" and best at creating a sense of pity and fear in the audience. Euripides' plays challenged Athenian audiences and even readers today with their intense realism. In the *Trojan Women*, written in 415 amid the turmoil of the Peloponnesian War (particularly the siege of Melos), Euripides focuses on the savagery of war and relates with shock and vividness what happens to a city and its women when it falls. In the *Medea* as well as other dramas (e.g., *Orestes, Hippolytus*), Euripides explores human psychology, especially the feminine mind. A line he assigns to Medea must have shocked the largely male audience who took such pride in their military service and glories: "I'd rather stand in battle three times than give birth once" (lines 250–51). *Bacchae*, his last play written while in self-imposed exile in Makedonia, turns to a theme of spirituality and divine revenge clashing with human arrogance that knows all.

Euripides was unconventional as well in other respects. His plays often focused on those marginalized in Greek society, particularly women and slaves. *Medea* and *Hippolytus* particularly illustrate this, depicting the plight of a woman rejected by her husband for a younger woman and a woman falling in love with a stepson. Such stories seem very modern to the contemporary reader, but they suggest that such issues are universal; clearly Euripides was ahead of his time in probing them. Dramas such as these also appealed to the modern era, especially the nineteenth century, which saw Euripides as a "rationalist" who broke not only with conventional attitudes regarding gender issues but also religion.

The condition of slaves was also an issue that drew Euripides' interest. In *Andromache* and *Hecuba* (as well as *Trojan Women*), he combines his thought on women with the brutalities of war and the transition from freedom to slavery. In other plays such as *Ion*, he examines a more domestic version of slave status, in this case a young man whose father is Apollo but who is abandoned all the same. This confirms Aristotle's statement that Euripides aimed not just to show people as they are, but to reveal their underlying humanity as well. Possibly more than any of the other dramatists from classical Greece (those whose works survive or not), Euripides succeeds in speaking across the ages and remains an author whose views challenge the reader.

Gorgias (c. 485–380)

Born in Leontini in Greek Sicily, Gorgias is usually regarded as one of the most important of the Sophists in terms of philosophical thought and rhetorical style. It is thought that he was a student of the philosopher Empedokles, one of the pre-Sokratics who laid the foundations for the Greek Enlightenment. Gorgias' work *On the Non-existent*, in which he argued that "nothing is," may owe some of its inspiration to Empedokles' influence. Gorgias perhaps came to Athens in 427 on a diplomatic mission, but caused quite a stir with his flowery rhetoric with its balanced clauses, rhymes, and other features. Authors such as Plato imitated his style (see the *Symposium* and the Gorgianic speech there by Agathon) as well as politicians even in the nineteenth century. Abraham Lincoln's famous Gettysburg Address is just one such speech that Gorgias' style influenced (see Garry Wills, *Lincoln at Gettysburg: The Words That Remade America* [New York: Simon & Schuster, 1992], pp. 58, 212, 257–59). Another of Gorgias' work that we know of is the *Encomium of Helen* (about 414), in which he discusses the power of the spoken word, and in doing so alludes to the impact and trauma of war on combatants.

Gylippos

A Spartan officer sent with modest reinforcements from Corinth to the aid of Syracuse in 415. He took over the defense of Syracuse from its own generals, and his presence restored morale and bolstered Syracusan defenses. Gylippos organized the building of the counter-walls that prevented the Athenians from besieging the city, forcing them to attack Syracuse, at which they failed. In the retreat of the Athenian forces, Gylippos attempted to save the lives of the two Athenian generals captured, Nikias and Demosthenes, but failed. Gylippos then returned to the Aegean where he joined Lysander's staff in the war against the Athenians. At the end of the war, he brought back to Sparta Persian-supplied gold as well as loot seized from the Athenians at Aigospotami. He embezzled a large sum (reportedly three hundred talents), was detected, and fled into exile. His career reflects the extremes of Spartan soldiery: brave and resourceful, but also corruptible.

Kleon (c. 462–421)

The best known political figure in Athens after the death of Perikles, Kleon came from a wealthy industrial family (his father was a rich tanner). Kleon may have already challenged Perikles' leadership over the defense of Attika after the war began, arguing that the Spartans should not be allowed to ravage the land unopposed. He took a prominent part in the debate over Mytilene (427) and proposed that all the men of that city be executed, a decree overturned the next day. It was in the struggle against the Spartans at Pylos that Kleon became a major figure. As the Athenians debated the proper tactics and strategy to use in defeating the Spartan garrison on Sphakteria Island, Nikias challenged Kleon to make good on his promise to accomplish this in three weeks and offered to resign his appointment as general and give it to Kleon. This greatly amused the assembled Athenians, and Kleon could do nothing other than accept. In a stunning success, Kleon kept his promise and brought to Athens 292 Spartan prisoners (of whom 120 were Spartiates), who were held as hostages. Kleon stopped the annual Spartan invasions by threatening to bring the prisoners out and execute them. What needs to be remembered is that the general Demosthenes was already at Pylos employing the tactics that would bring the Athenians their victory. As Aristophanes tells in *Knights* (through a character named after the general), Demosthenes complains about Kleon's theft of the dinner—the Spartans on Sphakteria Island—he was preparing for the *demos*. Aristophanes' reference follows Athenian opinion that saw Kleon literally stealing Demosthenes' victory and the accompanying fame.

Pylos made Kleon, and in the following years he enacted legislation to increase daily payments for jury service and to improve the collection of tribute from the subject states. In 423 he proposed a decree that the citizens of Skione (in northern Greece) be executed after they defected to Brasidas. The next year (422) Kleon, holding the generalship again, took an expedition to the north to turn back Brasidas. In a battle before the walls of Amphipolis, Kleon proved an unworthy opponent: his army was defeated, and he was killed (and Thucydides seems to relate with some satisfaction that Kleon was stabbed in the back as he ran away).

In many respects Kleon was a product of the Athenian democracy and empire that gave him birth. His speeches to the *demos* were typically brash and arrogant, and as Thucydides relates, he had a habit of making extreme statements and charges. This is the sort of character that typifies the democracy and that saw the empire as property to be used for the enrichment and greater power of Athens.

Kyros (c. 430–401)

The younger son of the Persian king Darios II and Parysatis, Kyros was ambitious and favored by his mother. Placed in general command of Asia by his father in 408, Kyros moved to support the Spartans against the Athenians and did so effectively, probably causing a certain amount of resentment among the satrap Tissaphernes. Upon the accession of his older brother, Arsikas, who took the regnal name Artaxerxes (II), Kyros returned to Asia where he soon began plotting against his brother. He organized a large army, including ten thousand Greek mercenaries, with whom he launched an attack to overthrow his brother and take his place. While his Greeks won the battle (at Kunaxa), Kyros himself was killed as he attacked his brother, leaving the Greeks leaderless in the middle of the Persian Empire. After Tissaphernes treacherously killed many of their officers and seized their generals, the Greeks calmly elected new leaders, including Xenophon the Athenian, and proceeded to march home. The exploits of these men reveal much of the state of affairs in Greece after the Peloponnesian War, as well as the weakness of Persia, a lesson not lost on Alexander the Great seventy years later.

Lamakhos (d. 414)

One of the better known generals (*strategoi*) that Athens produced during the war, Lamakhos was famous enough for Aristophanes to caricature in his play *Acharnians* (425) and to figure in Thucydides' account of the war, particularly the disastrous campaign in Sicily. A veteran commander of some twenty years' experience, Lamakhos was appointed along with Nikias and Alkibiades to command that expedition's invasion of the island in 415. He argued but could not persuade his colleagues to attack a still unprepared Syracuse, and as a result, the Athenians became bogged down in positional warfare, attempting to starve Syracuse into surrender. In a minor skirmish around the walls and counter-walls outside the city, Lamakhos was killed. The Athenian effort, now led by the sick and disheartened Nikias (Alkibiades had been recalled to Athens to stand trial; see the entry starting on p. 105), stalled. In *Acharnians* Aristophanes made fun of Lamakhos as a blustering braggart soldier (lines 572–623), but after his death he praised him as a hero in *Frogs* (line 1040).

Lysander (c. 440–395)

The Spartan commander who finally defeated Athens in spring 404, Lysander rose from poverty to become king-maker. Of an impoverished

Spartiate family (classified as *mothakes*, singular *mothax*), Lysander re-quired help in gaining admission to the *agoge*, the Spartan education sys-tem. He later became the lover of Agesilaos, the younger son of King Archidamos II, whom he would make king after the Peloponnesian War when his influence was at its height. Appointed to a naval command in the Aegean (408/7), he won the support of the Persian prince Kyros (and with it Persian money) and later defeated forces under the command of Alkibiades, which led to his exile from Athens. In 405 he destroyed the Athenian fleet at Aigospotami (where large numbers of Athenian pris-oners were executed) and then turned to the blockade of Athens, which led to the city's surrender in the following spring.

Lysander forced upon Athens a group of murderous oligarchs later known as the Thirty Tyrants, the precedent for which were the de-carchies (boards of ten and loyal friends) that he had created in the Aegean four years earlier. By now, however, Lysander was becoming too powerful. Several monuments commemorating his successes had been set up in the Aegean, and at Samos a cult in his name had been established where he may have received worship as a god. This and his victory over Athens made some in Sparta nervous, and so when the democrats in Athens rose against the Thirty Tyrants, the Spartan king Pausanias sup-ported them, not so much to help them as to weaken Lysander. Later, Spartan authorities abandoned the decarchies, but Lysander's influence remained, as seen in the election of Agesilaos to the kingship. In 395 the Spartans were attempting to reestablish control over central Greece. Lysander was to coordinate the movement of his force with King Pausa-nias, but rather than wait, Lysander made an unsuccessful attack on Haliartos and was killed in the fighting that followed.

When Lysander died, among his papers was found a plan to overthrow the Spartan kingship, which was hereditary, and replace it with an elec-tive one (and Lysander surely proposed himself!). The circumstances of this discovery and Lysander's supposed plot are obscure and clouded by substantial animosity designed to discredit him.

Lysimakhe

Priestess of Athena Polias for some sixty-four years (ending sometime in the late fifth century or early fourth), Lysimakhe belonged to the aris-tocratic family of the Eteoboutadai, and so to the old families of Athens.

As priestess of the cult of Athena Polias (centered on the acropolis where an ancient wood statue represented the goddess), Lysimakhe enjoyed social as well as religious prominence in the city. The cult over which she presided was the most important in the city, and her position was the most significant that an Athenian woman could occupy.

Lysimakhe's stature may have given Aristophanes the initial inspiration for his drama *Lysistrata* (411), perhaps his best known play. In this drama, the title character, an Athenian woman named Lysistrata, leads the women of Greece on a sex strike in order to bring an end to the Peloponnesian War, now in its twentieth year. The names Lysimakhe and Lysistrata both mean virtually the same thing—Lysimakhe, "Dissolving battles," Lysistrata, "Dissolving armies." In the drama, Lysistrata is assisted by another Athenian woman, Myrrhine, who also has a real-life contemporary of the same name, the priestess of Athena Nike, another cult located on the acropolis. When the Athenian audience watched this play, then, reality and fiction would have been rather blurred. This suited Aristophanes, for he could then safely address issues that might have been otherwise controversial or even risky.

Nikias (c. 470–413)

Athenian general and politician who rose to prominence after the death of Perikles. He was a moderate and seems to have opposed the aggressive form of imperialism advocated by Perikles and Kleon. One of the richest men in Athens, he reportedly owned a thousand slaves who worked the silver mines in Laureion in southern Attika. He shared his wealth generously, among other things funding a public festival on the island of Delos for his fellow Athenians.

On the death of Kleon (422), he was able to assert his moderate views and persuade the combatants to accept a peace that has since carried his name, the Peace of Nikias (421). Afterward Nikias found an even greater challenge in Alkibiades who promoted the ambitious scheme to invade Sicily, an action he opposed. Much against his advice, the Athenians voted approval of the expedition to Sicily and appointed him to share the command. One can imagine he did so without a great deal of enthusiasm. Alkibiades' recall to Athens and flight left the expedition in the hands of Nikias and Lamakhos; Syracuse, the expedition's principal target, nearly fell to them. The arrival of Spartan and Corinthian aid (see Gylippos,

p. 112), however, and Lamakhos' death and Nikias' poor health (he had by now begun to suffer from kidney failure or related disease) rallied the defenders, and Athenian fortunes rapidly declined. A relief force from Athens arrived under the command of Demosthenes, but setbacks continued to weaken the Athenian cause. A naval battle fought in the Great Harbor of Syracuse resulted in the defeat and destruction of the Athenian fleet, and soon, but not soon enough, Nikias and Demosthenes attempted a retreat. The retreat turned into a rout, and the Athenian and allied force of some twenty thousand men was annihilated. Sick and demoralized, Nikias surrendered the remnants of his army to save them from slaughter. Not long after his capture, the Syracusans executed Nikias, and the Athenians later omitted his name—because of this surrender—from the casualty list that memorialized the Athenian dead of Sicily.

Perikles (c. 495–429)

Athenian politician, the son of Xanthippos and the Alkmeonid Agariste, Perikles came from the most notable circle of Athenians, as he was related to Kleisthenes, the "founder" of Athenian democracy. It is not until mid–fifth century that Perikles becomes truly prominent in Athens. Before then he is known for sponsoring the chorus in Aeschylus' play *Persians* (472) and as one of the elected prosecutors of Kimon (462/1), whom he seems not to have attacked vigorously. He seems to have joined the reformer Ephialtes in reducing the authority of the Areopagos Council, an ancient legislative body with conservative leanings (c. 461/0).

In the twenty years before the Peloponnesian War, Perikles enacted several decrees that had an impact on the democracy. He introduced pay for jury service, which prompted critics to say he bribed the Athenians with their own money (as the funds used for this came from imperial revenue), and in 451/0 he established Athenian legal identity: henceforth Athenian citizenship would be restricted to those who had an Athenian-born father and mother. Abroad he sponsored the creation of Athenian colonists (called *cleruchs*) in the territories of subject states and took an energetic role in suppressing revolts in Euboia (446/5) and in Samos (440). It was this policy that frightened and intimidated the other Greeks, as Thucydides notes in his history.

Perikles took an interest in and facilitated the rebuilding of Athens after the war with Persia officially ended. The great monuments of Athens on the acropolis—the Parthenon, Erechtheion—as well as other buildings owe their creation to his influence. This policy found an opponent in Thucydides, the son of Melesias (related to Kimon, whom Perikles had helped prosecute, and Thucydides the historian), but Perikles prevailed and brought about the ostracism or exile of his opponent. Other critics, however, brought various charges against Aspasia, his mistress; Anaxagoras, a philosopher and friend; and even Perikles himself. But Perikles emerged stronger and more influential than ever from these attacks. He was elected general nearly every year from then until his death, which gave him extensive authority (he could summon the council to convene for example) as well as prestige (he received first-row seats at the theater and helped select the winners of the dramatic competitions). Thucydides (the historian) in reflecting on this later said that in theory Athens was a democracy, but in reality it was the rule of one man—Perikles.

In foreign affairs Perikles advocated an aggressive policy for the Athenians and their empire, and he took a tough-minded course in refusing to negotiate with the Spartans in the events leading up to the Peloponnesian War. When things went badly after the war began, Perikles was forced from office, though the Athenians later changed their minds and reinstated him. A talented orator, Perikles led the democracy through his vision of Athenian greatness rather than pandering to the crowd as did the politicians who came after him. His private life was not always easy—problems with his nephew and ward Alkibiades, the divorce of his wife, and his affair with Aspasia are just some of the highlights. Two sons by his first wife also died in the plague. This led the Athenians to legitimize Aspasia's son Perikles, though he too would not see the end of the war. (He was later executed for dereliction of duty after the battle of Arginusai, 406.)

Pheidias (c. 485–425)

Athenian sculptor and son of Kharmides, Pheidias was one of the great artists of the classical Greek world. He may have been a pupil of Hegias and Hageladas, though the relationships are poorly known. Pheidias was regarded as the most accomplished of Greek sculptors, and his students (e.g., Alkamenes, Kallimachos) were influential into the following generations.

Among Pheidias' earliest works was the colossal bronze statue of Athena Promachos, or "Champion" (derived from the word for a hero who fights in front of others). Thirty feet high, the spear and helmet were said to be visible to sailors rounding Cape Sounion as they approached Athens. It stood on the acropolis into late Roman times when the emperor Constantine moved it to Constantinople (modern-day Istanbul). There it was destroyed in January 1204 because the superstitious populace believed that it had summoned from the west the approaching Crusader armies of the Fourth Crusade (its now spearless hand pointed in that direction). Other early works include the Athena Lemnia and a Marathon group, which some scholars have identified with two bronze statues found in 1972 off the southern Italian coast and now known as the Riace Bronzes.

It was in association with Perikles, however, that Pheidias and his work became best known. Pheidias belonged to Perikles' circle and played a major part in the building program associated with Perikles in the 440s and 430s. He crafted the large cult statue of Athena, nearly forty feet in height and made of gold and ivory, that was placed in the Parthenon. Work on this statue began in 447 and was completed in 438. Descriptions of later eyewitnesses have enabled identification of surviving Roman copies of Pheidias' Athena: in her right hand stood a Nike (or symbol of victory), and in her left was a spear, and both sides of her shield were decorated with heroic scenes. Pheidias may well have had overall responsibility for Perikles' building program and certainly had responsibility for the Parthenon's exterior sculptures.

Pheidias was prosecuted along with other friends of Perikles. Charges were brought against him for embezzlement (of the gold used to decorate the cult statue of Athena) as well as impiety. There are several stories regarding his fate, but it seems most likely that he left (or fled) Athens upon being put on trial (perhaps 438). He then went to Olympia where he crafted the even larger cult statue of Zeus (one of the "seven" wonders of the ancient world) adorned, like the Athena, with a Nike in his right hand and a scepter in his left, and further decorated with multiple scenes drawn from mythology. Archaeologists excavating in Olympia have found the remains of his shop, including tools and moulds and even a cup inscribed with his name. It is believed that he died in Elis, killed by a mob after he had sculpted the Zeus.

Plato (c. 429–346)

Plato belonged to one of the ancient families of Athens, reportedly descended from the early kings of Athens and mentioned in the poems of Solon, founder of the Athenian state. In the fifth century Plato's family was well placed politically and enjoyed elite status, though the early death of his father Ariston did not help family fortunes. Upon Ariston's death, his widow Periktione married her uncle, Pyrilampes, who was a friend of Perikles, a democrat and ambassador to the Persian court. Yet within this extended family there were family members among the radical oligarchs, most notably Plato's cousin Kritias and uncle Kharmides, who would later be among the more vicious of the Thirty Tyrants who ruled Athens briefly after the Peloponnesian War. Born at the start of the war, Plato would have been old enough to listen to Sokrates debate ideas with the great Sophists of the day, men like Gorgias and Protagoras, as a young man. Later, when Plato began to write philosophy, these arguments would often provide the dramatic background and title to his ideas and famous dialogues. Plato would also have been of age to have served in military campaigns late in the war (and into the 390s), though there is no information on this.

That Sokrates made a great impression on Plato would be an understatement. It is more likely that Plato idolized Sokrates and that the martyr's death that claimed his teacher shaped his life in various ways. Sokrates' death was controversial, and a number of writers took various positions on it. Plato wrote in defense of Sokrates, as is evident in his early dialogues, *The Apology*, *Euthyphro*, and *Crito*, in which he outlined Sokrates' ideas and famous style of teaching by question and answer, the Sokratic method. But the death of Sokrates also turned Plato against any idea of a political career (not to mention, too, the activities of his relatives) for himself. More than a decade after Sokrates' death (probably in 387), Plato opened the Academy (in Athens) where he hoped to reach out to others who might act politically in his place. Although he did not enjoy much success in this area, he was more successful in developing what might be termed "higher education," something that survives into the modern world.

With his so-called middle dialogues, works such as the *Gorgias* and *Meno*, Plato began to carve out his own philosophical ideas and continued to do so the rest of his life. By the time of his "late" dialogues, for example, *Sophist*, *Statesman*, and *Laws*, his work had become more technical. Plato founded Western philosophy, but before that he provided a moving portrait of a great and original thinker, his teacher Sokrates.

Plutarch (C.E. 50–120)

The famous Greek author, essayist, and biographer provides such a great mass of material on the Peloponnesian War, especially some of the key individuals who figured in it, that his inclusion is warranted here. Plutarch was born in central Greece near the town of Khaironeia, a town that was already in his time known for two great battles—one between the Greeks and Macedonians in 338/7 and the second between the Romans and their feared enemy, King Mithridates of Pontos, fought in 87/6. His family was well established, which enabled him to move easily in elite circles, bringing him into contact with members of the Roman ruling class. Plutarch also traveled a good deal, visiting nearby Athens frequently, Rome, and such distant places as Egypt. He was then a member of the leisured class and was able not only to travel, but also to read extensively and write. In doing so, he provides material to us today that otherwise would be lost.

Among his many works are the "lives" or biographies of famous Greeks and Romans, including several figures of Peloponnesian War fame. These include the great Athenian statesman Perikles as well as his nephew Alkibiades and the unfortunate Nikias who became the scapegoat for the disaster that befell the Athenians in Sicily. His account of the Spartan commander Lysander provides information about the Spartan general who brought Athens to its knees and so ended the great war. Additional information is given in such essays as "The Glory of Athens" and, in anecdotal form, the "Sayings of Famous Commanders" and those of Spartan kings and women (the latter discussed in Chapter 5).

Plutarch remains an important source of information, and while it is often difficult to know where he found his information, he plays an important part in showing readers today what the ancient Greek world was like.

Protagoras (c. 490–420)

From Abdera in northern Greece, Protagoras was the best known of the Sophists, or itinerant teachers (regarded today as philosophers), who traveled throughout the Greek world but mostly frequented Athens. While in Athens, Perikles asked Protagoras to write the constitution for Thurii, a pan-hellenic colony founded in southern Italy in 444/3 but sponsored and largely developed by Athens. (Among its population was Herodotus the historian.) Protagoras was famous for his religious beliefs, namely the conviction that knowledge of the gods was not possible. Of greater significance perhaps was his criticism of the existence of "truth," as expressed in his saying, "Man is the measure of all things." By this he seems to have meant everything is to be regarded from the subjective view of the individual (which implicitly omits the idea of a divine standard as well), thus denying truth and objectivity. Opposition to this idea came from Demokritos and Plato, who countered that the theory contradicts itself: that if all beliefs are true then the opposite is too. Protagoras' critics may have missed his point. Placed in the larger context of Greek discoveries of the world in the fifth century, Protagoras may have been hinting that what one culture values is truth for it even if not for another (as reflected in Herodotus' story of disposing of the dead in Book Three).

Protagoras was an important figure in the development of thought in the mid–fifth century. He stimulated moral and political thinking, the art of persuasive speaking (especially the ability to argue both sides of a question), as well as the value of a practical education. Others, including Sokrates, would follow his example, and the age of Greek "Enlightenment" resulted.

Sokrates (c. 469–399)

Perhaps the most famous Greek of the classical age, Sokrates of Athens was the son of Sophroniskos, a stonemason or sculptor, and Phainarete, famous for her skills as a midwife. His father's occupation argues for a moderate, though not elite, economic status, and this is seen further in Sokrates' military service in the Peloponnesian War. He served as a hoplite in numerous campaigns in the Archidamian War (i.e., the campaigns of Potidaia, Delion, and Amphipolis), after which he would have served only as a "reservist" called out for home defense. This status is also supported by his membership in the Council of 500 in 406 where he defended the generals placed on trial for their supposed dereliction of duty in failing to rescue shipwrecked sailors after the battle of Arginusai. Sokrates was probably married at least twice, for at the time of his execution he told those waiting with him to take his final words to his wife, Xanthippe, and three young sons.

It was probably in and after the 420s that Sokrates' life as a philosopher and noted intellectual in Athens developed. His students Plato and Xenophon identify his friends and followers, those who made up his "circle" of students. These included two relatives of Plato's, his uncle Kharmides and cousin Kritias, both of whom later gained infamy for their participation among the Thirty Tyrants who terrorized Athenians after the war when an oligarchic regime ruled Athens. Sokrates' association with these men would later be turned against him when he was placed on trial for "corrupting the youth" of Athens. In the same category, certainly in the views of many Athenians, was Alkibiades, who soldiered with Sokrates and attended some of the famous symposia as told by Plato in his dialogue *Symposium*, and Xenophon, whose "memoirs" of Sokrates provide some of what is known of him. Another Athenian who seems to have idolized Sokrates was his friend Khairephon, who once went to Delphi and asked the oracle if Sokrates was not the wisest man in Greece. The oracle replied yes to this leading question, and though Sokrates rejected the label and mildly rebuked Khairephon for asking, he then proceeded to demonstrate the wisdom of the god. As it turned out, he was the wisest man in Greece. When questioned about what they knew, Sokrates found that most people either did not know or attempted to obscure the fact, while he admitted to knowing nothing but then worked on correcting his ignorance. Thus developed the idea of Sokratic ignorance—real knowledge begins with the admission that one does not really know. Sokrates characterized himself as a "gadfly"—buzzing around and questioning people, trying to get at the truth of things, as he saw it, or bothering and annoying people, as most others did. It was this perhaps that supplied some of the inspiration for Aristophanes' attack on him in his play *Clouds*.

Sokrates' great concern was others, and in this light his prosecution and execution seem a contradiction. Yet in 399 the Athenians prosecuted him for impiety—"corrupting the youth" and "worshiping strange gods." His prosecutors included Anytos and Meletos, democratic politicians seeking to make names for themselves and critical of Sokrates for his antidemocratic attitudes, as well as his supposed influence over the Thirty Tyrants, oligarchic enemies of Athens. Plato's dialogue *The Apology* offers a rather partisan view of the trial, where it seems that Sokrates antagonized his jury of fellow citizens who condemned him to death. Although he could have slipped away into a life of exile, Sokrates chose to abide by the laws of his city and accept its judgment.

His death gave birth to the "Sokratic Legend," which influenced both later philosophy and literature. His political views and criticisms of democracy influenced those of Plato, who some modern political theorists (e.g., Karl Popper, *The Open Society and Its Enemies*, 5th ed., 2 vols., Princeton, NJ: Princeton University Press, 1966) have argued provided the inspiration for such modern ideas as totalitarianism.

Sophocles (c. 496–406)

Arguably the greatest of the Athenian playwrights, Sophocles began his literary career around 468 when he competed with Aeschylus; his career ended in 401 when his grandson, also named Sophocles, posthumously staged his last play, *Oedipus at Colonus*, which won first prize (out of three). Sophocles was prolific, writing more than one hundred twenty plays, and was more often victorious than any other playwright, winning first prize twenty times. He also played an active role in affairs of state throughout his life, including several positions of responsibility and influence during the Peloponnesian War. Yet his life also appears to have been one of little controversy. In 406/5, Aristophanes staged his comedy *Frogs* in which he created a poetic battle between Aeschylus and Euripides for the title of poet laureate of Athens. (The play also gave Aristophanes the opportunity to make certain statements about politics and the moral value of literature.) The play followed shortly after the deaths of both Sophocles and Euripides (Aeschylus had died some time before), and so the setting for the drama is Hades. Aristophanes explains the absence of Sophocles in the play by noting that Sophocles was contented wherever he happened to be!

In the years before the Peloponnesian War, Sophocles belonged to the board of officials called the Treasurers of Athena (e.g., 443/2). These officials were responsible for supervising the collection of tribute from the member states of the Delian League, later the Athenian Empire. Although this post was filled by lot, the fact that Sophocles could be available for such officeholding suggests a certain social-economic status. This also holds true for his election to the office of general, probably in the next year (441/0), when he served in the Athenian expedition that suppressed the revolt of Samos. The evidence is obscure, but it suggests that he also served as general in the early years of the war as well as on several embassies. This service points to a man of influence, and it was as a result of this service that he was appointed to the board of supervisors (*symbouloi*) given the authority to deal with the crisis that followed the disastrous defeat in Sicily (413). Sophocles regarded the gods with awe and respect, as a reading of his plays will also suggest. This is attested in real life by his hosting in his own home of the god Asklepios—and his snake—while the god's sanctuary was built (c. 420/19); in addition, he was priest of the hero Halon.

Although Sophocles performed many public duties for his city, it was for his dramas that he is remembered, and this is as true today as in antiquity. Later critics characterized Sophocles' style as one between that of Aeschylus and Euripides, neither complex nor simple but just right. In reality, Sophocles was much more sophisticated than these descriptions suggest. Aristotle admired the structure of his *Oedipus the King*, which he thought was a model for a drama (in *Poetics* 1452A 17–32), as the revelations of Oidipous were brought forth one by one. Other dramas, however, such as *Antigone*, cannot be so characterized. Other defining features of Sophoclean drama include rich imagery of language such as blindness in *Oedipus the King*. The blind seer Teiresias can "see" that Oidipous is guilty of wrongdoing, while the seeing Oidipous is blind to the past that will punish and blind him in the end. Of importance also to Sophoclean drama were his use of objects and the movement of actors into and out of the drama's action. Good examples of the former include the sword that will take Ajax's life (in *Ajax*) and, of the latter, the entry of Oidipous after he has blinded himself. Sophocles enjoyed enduring success in later antiquity and provided the inspiration (along with Aeschylus' trilogy *Oresteia*) for such modern-day classics as Eugene O'Neill's *Mourning Becomes Electra*.

Thucydides (c. 460–400)

The great Athenian historian of the Peloponnesian War, Thucydides was the son of Oloros and so was related to the influential family of Miltiades and Kimon (whose grandfather carried the same name). That his family possessed substantial wealth seems to be suggested by the ease of his travels during his life of exile. Thucydides served as general at least in the year 424, the year in which he failed to arrive in time and save Amphipolis from the Spartan commander Brasidas. It was this failure that forced him into a life of exile rather than return home to Athens and explain himself to the likes of Kleon, who may have introduced an en-actment making his exile legal. Thucydides clearly did not like Kleon, as evidenced by his introduction of him in the *History* as the most violent man in Athens (3.36.6) and by his apparent satisfaction in describing Kleon's cowardly death fighting Brasidas (5.10.9). Subsequently, Thucy-dides traveled around the Greek world, talking to those who participated in and/or observed the events of the war, including Alkibiades, a fellow exile from Athens, and then wrote down what he learned, as he an-nounced in the opening of his *History*.

Tissaphernes

The Persian satrap of Sardis after 413, Tissaphernes belonged to an old Persian family that had supported Darios I, who seized power in 522. Both his father and grandfathers were named Hydarnes, the latter participat-ing in the Persian Wars of 480/79. Upon arriving in Asia Minor, Tissa-phernes had responsibility over the entire region. His orders were to cooperate with Sparta, thereby ignoring the existing treaty with Athens, and to enforce payment of the tribute owed the Persians by the Greek cities in the area. His efforts to cooperate with the Spartans, however, were stymied by the arrival first of Alkibiades and then Kyros, the Per-sian "crown prince" who took over Persian intriguing, which resulted in Sparta's victory in the Ionian War.

Possibly Tissaphernes always hated Kyros for his success and contri-butions to the Spartan victory and had denounced him to his brother, King Artaxerxes, even before the war was over. When the royal broth-ers finally broke irrevocably as Kyros attempted to seize the throne (401), Tissaphernes won royal favor by supporting the King. Later when Sparta and Persia broke relations and went to war, Tissaphernes attempted a dangerous game of bluff and deceit that in the end lost him his royal favor and brought about his death soon after 395.

Xanthippe

The wife of Sokrates and the mother of his three young sons at the time of his execution in 399, Xanthippe was best known in antiquity for her bad temper and nagging ways. In his dialogue *Phaedo*, Plato has her tell Sokrates on the day of his execution that this would be the last day he would spend talking with his friends! Other writers such as Xenophon who also provide testimony on Sokrates agree that she was difficult to live with, which prompted one critic, Antisthenes, to ask Sokrates why, if women were as capable as men of being educated, he had not yet educated his wife. Sokrates' reply was that this was the reason he had married Xanthippe in the first place—to achieve that goal by starting with her. Yet Xanthippe reacted with the grief typical of a Greek woman when she last parted with Sokrates, though the tears and beating of her breasts were expected of a woman at the time.

W.K.C. Guthrie (*Socrates* [Cambridge: Cambridge University Press, 1969/71], p. 66, n.) has made the intriguing suggestion that the humorous criticism (or attack) made on Sokrates in Aristophanes' *Clouds* extended to Xanthippe. The critique of Sokrates and his philosophizing has long been known, but it is seldom noticed that the wife of Strepsiades in the drama was of aristocratic birth and that she had a liking for aristocratic names, especially those ending in *-ippos*, or "horsie." As Strepsiades tells and complains of all this, the first aristocratic name he mentions that his wife liked is Xanthippos, the masculine equivalent of Xanthippe. The line might well have produced a huge laugh in the audience as a subtle reference to Sokrates' wife. But it might also reveal something regarding their marriage—that Sokrates had married into an aristocratic family, and it was this that led to Xanthippe's famous nagging as she groused at Sokrates spending time talking with his friends rather than providing more for the family. Lamprokles, the known name of one son of Sokrates, is an aristocratic name, which supports the argument. This is all very speculative, but it provides some explanation of how it was that Sokrates came to be associated with individuals such as Alkibiades and Plato's relatives Kritias and Kharmides, aristocrats all. Upon Sokrates' death, Xanthippe would have disappeared into widowhood, as she fell back upon her own family for support in raising her sons.

Xenophon (c. 430–360?)

The son of Gryllos, Xenophon belonged to an old and elite Athenian family. As a young man he associated with Sokrates, a connection that perhaps influenced his political beliefs. His social-economic standing qualified him for service in the Athenian cavalry, which played a con-

troversial role in the events in Athens after the Peloponnesian War, supporting the Thirty Tyrants against the democracy. Xenophon may have
fought in this civil war and then afterward, in spite of the proclaimed
amnesty, decided to leave Athens. His life after 402 was spent in many
places but not home. He served in the famous and unsuccessful expedition of Kyros against his brother Artaxerxes, which ended in Kyros' death
and the heroic march home of the stranded Greek mercenary army of
which Xenophon was a part. Xenophon recounted this story in the *Anabasis*, the "march up country"—a work that reveals much of Greek life
and attitudes, as well as the Persian Empire, its peoples, and those living
around it. He settled for a time in Sparta where he became friends with
its fighting king, Agesilaos, and he reportedly enrolled his sons in the
renowned *agoge*, the Spartan system of military education. The Spartan
defeat at Leuktra (371) left Sparta in turmoil (as it was now invaded
three times), and he relocated to Corinth. Later Xenophon reconciled
with the Athenians, and one of his sons, Gryllos, died fighting for Athens
at the battle of Mantineia (362). His own death came some time afterward.

Xenophon lived at the end of the Peloponnesian War and remains an
important source of information for its later course. Thucydides' history
of the war breaks off in 411/10, and Xenophon picks up the narrative in
his work *Hellenica* (or "Affairs in Greece" or "Greek Things"). Xenophon
did not attempt to re-create the style and structure used by Thucydides,
and the two works are quite distinct. Xenophon focused his story on
Sparta, and often his partisan pro-Spartan inclination can be seen clearly.
That said, the *Hellenica* remains essential to reconstructing the events
leading to the end of the Peloponnesian War.

A friend and "student" of Sokrates (the term should be used generally
and without modern definitions), Xenophon relates how he told Sokrates
of his question to the Delphic oracle regarding his proposed enlistment in
Kyros' mercenary army. Sokrates told him that he had not phrased the
question well, but since the god had given his blessing, Xenophon should
go ahead with his plans. This little story reveals the relationship between
the two men that Xenophon explored in three "Sokratic" works that add
to the information provided by Plato and Aristophanes. These accounts—
Apology, *Symposium*, and *Memorabilia* (or "Memoirs of Sokrates")—present a like problem in drawing the line between Sokrates and Xenophon.
They also provide useful information relating to the nature of Athenian

legal procedure, personal relationships, as well as the nature of Sokratic discourse. Additional works of his treat various topics (e.g., military affairs, economics) that relate to the era after the Peloponnesian War. Xenophon is sometimes criticized as a simple and mundane author, but the body and range of his work are impressive and full of interest, a fact underlined by its survival into modern times.

Primary Documents of the War

DOCUMENT 1
The Plague in Athens

In the year 430 a plague broke out in the city of Athens. As part of his strategy to fight Sparta, Perikles yielded the Attic countryside to the Spartan-led Peloponnesian army, which devastated the empty countryside, as the rural population had been brought in behind the city walls. Thucydides, the war's historian, was in Athens during the plague and suffered from it himself. His scientific and exact description of symptoms of the plague may have been influenced by contemporary Greek scientists including Hippokrates (of the famous doctors' oath), as the following selection shows. Thucydides' detailed description has inspired various efforts over the years to identify it as measles, small pox, or typhus, for example. More recent thought, however, suggests that the disease described by Thucydides has died out or changed its form, something that also occurred with the Black Death during the Middle Ages.

That year then is admitted to have been otherwise unprecedently free from sickness; if someone had a previous illness it ended in this alone. As a rule, however, there was no ostensible cause; but people in good health were suddenly attacked by violent heats in the head, and redness and inflammation in the eyes, the inward parts, such as the throat or tongue, becoming bloody and emitting an unnatural and fetid breath. These symptoms were followed by sneezing and hoarseness, after which the pain soon reached the chest, and produced a hard cough. When it fixed in the stomach, it upset it; and discharges of bile of every kind named by physicians ensued, accompanied by very great distress. In most cases also an ineffectual retching followed, producing violent spasms, which in some cases ceased soon after, in others much later. Externally the body was not very hot to the touch, nor pale in its appearances, but reddish, livid, and breaking out into small pustules and ulcers. But internally it burned so that the patient could not bear to have on him clothing or linen even of the very lightest description; or indeed to be otherwise than stark naked. What they would have liked best would have been to throw themselves into cold water; as indeed was done by some of the neglected sick, who plunged into the rain-tanks in their agonies of unquenchable thirst; though it made no difference whether they drank little or much. Besides this, the miserable feeling of not being able to rest or sleep never ceased to torment them. The body meanwhile did not waste away so long as the distemper was at its height, but held out to a marvel against its ravages; so that when they succumbed, as in most cases, on the seventh or eighth day to the internal inflammation, they had still some strength in them. But if they passed this stage, and the disease descended further into the bowels, inducing a violent ulceration there accompanied by severe diarrhea, this brought on a weakness which was generally fatal. For the disorder first settled in the head, ran its course from thence through the whole of the body, and even where it did not prove mortal, it still left its mark on the extremities; for it settled in the private parts, the fingers and the toes, and many escaped with the loss of these, some too with that of their eyes. Others again were seized with an entire loss of memory on their first recovery, and did not know either themselves or their friends.

But while the nature of the disease was such as to baffle all description, and its attacks almost too grievous for human nature to endure, it was still in the following circumstance that its difference from all ordinary disorders was most clearly shown. All the birds and beasts that prey upon human bodies, either abstained from touching them (though there were many lying unburied), or died after tasting them. In proof of this it was noticed that birds of this kind actually disappeared; but they were not about the bodies, or indeed to be seen at all. But of course the effects which I have mentioned could best be studied in a domestic animal like the dog.

Such then, if we pass over the varieties of particular cases, which were many and peculiar, were the general features of the disease. Meanwhile the town enjoyed an immunity from all the ordinary disorders; or if any case occurred, it ended in this. Some died in neglect, others in the midst of every attention. No remedy was found that could be used as a specific; for what did good in one case, did harm in another. Strong and weak constitutions proved equally incapable of resistance, all alike being swept away, although dieted with the utmost precaution. By far the most terrible feature in the malady was the dejection that ensued when any one felt himself sickening, for the despair into which they instantly fell took away their power of resistance, and left them a much easier prey to the disorder; besides which, there was the awful spectacle of men dying like sheep, through having caught the infection from nursing each other. This caused the greatest mortality. On the one hand, if they were afraid to visit each other, they perished from neglect; indeed many houses were emptied of their inhabitants for want of a nurse: on the other, if they ventured to do so, death was the consequence.

An aggravation of the existing calamity was the influx from the country into the city, and this was especially felt by the new arrivals. As there were no houses to receive them, they had to be lodged at the hot season of the year in stifling cabins, where the mortality raged without restraint. The bodies of dying men lay one upon another, and half-dead creatures reeled about the streets and gathered round all the fountains in their longing for water. The sacred places also in which they had quartered themselves were full of corpses of persons that had died there, just as they were; for the disaster passed all bounds, men, not knowing what was to become of them, became utterly careless of everything, whether sacred or profane. All the burial rites before in use were entirely upset, and they buried the bodies as best they could. Many from want of proper appliances, through so many of their friends having died already, had recourse to the most shameless graves: sometimes getting the start of those who had raised a pile, they threw their own dead body upon the stranger's pyre and ignited it; sometimes they tossed the corpse which they were carrying on the top of another that was burning, and so went off.

Source: Thucydides, *The Peloponnesian War*. Translated by R. Crawley. London: Longmans, 1874 (= Bk. 2. 49–51.5, 52); slightly adapted by L. Tritle.

DOCUMENT 2
Brasidas and Kleon, Two Warlovers

In the spring of 421, Aristophanes staged a drama called Peace, *in which an Athenian named Trygaios decides to petition Zeus himself to put an end to the ten-year-long war with Sparta. To make his flight to Olympos, Trygaios uses as his "heroic" mount a dung-beetle, which he has found in his backyard. Upon reaching Olympos, Trygaios finds that the gods have given up on humankind and have allowed War to do what he likes, accompanied by his servant Riot (which explains why he is ordered about by War in the excerpt). In the following scene from the play, Trygaios observes War and Riot in action, as they attempt to keep the Greeks killing each other in the war by mixing up yet another "salad," which to stir they require a pestle, or a serving spoon. Aristophanes makes clear that the pestles used most recently have been an Athenian one, Kleon, or a Spartan one, Brasidas. Riot searches for them, only to find that they are both lost (and as we have seen, killed in battle), a fact that encourages Trygaios, as he notes, that "all might yet be well."*

Riot: What's your will?

War: You'll catch it, you rascal, standing idle there! Take that!

Riot: Oh, how it stings. O me, O me! Why master,
Sure you've not primed your knuckles with the garlic?

War: Run in and get a pestle.

Riot: We've not got one;
We only moved in yesterday, you know.

War: Then run at once and borrow one from Athens.

Riot: I'll run by Zeus; or else I'm sure to catch it.

Trygaios: What's to be done, my poor dear mortals, now?
Just see how terrible our danger is:
For if that scoundrel brings a pestle back,
War will sit down and pulverize our cities.
Heavens! May he perish, and not bring one back.

Riot: You there!

War: What? Don't you bring it?

Riot: Just look here, sir:

The pestle the Athenians had is lost,
The tanner fellow that disturbed all Greece.

Trygaios: O well done he, Athene, mighty mistress:
Well is he lost, and for the state's advantage,
Before they've mixed us up this bitter salad.

War: Then run away and fetch from Sparta
Another pestle.

Riot: Yes, sir.

War: Don't be long.

Trygaios: Now is the crisis of our fate, my friends.
And if there's here a man initiate
In Samothrake, it's now the hour to pray
For the averting of—the scoundrel's feet.

Riot: Alas, alas! And yet again alas!

War: What ails you? Don't you bring one now?

Riot: O Sir,
The Spartans too have lost their pestle now.

War: How so, you rascal?

Riot: Why, they lent it out
To friends up Thraceward, and they lost it there.

Trygaios: And well done they! Well done! Twin sons of Zeus!
Take courage, mortals: all may yet be well.

Source: Aristophanes, *Peace*. Translated by B. B. Rogers. Loeb Classical Library. London: William Heinemann, 1924, pp. 25–27 (= lines 254–86); slightly adapted by L. Tritle.

DOCUMENT 3
The Peace of Nikias

The Peace of Nikias ended the first phase of the Peloponnesian War, the so-called Archidamian War. Thucydides' account here is of interest for several reasons. First, it gives us some idea of how he went about researching and writing his account of the war. In the following passage he refers to the placing of inscribed pillars recording the treaty terms in both Athens and Sparta, as well as the principal religious sanctuaries of the Greeks. The detail he gives argues that he actually saw at least one of these. This clearly verifies his account and tells us that he is trying to be accurate and reliable with the information he gives us. The text is also important, for it gives us some idea about how the Greeks attempted to resolve inter-city conflict and to control the passions and violence that arise from war— that is, that it was better to sit down and discuss differences rather than fight about them. The terms of the treaty also reveal several important things about Sparta at war: the stress upon the return of prisoners of war (especially the men captured at Sphakteria), and Sparta's inability to con-trol the member states of the Peloponnesian League. As Thucydides notes, Corinth, Megara, and Thebes (among others) refused to accept the treaty, and Sparta could do nothing to force their compliance.

Accordingly this winter was employed in conferences; and as spring rapidly approached, the Lacedaemonians sent round orders to the cities to prepare for a fortified occupation of Attica, and held this as a sword to the heads of the Athenians to induce them to listen to their overtures; and at last, after many claims had been urged on either side at the conferences, a peace was agreed on upon the following basis. Each party was to restore its conquests, but Athens was to keep Nisaea; her demand for Plataea being met by the Thebans asserting that they had acquired the place not by force or treachery, but by the voluntary adhesion upon agreement of its citizens; and the same, according to the Athenian account, being the history of her acquisition of Nisaea. This arranged, the Lacedaemonians summoned their allies, and all voting for peace except the Boeotians, Corinthians, Eleans, and Megarians, who did not approve of these proceedings, they concluded the treaty and made peace, each of the contracting parties swearing to the following articles:

The Athenians and Lacedaemonians and their allies made a treaty, and swear to it, city by city, as follows:

1. Touching the national temples, there shall be a free passage by land and sea to all who wish it, to sacrifice, travel, consult, and attend the oracle or games according to the customs of their countries.
2. The temple and shrine of Apollo at Delphi and the Delphians shall be governed by their own laws, taxed by their own state, and judged by their own judges, the land and the people, according to the custom of their country.

3. The treaty shall be binding for fifty years upon the Athenians and the allies of the Athenians, and upon the Lacedaemonians and the allies of the Lacedaemonians, without fraud or harm by land or by sea.

4. It shall not be lawful to take up arms, with intent to do harm, either for the Lacedaemonians and their allies against the Athenians and their allies, or for the Athenians and their allies against the Lacedaemonians and their allies, in any way or means whatsoever. But should any difference arise between them they are to have recourse to laws and oaths, according as may be agreed between the parties.

5. The Lacedaemonians and their allies shall give back Amphipolis to the Athenians. Nevertheless, in the case of cities given up by the Lacedaemonians to the Athenians, the inhabitants shall be allowed to go where they please and to take their property with them; and the cities shall be independent, paying only the tribute of Aristides. And it shall not be lawful for the Athenians or their allies to carry on war against them after the treaty has been concluded, so long as the tribute is paid. The cities referred to are Argilus, Stagirus, Acanthus, Scolus, Olynthus, and Spartolus. These cities shall be neutral, allies neither of the Lacedaemonians nor of the Athenians; but if the cities consent, it shall be lawful for the Athenians to make them allies, provided always that the cities wish it. The Mecybernaeans, Sanaeans, and Singaeans shall inhabit their own cities, as also the Olynthians and Acanthians; but the Lacedaemonians and their allies shall give back Panactum to the Athenians.

6. The Athenians shall give back Coryphasium, Cythera, Methana, Pteleum, and Atalanta to the Lacedaemonians, and also all Lacedaemonians that are in the prison at Athens or elsewhere in the Athenian dominions, and shall let go the Peloponnesians besieged in Scione, and all others in Scione that are allies of the Lacedaemonians, and all whom Brasidas sent in there, and any others of the allies of the Lacedaemonians that may be in the prison at Athens or elsewhere in the Athenian dominions.

7. The Lacedaemonians and their allies shall in like manner give back any of the Athenians or their allies that they may have in their hands.

8. In the case of Scione, Torone, and Sermylium, and any other cities that the Athenians may have, the Athenians may adopt such measures as they please.

9. The Athenians shall take an oath to the Lacedaemonians and their allies, city by city. Every man shall swear by the most binding oath of his country, seventeen from each city. The oath shall be as follows: "I will abide by this agreement and treaty honestly and without deceit." In the same way an oath shall be taken by the Lacedaemonians and their allies to the Athenians; and the oath shall be renewed annually by both parties. Pillars shall be erected at Olympia, Pythia, the Isthmus, at Athens in the Acropolis, and at Lacedaemon in the temple at Amyclae.

10. If anything be forgotten, whatever it be, and on whatever point, it shall be consistent with their oath for both parties the Athenians and the Lacedaemonians to alter it, according to their discretion.

The treaty begins from the ephorate of Pleistolas in Lacedaemon, on the 27th day of the month of Artemisium, and from the archonship of Alcaeus at Athens, on the 25th day of the month of Elaphebolion. Those who took the oath and poured the libations for the Lacedaemonians were [17 men]; for the Athenians [17 men].

Source: Thucydides, *The Peloponnesian War*. Translated by R. Crawley. London: Longmans, 1874 (= Bk. 5. 17.2–19); slightly adapted by L. Tritle.

DOCUMENT 4
The Battle of Mantineia

The Archidamian War had seen some major clashes of armies (e.g., Delion and Amphipolis in 424 and 422, respectively), but that at Mantineia in 418 was, as Thucydides says, the biggest battle that so many Greek cities had fought for a long time. The following selection provides a basic introduction to the nature of Greek warfare: how opposing armies tended to drift right as men attempted to cover their unshielded sides and the problems this caused commanders, as it did the Spartan king Agis. His solution, when he realized the gap forming in his ranks, was to order several companies to move into the gap from their original place, but in doing so, he nearly caused disaster, as the two Spartan officers so ordered (Aristokles and Hipponoidas) refused to move, probably thinking that such a late shift in the line would cause disaster (they were later tried and condemned for cowardice, and may be seen as scapegoats for Agis' near bungling of the command). The passage also gives some idea of the ferocity of hoplite battle: at least fourteen hundred men were killed this day, and one can infer from this that hundreds more were wounded, with many dying days and weeks later from infection.

After this [i.e., words of encouragement] they joined battle, the Argives and their allies advancing with haste and fury, the Lacedaemonians slowly and to the music of many flute-players—a standing institution in their army, that has nothing to do with religion, but is meant to make them advance evenly, stepping in time, without breaking their order, as large armies are apt to do in the moment of engaging.

Just before the battle joined, King Agis resolved upon the following maneuver. All armies are alike in this: on going into action they get forced out rather on their right wing, and one and the other overlap with this their adversary's left; because fear makes each man do his best to shelter his unarmed side with the shield of the man next to him on the right, thinking that the closer the shields are locked together the better will he be protected. The man primarily responsible for this is the first upon the right wing, who is always striving to withdraw from the enemy his unarmed side; and the same apprehension makes the rest follow him. On the present occasion the Mantineans reached with their wing far beyond the Sciritae, and the Lacedaemonians and the Tegeans still farther beyond the Athenians, as their army was the largest. Agis, afraid of his left being surrounded, and thinking that the Mantineans outflanked it too far, ordered the Sciritae and the Brasideans to move out from their place in the ranks and make the line even with the Mantineans, and told the polemarchs Hipponoidas and Aristocles to fill up the gap this formed, by throwing themselves into it with two companies taken from the right wing; thinking that his right would still be strong enough and to spare, and that the line fronting the Mantineans would gain in solidity.

However, as he gave these orders in the moment of the onset, and at short notice, it so happened that Aristocles and Hipponoidas would not move over, for which offense they were afterwards banished from Sparta, as having been guilty of cowardice; and the enemy meanwhile closed before the Sciritae (whom Agis on seeing that the two companies did not move over ordered to return to their place) had time to fill up the breach in question. Now it was, however, that the Lacedaemonians, utterly worsted in respect of skill, showed themselves superior in point of courage. As soon as they came to close quarters with the enemy, the Mantinean right broke the Sciritae and Brasideans, and bursting in with their allies and the thousand picked Argives into the unclosed breach in their line cut up and surrounded the Lacedaemonians, and drove them in full rout to the wagons, killing some of the older men on guard there. But the Lacedaemonians, worsted in this part of the field, with the rest of their army, and especially the center, where the three hundred knights as they are called, fought round King Agis, fell on the Cleonaeans, the

Orneans, and the Athenians next to them, and instantly routed them; the greater number not even waiting to strike a blow, but giving way the moment that they came on, some even being trodden under foot, in their fear of being overtaken by their assailants. The army of the Argives and their allies having given way in this quarter was now completely cut in two, and the Lacedaemonian and Tegean right simultaneously closing round the Athenians with the troops that outflanked them, these last found themselves placed between two fires, being surrounded on one side and already defeated on the other. Indeed they would have suffered more severely than any other part of the army, but for the services of the cavalry which they had with them. Agis also on perceiving the distress of his left opposed to the Mantineans and the thousand Argives, ordered all the army to advance to the support of the defeated wing; and while this took place, as the enemy moved past and slanted away from them, the Athenians escaped at their leisure, and with them the beaten Argive division. Meanwhile the Mantineans and their allies and the picked body of the Argives ceased to press the enemy, and seeing their friends defeated and the Lacedaemonians in full advance upon them, took to flight. Many of the Mantineans perished; but the bulk of the picked body of the Argives made good their escape. The flight and retreat, however, were neither hurried nor long; the Lacedaemonians fighting long and stubbornly until the rout of their enemy, but that once effected, pursuing for a short time and not far.

Such was the battle, as nearly as possible as I have described it; the greatest battle that had occurred for a very long time among the Hellenes, and joined by the most considerable states. The Lacedaemonians took up a position in front of the enemy's dead, and immediately set up a trophy and stripped the dead; they took up their own dead and carried them back to Tegea, where they buried them, and restored those of the enemy under truce. The Argives, Orneans, and Cleonaeans had seven hundred killed; the Mantineans two hundred, and the Athenians and Aeginetans also two hundred, with both their generals. On the side of the Lacedaemonians, the allies did not suffer any loss worth speaking of: as to the Lacedaemonians themselves it was difficult to learn the truth; it is said, however, that there were slain about three hundred of them.

Source: Thucydides, *The Peloponnesian War*. Translated by R. Crawley. London: Longmans, 1874 (= 5. 70–74); slightly adapted by L. Tritle.

DOCUMENT 5
The Melian Dialogue

Thucydides was not present at the discussion between the Athenian commanders and the Melian council, but it is possible that he learned from one or two of those present some of what was said. But the words in the Dialogue that Thucydides assigns to both the Athenians and the Melians are his, however well he may have been informed as to what was said in the Melian council chambers. The dramatic form of dialogue that he uses here (later made famous by Plato) reflects literary experiments practiced by a number of authors at the time, including Antiphon and the anonymous author of a pamphlet called the Dissoi Logoi *("Double Arguments" or "Double Speeches"). The brief exchange may also reflect the give and take that would have occurred in political debates. In the passage reproduced here, Thucydides focuses on the nature of power and justice—that right depends on might—and the idea of expediency, or doing that which is useful. Intellectuals active in Athens and the rest of Greece at this time, including Sokrates, debated the merits of these ideas, and Thucydides' use of them here reflects the influence of philosophical ideas and argumentation on historical writing. Finally, the closing long statement by the Athenians cited here indicates that Thucydides lived to see the defeat of Athens by the Spartans, after which he began the final revisions on his account of the war.*

The Athenian envoys spoke as follows:

Athenians. "Since the negotiations are not to go on before the people, in order that we may not be able to speak straight on without interruption, and deceive the ears of the multitude by seductive arguments which would pass without refutation (for we know that this is the meaning of our being brought before the few), what if you who sit there were to pursue a method more cautious still! Make no set speech yourselves, but take us up at whatever you do not like, and settle that before going any further, and first tell us if this proposition of ours suits you."

The Melian commissioners answered:

Melians. "To the fairness of quietly instructing each other as you propose there is nothing to object; but your military preparations are too far advanced to agree with what you say, as we see you are come to be judges in your own cause, and that all we can reasonably expect from this negotiation is war, if we prove to have right on our side and refuse to submit, and in the contrary case, slavery."

Athenians. "If you have met to reason about predicting the future, or for anything else than to consult for the safety of your state upon the facts that you see before you, we will give over; otherwise we will go on."

Melians. "It is natural and excusable for men in our position to turn more ways than one both in thought and utterance. However, the question in this conference is, as you say, the safety of our country; and the discussion, if you please, can proceed in the way which you propose."

Athenians. "For ourselves, we shall not trouble you with specious pretences—either of how we have a right to our empire because we overthrew the Persians, or are now attacking you because of wrong that you have done us—and make a long speech which would not be believed; and in return we hope that you, instead of thinking to influence us by saying that you did not join the Lacedaemonians, although their colonists, or that you have done us no wrong, will aim at what is feasible, holding in view the real sentiments of us both: since you know as well as we do that right, as the world goes is only a question between equals in power, while the strong do what they can and the weak suffer what they must."

Melians. "As we think, at any rate, it is expedient—we speak as we are obliged, since you enjoin us to let right alone and talk only of interest—that you should not destroy what is our common protection, the privilege of being allowed in danger to invoke what is fair and right, and even to profit by arguments not strictly valid if they can be got to pass current. And you are as much interested in this as any, as your fall would be a signal for the heaviest vengeance and an example for the world to meditate upon."

Athenians. "The end of our empire, if end it should, does not frighten us: a rival empire like Lacedaemon, even if Lacedaemon was our real antagonist, is not so terrible to the vanquished as subjects who by themselves attack and overpower their rulers. This, however, is a risk that we are content to take. We will now proceed to show you that we have come here in the interest of our empire, and that we shall say what we are now going to say, for the preservation of your country; as we would gladly exercise that empire over you without trouble, and see you preserved for the good of us both."

Melians. "And how, pray, could it turn out as good for us to serve as for you to rule?"

Athenians. "Because you would have the advantage of submitting before suffering the worst, and we should gain by not destroying you."

Melians. "So that you would not consent to our being neutral, friends instead of enemies, but allies of neither side?"

Athenians. "No; for your hostility cannot so much hurt us as your friendship will be an argument to our subjects of our weakness, and your enmity of our power."

Source: Thucydides, *The Peloponnesian War*. Translated by R. Crawley. London: Longmans, 1874 (= Bk. 5. 84–95); slightly adapted by L. Tritle.

DOCUMENT 6
The End of the Athenian Sicilian Expedition

The Athenian fleet's failure to break out of the Great Harbor of Syracuse was a demoralizing setback. With no hope of withdrawing by sea, the only hope of salvation was by land. In a highly emotional passage, Thucydides relates how the Athenians broke camp as they attempted to escape the closing net of the Syracusans; many sick and injured men had to be left behind as they could not march with the army, and the camp was littered with the unburied bodies of the dead (Thucydides 7.75). Some forty thousand men, including sailors who would be of little use in land warfare now, set out, but the Syracusans managed to trick them into delaying their withdrawal with false information. Any sense of order and cohesion in the retreating army broke down under the relentless pressure of Syracusan attack until finally the army broke in roughly two unequal halves under Demosthenes and Nikias. Demosthenes' force collapsed and surrendered first, which meant that the full fury of the attack then descended on Nikias and his men. A vicious attack caught them as they attempted to cross the Assinaros River, and here they were literally slaughtered. (One of the verbs Thucydides uses to describe this is sphazein, used to describe sacrificial slaughter as in cutting throats.) As Thucydides states at the end of book seven, few of these forty thousand men returned home.

The following passage records the destruction of that portion of the Athenian army commanded by Nikias, that of Demosthenes already being overtaken and forced into surrender by the Syracusans. Note how the cap-

tured Athenians and their allies were enslaved, some of them through the legal distribution of the spoils of war, but others by being captured and held by individual Syracusans who then turned the captives into slave laborers. Some of these later escaped, and a few, able to recite lines of poetry from recent plays of Euripides, would be able to gain their freedom (Plutarch, Life of Nicias 29.3).

Meanwhile, Nicias with his division arrived that day at the river Erineus, crossed over and posted his army upon some high ground upon the other side. The next day the Syracusans overtook him and told him that the troops under Demosthenes had surrendered, and invited him to follow their example. Incredulous of the fact, Nicias asked for a truce to send a horseman to see and upon the return of the messenger with the news that they had surrendered, sent a herald to Gylippus and the Syracusans, saying that he was ready to agree with them on behalf of the Athenians to repay whatever money the Syracusans had spent upon the war if they would let his army go; and offered until the money was paid to give Athenians as hostages, one for every talent. The Syracusans and Gylippus rejected this proposition, and attacked this division as they had the other, standing all round and shooting them with missiles until the evening. Food and necessities were as miserably wanting to the troops of Nicias as they had been to those of Demosthenes; nevertheless they watched for the quiet of the night to resume their march. But as they were taking up their arms the Syracusans perceived it and raised the war cry, upon which the Athenians, finding that they were discovered, laid them down again, except about three hundred men who forced their way through the guards and went on during the night as they were able.

As soon as it was day Nicias put his army into motion, pressed, as before, by the Syracusans and their allies, pelted from every side by their missiles, and struck down by their javelins. The Athenians pushed on for the Assinarus, impelled by the attacks made upon them from every side by numerous cavalry and the swarm of other arms, fancying that they should breathe more freely if once across the water. Once there they rushed in, and all order was at an end, each man wanting to cross first, and the attacks of the enemy making it difficult to cross at all; forced to huddle together, they fell against and trod down one another, some dying immediately upon the javelins, others getting entangled together and stumbling over the articles of baggage, without being able to rise again. Meanwhile the opposite bank, which was steep, was lined by the Syracusans, who showered missiles down upon the Athenians, most of them drinking greedily and heaped together in disorder in the hollow bed of the river. The Peloponnesians also came down and butchered them, especially those in the water, which was thus immediately spoiled, but which they went on drinking just the same, mud and all, bloody as it was, most even fighting to have it.

At last, when many dead now lay piled one upon another in the stream, and part of the army had been destroyed at the river, and the few that escaped from there were cut off by the cavalry, Nicias surrendered himself to Gylippus, whom he trusted more than he did the Syracusans, and told him and the Lacedaemonians to do what they liked with him, but to stop the slaughter of the soldiers. Gylippus, after this, immediately gave orders to make prisoners; upon which the rest were brought together alive, except a large number secreted away by the soldiers, and a party was sent in pursuit of the three hundred who had got through the guard during the previous night, and who were now taken with the rest. The number of the enemy collected as public property was not considerable; but those taken away secretly was very large, and all Sicily was filled with them, no convention having been made in their case as for those taken with Demosthenes. Besides this, a large portion were killed outright, the carnage being very great, and not exceeded by any in this Sicilian war. In numerous other encounters upon the march, not a few had also fallen. Nevertheless many escaped, some at the moment, others served as slaves, and then ran away subsequently. These found refuge at Catana.

· · ·

This was the greatest Hellenic achievement of any in this war, or, in my opinion, in Hellenic history; at once most glorious to the victors, and most calamitous to the conquered. They were beaten at all points and altogether; all that they suffered was great; they were destroyed, as the saying is, with a total destruction, their fleet, their army—everything was destroyed, and few out of many returned home.

Source: Thucydides, *The Peloponnesian War*. Translated by R. Crawley. London: Longmans, 1874 (= 7. 82–85, 87); slightly adapted by L. Tritle.

DOCUMENT 7
Civil War in Corcyra

The horrors of war descended on the Greeks in all forms—death from plague, death in battle, and death at the hands of fellow citizens, or civil war. In a famous discussion, Thucydides relates the horrors of civil war that struck Corcyra in 427. This narrative he uses as an example of the destructiveness of civil war (what the Greeks called stasis*), and from his account one can see that the viciousness of the civil war in ancient Greek times was no less severe than in modern (cf. the U.S. Civil War, or any other more recent example such as Rwanda in 1994 and the brutal Hutu attacks on the Tutsi there).*

In this passage, Thucydides first relates the viciousness of the violence, how it knew no limits, and how war, which had unleashed the violence, became in his eyes "a violent teacher," bringing people down to the level of conduct according to the situation in which they found themselves. This analysis of war's impact has to be seen as one of Thucydides' lasting judgments on what war does to people.

During seven days . . . the Corcyraeans were engaged in butchering those of their fellow-citizens whom they regarded as their enemies: and although the crime imputed was that of attempting to put down the democracy, some were killed also for private hatred, others by their debtors because of the monies owed them. Death thus raged in every shape; and, as usually happens at such times, there was no length to which violence did not go; sons were killed by their fathers, and suppliants dragged from the altar or slain upon it; while some were even walled up in the temple of Dionysus and died there.

So bloody was the march of the revolution, and the impression which it made was the greater as it was one of the first to occur. Later on, one may say, the whole Hellenic world was convulsed; struggles being everywhere made by the popular chiefs to bring in the Athenians, and by the oligarchs to introduce the Lacedaemonians. In peace there would have been neither the pretext nor the wish to make such an invitation; but in war, with an alliance always at the command of either faction for the harm of their adversaries and their own corresponding advantage, opportunities for bringing in the foreigner were never wanting to the revolutionary parties. The sufferings which revolution entailed upon the cities were many and terrible, such as have occurred and always will occur, as long as the nature of mankind remains the same; though in a severer or milder form, and varying in their symptoms, according to the variety of the particular cases. In peace and prosperity states and individuals have better sentiments, because they do not find themselves suddenly confronted with imperious necessities; but war takes away the easy supply of daily wants, and so proves a violent teacher, that brings most men's characters to a level with their fortunes.

. . .

The cause of all these evils was the lust for power arising from greed and ambition; and from these passions proceeded the violence of parties once engaged in contention. The leaders in the cities, each provided with the fairest professions, on the one side with the cry of political equality of the people, on the other of a moderate aristocracy, sought prizes for themselves in those public interests which they pretended to cherish, and, recoiling from no means in their struggles for ascendancy, engaged in the direct excesses; in their acts of vengeance they went to even greater lengths, not stopping at what justice or the good of the state demanded, but making the party caprice of the moment their only standard, and invoking with equal readiness the condemnation of an unjust verdict or the authority of the strong arm to glut the animosities of the hour. Thus religion was in honor with neither party; but the use of fair phrases to arrive at guilty ends was in high reputation. Meanwhile the moderate part of the citizens perished between the two, either for not joining in the quarrel, or because envy would not suffer them to escape.

Thus every form of iniquity took root in the Hellenic countries by reason of the troubles. The ancient simplicity into which honor so largely entered was laughed down and disappeared; and society became divided into camps in which no man trusted his fellow.

Source: Thucydides, *The Peloponnesian War*. Translated by R. Crawley. London: Longmans, 1874 (= 3. 81.4–82.2, 82.8–83.1); slightly adapted by L. Tritle.

DOCUMENT 8
Aristophanes on the Causes of War

In his play Acharnians, Aristophanes has some fun with historians like Herodotus and Thucydides, as well as the great poet Homer, in ridi-

culing the historians' efforts to make sense of the causes of war. His references to the kidnapping of prostitutes is an updating of Homer's Trojan War in which Helen was lured away to Troy by Paris, which set into motion that great war (and which Herodotus also mentioned in his account of the Persian Wars). But Aristophanes can also be serious here, that is, using comedy to disguise a critical appraisal of what happened to set off war among the Greeks in 431. Most important here are his remarks on the Megarian Decree and the stubbornness with which Perikles defended it, to the point that war with Sparta erupted, and so in his mind, Perikles bears as much responsibility for what happened as the Spartans, whom he clearly does not like. The speaker here is Dikaiopolis, who sets out in the play to make his own private peace with the enemy.

Bear me no grudge, spectators, if, a beggar
I dare to speak before the Athenian people
About the city in a comic play.
For what is true even comedy can tell.
And I shall utter startling things but true.
Nor now can Cleon slander me because
With strangers present, I defame the State.
It's the Lenaea, and we're all alone;
No strangers yet have come; nor from the states
Have yet arrived the tribute and allies.
We're quite alone clean-winnowed; for I count
Our alien residents the civic bran.
The Lacedaemonians I detest entirely;
And may Poseidon, Lord of Taenarum,
Shake all their houses down about their ears;
For I, like you, have had my vines cut down,
But after all—for none but friends are here—
Why the Lakonians do we blame for this?
For men of ours, I do not say the State,
Remember this, I do not say the State,
But worthless fellows of a worthless stamp,
Ill-coined, ill-minted, spurious little men,
Kept on denouncing Megara's little coats.
And if a cucumber or hare they saw,
Or sucking pig, or garlic, or lump salt,
All were Megarian, and were sold offhand.
Still these were trifles, and our country's way.
But some young drunken gamblers went

And stole from Megara town the fair Simaetha.
Then the Megarians, garlicked with the smart,
Stole, in return, two of Aspasia's whores.
From these three Wantons over the Hellenic race
Burst forth the first beginnings of the War.
For then, in wrath, the Olympian Pericles
Thundered and lightened, and confounded Hellas.
Enacting laws which ran like drinking songs,
That the Megarians presently depart
From earth and sea, the mainland, and the market.
Then the Megarians, slowly starving,
Besought their Spartan friends to get the Law
Of the three Wantons canceled and withdrawn.
And often they asked us, but we yielded not.
Then followed instantly the clash of shields.

Source: Aristophanes, *Acharnians*. Translated by B. B. Rogers. Loeb Classical Library. London: William Heinemann, 1924, pp. 29–30 (= lines 496–535); slightly adapted by L. Tritle.

DOCUMENT 9
Thucydides on His History and the Causes of the War

Thucydides was the reporter of the Peloponnesian War, and as a consequence his account of the war must be regarded carefully. As discussed earlier, however, he had certain ideas about the method he adopted to write about the war, and nowhere is this more important than in his first book. Here his statement marks a departure from the great poetical account of war provided by Homer in his Iliad and from the colorful but sometimes confusing account of his older contemporary Herodotus who wrote his account of the Persian Wars about the same time as the Peloponnesian War broke out. It is clear from this statement that Thucydides believed it was possible to find the "truth" if all the evidence was subjected to careful examination. Historians today are somewhat more skeptical of proclaiming the "truth" and instead attempt to give a broader view of what happened based on different perspectives and a balanced assessment of the evidence. Some historians have argued that Thucydides was more like a journalist who was telling (or even selling) a particular story, while Herodotus' technique was more like that of the modern researcher who gives variant ac-

counts and leaves it up to the reader to decide where the "truth" lies. Yet
it must be noted that Thucydides took the time and made the effort to lo-
cate eyewitnesses to the events he recorded (as is evident in his account
of the Peace of Nikias, for which see Document 3) and actual documents
that he incorporated into his history.

Having now given the result of my inquires into early times, I grant that there will be a difficulty in believing every particular detail. The way that most men deal with traditions, even traditions of their own country, is to receive them all alike as they are delivered, without applying any critical test whatever. The general Athenian public imagines that Hipparchus was tyrant when he fell by the hands of Harmodius and Aristogeiton; not knowing that Hippias, the eldest of the sons of Pisistratus, was really supreme, and that Harmodius and Aristogeiton suspecting, on the very day, literally at the very moment fixed on the deed, that information had been conveyed to Hippias by their accomplices, concluded that he had been warned, and did not attack him, yet, not liking to be apprehended and risk their lives for nothing, fell upon Hipparchus near the temple of the daughters of Leos, and killed him as he was arranging the Panathenaic procession.

There are many other unfounded ideas current among the rest of the Hellenes, even on matters of contemporary history which have not been obscured by time. For instance; there is the notion that the Lacedaemonian kings have two votes each, the fact being, that they have only one; and that there is a company of Pitane, there being no such thing. So little pains do the simple take in the investigation of truth, accepting readily the first story that comes to hand. On the whole, however, the conclusions I have drawn from the proofs quoted may, I believe, safely be relied on. Assuredly they will not be disturbed either by the works of a poet displaying the exaggeration of his craft, or by the compositions of the chroniclers that are attractive at truth's expense; the subjects they treat of being out of the reach of evidence, and time having robbed most of them of historical value by enthroning them in the region of legend. Turning from these, we can rest satisfied with having proceeded upon the clearest data, and having arrived at conclusions as exact as can be expected in matters of such antiquity. To come to this war; despite the known disposition of the actors in a struggle to overrate its importance, and when it is over to return to their admiration of earlier events, yet an examination of the facts will show that it was much greater than the wars that preceded it.

With reference to the speeches in this history, some were delivered before the war began, others while it was going on; some I heard myself, others I got from various quarters; it was in all cases difficult to carry them word for word in one's memory, so my habit has been to make the speakers say what was in my opinion demanded of them by the various occasions, of course adhering as closely as possible to the general sense of what was really said. And with reference to the narrative of events, far from permitting myself to derive it from the first source that came to hand, I did not even trust my own impressions, but it rests partly on what I saw myself, partly on what others saw for me, the accuracy of the report being always tried by the most severe and detailed tests possible. My conclusions have cost me some labors from the want of coincidence between accounts of the same events by different eyewitnesses, arising sometimes from imperfect memory, sometimes from undue partiality for one side or the other. The absence of romance in my history will, I fear, detract somewhat from its interest; but if it be judged useful by those inquirers who desire an exact knowledge of the past as an aid to the interpretation of the future, which in the course of human things must resemble if it does not reflect it, I shall be content. In conclusion, I have written my work, not as an essay which is to win the applause of the moment, but as a possession for all time.

Source: Thucydides, *The Peloponnesian War*. Translated by R. Crawley. London: Longmans, 1874 (= Bk. 1. 20–22); slightly adapted by L. Tritle.

DOCUMENT 10
Plutarch on Perikles and the Causes of War

In his comedy Acharnians, *Aristophanes reflected the popular view in Athens that the primary cause of the Peloponnesian War was the Megarian Decree and the stubbornness with which Perikles held to its defense against the Spartans, who interceded on behalf of the Megarians. The later Greek writer Plutarch (second century* C.E.*) wrote a series of biographies or lives of Greeks (and Romans) in which he preserves much information that otherwise would have been lost, including traditions and accounts*

from outside Athens. One of those lives was of Perikles, and in this ac-
count Plutarch supplements what Aristophanes reports (he also includes
what Aristophanes told), including information regarding the diplomatic
exchanges between Athens and Sparta as they attempted to defuse the cri-
sis. This excerpt adds to the information regarding the Megarian Decree
as well as some of what the Spartans reportedly told the Athenians, espe-
cially Perikles, about the decree and how to deal with the law.

Despite all the complaints, embassies were being sent to Athens, and
Archidamos, king of the Lakedaimonians, was trying to resolve the many
complaints of the allies and calm them. It appears that war with the
Athenians would not have followed from the other complaints, if the
Athenians could have been persuaded to repeal the resolution against
the Megarians [the Megarian Decree] and be reconciled with them. And
since Perikles was most opposed to this and urged the people to hold fast
to their rivalry with the Megarians, he alone was the cause of the war.

They say that an embassy arrived in Athens from Lakedaimon to discuss this matter, and when Perikles put forward as an excuse some law
preventing the repeal of the tablet on which the decree happened to be
written, Polyalkes, one of the Spartan ambassadors, said, "You don't have
to repeal it, but turn it to the wall. There's no law that prevents that is
there?" While a witty remark, Perikles was not moved at all. It may have
been that he had some private ill-feelings against the Megarians, but in
public he openly charged them with appropriating part of the sacred lands
on the frontier between the two states. He proposed a decree sending a
herald to them, and the same also to the Lakedaimonians, to denounce
the Megarians. This decree of Perikles' presented a reasonable and cour-
teous claim for justice. But after the herald, Anthemokritos, was sent and
killed, and it appeared that the Megarians were responsible, Charinos
proposed a decree against them, that there should be an implacable hatred and a state of truceless war between the two states; that any Megarian who should cross into Attika should be condemned to death; that
the generals, when taking the traditional oaths, should swear in addition
that twice a year they would invade Megarian territory; and that Anthemokritos should be buried beside the Thriasian Gates, now called the
Dipylon, or Double Gate. But the Megarians denied the murder of Anthemokritos, throwing the blame on Aspasia and Perikles, appealing to
the famous and trite verses from Aristophanes' play *Acharnians* [see Document 8].

It is not so easy to find out the reasons for the decree against the Megarians, but all agree in blaming Perikles that it was not repealed. Except some say he held fast to his position out of high-mindedness with regard to the best interests of Athens, that he thought yielding on the decree was a test and that any agreement or concession would be an admission of weakness; but others say that it was out of his stubbornness and contentiousness, his desire to demonstrate his strength, that he showed contempt to the Lakedaimonians.

Source: Plutarch, *Life of Pericles* 29.7–31.1. Translated by L. Tritle.

DOCUMENT 11
Kleon and Diodotos on Democracy and Power

> *The debate over Mytilene that Thucydides provides in his account of the Peloponnesian War is one of the most studied and important parts of his* History, *as it reveals the fundamental problem a democratic society faces when it rules others or seeks to use its power. It is also clear from what Thucydides tells us that the decision taken by the Athenians to punish their former friends and allies with a blanket sentence of death (remember, a first vote had decreed death for all adult males of Mytilene, probably meaning those above age eighteen, while everyone else would be enslaved) was viewed by many as too vindictive and if carried out might well stiffen opposition to Athenian rule rather than facilitate it.*
>
> *In the following selection, note how Thucydides constructs matching pairs of speeches for his two speakers, Kleon and Diodotos, who offer conflicting pictures first of democratic debate, and then of how an imperial state should exercise rule over its subjects.*

Cleon, son of Cleaenetus, . . . the most violent man at Athens, and at that time by far the most powerful with the commons, came forward again and spoke as follows:

"I have often before now been convinced that a democracy is incapable of empire, and never more so than by your present change of mind in the matter of Mytilene. Fears or plots being unknown to you in your daily relations with each other, you feel just the same with regard to your allies, and never reflect that the mistakes into which you may be led by listening to their appeals, or by giving way to your own compassion, are full of danger to yourselves, and bring you no thanks for your weakness from your allies; entirely forgetting that your empire is a tyranny and your subjects disaffected conspirators, whose obedience is insured not by your suicidal concessions, but by the superiority given you by your own strength and not their loyalty. The most alarming feature in the case is the constant change of measures with which we appear to be threatened, and our seeming ignorance of the fact that bad laws which are never changed are better for a city than good ones that have no authority; that unlearned loyalty is more serviceable than quick-witted insubordination; and that ordinary men usually manage public affairs better than their more gifted fellows. The latter are always wanting to appear wiser than the laws, and to overrule every proposition brought forward, thinking that they cannot show their wit in more important matters, and by such behavior too often ruin their country; while those who mistrust their own cleverness are content to be less learned than the laws, and less able to pick holes in the speech of a good speaker; and being fair judges rather than rival athletes, generally conduct affairs successfully. These we ought to imitate, instead of being led on by cleverness and intellectual rivalry to advise you contrary to your real opinions.

. . .

The truth is that great good fortune coming suddenly and unexpectedly tends to make a people insolent: in most cases it is safer for mankind to have success in reason than out of reason; and it is easier for them, one may say, to stave off adversity than to preserve prosperity. Our mistake has been to distinguish the Mytilenians as we have done: had they been long ago treated like the rest, they never would have so far forgotten themselves, human nature being as surely made arrogant by consideration, as it is awed by firmness.

. . .

To sum up shortly, I say that if you follow my advice you will do what is just towards the Mytilenians, and at the same time expedient; while by a different decision you will not oblige them so much as pass sentence upon yourselves. For if they were right in rebelling, you must be wrong in ruling. However, if, right or wrong, you determine to rule, you must carry out your principle and punish the Mytilenians as your interest requires; or else you must give up your empire and cultivate honesty with danger. Make up your minds, therefore, to give them like for like; and do not let the victims who escaped the plot be more insensible than the conspirators who hatched it; but reflect what they would have done if victorious over you, especially as they were the aggressors. It is they who wrong their neighbor without a cause, that pursue their victim to the death, on account of the danger which they foresee in letting their enemy survive; since the object of a wanton wrong is more dangerous, if he escape, than an enemy who has not this to complain of. Do not, therefore, be traitors to yourselves, but recall as nearly as possible the moment of suffering and the supreme importance which you then attached to their reduction; and now pay them back in their turn, without yielding to present weakness or forgetting the peril that once hung over you. Punish them as they deserve, and teach your other allies by a striking example that the penalty for rebellion is death. Let them once understand this and you will not have so often to neglect your enemies while you are fighting with your own allies.

Such were the words of Cleon. After him Diodotus, son of Eucrates, who had also in the previous assembly spoken most strongly against putting the Mytilenians to death, came forward and spoke as follows:

I do not blame the persons who have reopened the case of the Mytilenians, nor do I approve the protests which we have heard against important questions being frequently debated. I think the two things most opposed to good counsel are haste and passion: haste usually goes hand in hand with folly, passion with coarseness and narrowness of mind. As for the argument that speech ought not to be the exponent of action, the man who uses it must be either senseless or interested: senseless if he believes it possible to treat of the uncertain future through any other medium; interested if wishing to carry a disgraceful measure and doubting his ability to speak well in a bad cause, he thinks to frighten opponents and hearers by well-aimed slander. What is still more intolerable is to accuse a speaker of making a display in order to be paid for it. If ignorance only were imputed, an unsuccessful speaker might retire with a reputation for honesty, if not for wisdom; while the charge of dishonesty makes him suspected, if successful, and thought, if defeated, not only a fool but a rogue. The city is no gainer by such a system, since fear deprives it of its advisers; although in truth, if our speakers are to make such assertions, it would be better for the country if they could not speak at all, as we should then make fewer blunders. The good citizen ought to triumph not by frightening his opponents but by beating them fairly in argument; and a wise city without over-distinguishing its best advisers, will nevertheless not deprive them of their due, and far from punishing an unlucky counselor will not even regard him as disgraced. In this way successful orators would be least tempted to sacrifice their convictions to popularity, in the hope of still higher honors, and unsuccessful speakers to resort to the same popular arts in order to win over the multitude.

. . .

Only consider what a blunder you would commit in doing as Cleon recommends. As things are at present, in all the cities the people are your friend, and either do not revolt with the oligarchy, or, if forced to do so, becomes at once the enemy of the insurgents; so that in the war with the hostile city you have the masses on your side. But if you butcher the people of Mytilene, who had nothing to do with the revolt, and who, as soon as they got arms, of their own motion surrendered the town, first you will commit the crime of killing your benefactors; and next you will play directly into the hands of the higher classes, who when they induce their cities to rise, will immediately have the people on their side, through your having announced in advance the same punishment for those who are guilty and for those who are not. On the contrary, even if they were guilty, you ought to seem not to notice it, in order to avoid alienating the only class still friendly to us. In short, I consider it far more useful for the preservation of our empire voluntarily to put up with injustice, than to put to death, however justly, those whom it is in our interest to keep alive. As for Cleon's idea that in punishment the claims of justice and expediency can both be satisfied, facts do not confirm the possibility of such a combination.

Confess, therefore, that this is the wisest course, and without conceding too much either to pity or to poverty of thought, by neither of which motives do I any more than Cleon wish you to be influenced, upon the plain merits of the case before you, be persuaded by me to try calmly those of the Mytilenians whom Paches sent off as guilty, and to leave the rest undisturbed. This is at once best for the future, and most terrible to your enemies at the present moment; inasmuch as good policy against an adversary is superior to the blind attacks of brute force. Such were the words of Diodotus.

Source: Thucydides, *The Peloponnesian War*. Translated by R. Crawley. London: Longmans, 1874 (= Bk. 3. 37–39.4, 40.4–7, 41–42, 47–49.1); slightly adapted by L. Tritle.

DOCUMENT 12
Alkibiades and His Problems

> *Alkibiades is among the more colorful personalities of ancient Greece, and his role in the events of the Peloponnesian War is full of interest. At once charismatic, arrogant, and full of life, Alkibiades played a major role in both promoting and shaping the Athenian Expedition to Sicily. In the passage cited here from Plutarch's* Life of Alcibiades, *written in the second century* C.E., *Alkibiades' ambitions are clearly revealed, as is the suggested disapproval of the plan by Sokrates, who after the war would be blamed for actions taken by his supposed students and protégés like Alkibiades (see Chapter 5 and Document 18).*
>
> *Plutarch also provides information omitted by Thucydides and found in other now lost sources that tell what was happening in Athens as this great expedition formed. Plutarch reports that as the expedition was being prepared, Athenian women celebrated the feast of Adonis, a dying male god, which would have been unsettling as so many sons and husbands were about to sail off to war. Plutarch also gives details of the two religious-political controversies that shaped the outcome of the Sicilian Expedition on account of Alkibiades' supposed role in these, the Mutilation of the Hermai and the Profanation of the Mysteries of Demeter at Eleusis. Whether or not Alkibiades was involved in these scandals will never be known, but it is clear from what Plutarch says that many in Athens were prepared to believe the worst. Clearly, partisan politics became involved, and it is interesting to note that there were Athenians who placed political ambitions and rivalries before the welfare of the state. Allowing Alkibiades to sail with the invasion force was a bad idea: the decision later to recall him to Athens to stand trial for his alleged role in these sacrilegious acts simply compounded the mistake.*

The Athenians, even in the lifetime of Perikles, had set their hearts on Sicily, and after his death set to work to take it; they sent so-called "assistance" to their allies each time these were oppressed by the Syracusans, so laying stepping stones of a greater expedition. But all in all the one person inflaming this desire of theirs and persuading them neither in part nor in small ways, but to sail with a great armament and attempt to subdue the island was Alkibiades. While persuading the people to hope for great things, he reached for even greater: for the conquest of Sicily he had in mind not an end but the future. And while Nikias was trying to turn back the people, telling them that taking Syracuse would be a difficult thing, Alkibiades was dreaming of Carthage and Libya, and having expanded to these, from here adding Italy and the Peloponnese. He almost considered Sicily as only a supply base of war. The young men were at once stirred up by these hopes, while the old could be heard talking of the many wonders of the expedition, so that many in the wrestling schools and public meeting places could be seen sketching out the shape of Sicily and the position of Libya and Carthage.

Yet Sokrates the philosopher and Meton the astrologer, it is said, had little hope that any good would come to the city from this expedition; Sokrates being given a warning by his customary divine sign, while Meton, either fearing the future from rational calculation or his divinations, pretended madness and took a burning torch and acted as if he would set fire to his own house. [Plutarch adds in the following section (17.6) that some thought Meton did this in order to gain an exemption for his son on the planned expedition to Sicily and evidently succeeded in doing so.]

After the people had voted on the decree approving the expedition and preparations were being made to sail, some unlucky things happened, especially at the festival to be observed at that moment. This was the Adonia, at which women throughout the city were making statuettes for burial just like burying real dead men, and acted out funeral rituals, beating their breasts and singing funeral songs. The mutilation of the Hermai, however, the majority of which in one night had their faces disfigured, threw many into confusion, even those who thought little of such acts. A story was told that the Corinthians had carried out the deed as Syracuse was their colony, that from the omen the Athenians might hold back from the expedition or even change their minds about the war. But the story was not believed by many people, or the opinion of those who thought there was nothing dangerous in the matter, that it was only the sort of thing undisciplined young men do when carried away by unmixed wine into violence from child's play. Reacting angrily and at the same time in fear to what happened, thinking a group of conspirators were planning bold actions, they examined every suspicion closely, the Council and the assembly convening many times in a few days.

In these investigations, Androkles, a popular leader, produced some slaves and metics, who denounced Alkibiades and some of his friends for mutilating other statues and drunkenly imitating the Mysteries. They said someone named Theodoros represented the herald, Polytion the torch-bearer, and Alkibiades the hierophant, or chief priest, while others of his companions were present to be initiated and were addressed as Mystai. These were the charges in the impeachment brought by Thessalos, the son of Kimon, which accused Alkibiades for his impiety of the two goddesses [Demeter and Persephone]. The people were bitterly angry with Alkibiades, which Androkles—who was Alkibiades' most hated enemy—further provoked. In the beginning this troubled Alkibiades' friends, but learning that the sailors about to sail for Sicily were well disposed to him, and that the soldiers, especially the one thousand hoplites from Argos and Mantineia, being heard openly saying that it was on account of Alkibiades that they were campaigning far across the sea, and that were he treated unfairly, they would at once withdraw from the expedition, they regained their courage and taking the opportunity mounted a defense for him. At this his enemies lost heart and were afraid that the impending judgment of the people would be less harsh towards him on account of the need for his service. Therefore they contrived that some speakers, not known to be enemies of Alkibiades, but in reality hating him no less than those who admitted it, should stand up in the assembly and say that it was absurd that a general appointed with extraordinary powers of so great a force, the soldiers and allies gathered together, should lose the critical moment, between the casting of lots for the jury and the measuring of the water clock. "But," they said, "now let him sail with good fortune, and then when the war is finished, he can defend himself in person according to the laws."

The malice of this delay did not escape Alkibiades, and he argued it was terrible to be sent off with such a great force leaving behind charges and slanders against him; that he deserved to die, he said, if he could not clear himself of the charges directed against him; but being set free and openly cleared of guilt, he could prosecute the war unhindered by the accusations of informers and enemies. But he could not persuade the people, who ordered him to sail, and he put to sea with his fellow generals, being just short 140 triremes, 5100 hoplites, 1300 archers, slingers, and light-armed troops, and all noteworthy armaments.

Source: Plutarch, *The Life of Alcibiades* 17.1–5, 18.4–20.1. Translated by L. Tritle.

DOCUMENT 13
Sokrates and Parrhasios on Art

*Xenophon knew Sokrates well and probably wrote his memoirs of con-
versations held with Sokrates and others in Athens some twenty years or
more after Sokrates' death in 399. It is difficult to know (as in Plato's
writings on Sokrates) where Sokrates leaves off and Xenophon begins, but
as the discussion here focuses on art and imitation of life and nature, it
may be more Sokrates than Xenophon. As noted earlier, this passage provides some insight into the techniques of classical Greek artists and how
they were sensitive to questions of realism in art, one of the features of
the classical ideal.*

One day visiting Parrhasios the painter and entering into a conversation with him, Sokrates asked, "Parrhasios, is painting a representation
of those things that are seen? You painters represent hollows and heights,
darkness and light, hard and soft, rough and smooth, and young and old
bodies by use of color?" "In truth we do," he said. "And when portraying
a beautiful body, since it is not easy for one person to have perfect features, you bring together the best forms from many models and so make
the body appear beautiful?" "Yes, we do this," he said. "What about this
then? Do you represent the character of the soul, that which is most persuasive and pleasing, friendly and desirable, and loving? Or is this not capable of representation?" "How could it be represented, Sokrates, when
it has neither form nor color nor the other qualities you mentioned, nor
can it be seen?" "Is it possible," Sokrates said, "that one can look at someone in a friendly or hateful way?" "It seems so to me," Parrhasios said.
"Then this can be represented in the eyes?" "Definitely, he said." "Do you
think that those who care about good and bad things happening to their
friends have the same expressions on their faces?" "Not at all," he said:
for they become happy at the good things and unhappy at the bad." "And
it is possible to represent this?" "Definitely," Parrhasios said.

Source: Xenophon, *Memorabilia* ["Memories of Sokrates"] 3.10.1–4. Translated
by L. Tritle.

DOCUMENT 14
The Noble Death of Polyxena

In his drama Hecuba, *Euripides relates the death of Polyxena, one of two surviving daughters of Hekuba, the former queen of Troy. As discussed in Chapter 4, Euripides wrote this play during the Peloponnesian War, and while the audience (and reader today) watches a story taken from those of the legendary Trojan War saga, the ideas Euripides presents seem to be clearly influenced by contemporary events. It must be remembered that the audience of Athenians that attended the theater were mostly men, almost all of whom had served actively in the army or fleet, had fought battles, and had witnessed all the horrific things that accompany war. What Euripides does here then is all the more remarkable as he shows a young girl possessing all the courage that men value. This inversion of courage—that is, that women can be as brave as men, probably struck the men in the audience in very different ways. Some surely dismissed it as the nonsense of a poet, while more reflective individuals would have perhaps remembered the bravery of the Plataian women who remained behind in their city to cook for the defenders of that city holding out against their Theban and Spartan enemies (see Thucydides 3.68.2). Such displays of courage as this may have stuck in Euripides' mind and influenced him as here. Note also in the following passage how Euripides describes Polyxena tearing her own robes and "exposing her naked breasts, bare and lovely like a sculptured goddess." This passage also calls to mind several of the sculptures discussed in Chapter 4 and clearly points to the connection of literature and art during the Peloponnesian War era. Polyxena's noble death is related by Talthybios, the Greek herald, to her mother Hekuba.*

> There is a cost
> in telling too, a double price of tears,
> for I was crying when your daughter died,
> and I will cry again while telling you,
> lady. But listen.
> The whole army of the Greeks,
> drawn up in ranks, was present at the execution,
> waiting and watching while Polyxena was led
> by Achilles' son on slowly through the center of the camp
> and up to the tomb. I stood nearby, while behind her
> came a troop of soldiers purposely appointed

to prevent her struggles.
      Then Achilles' son
lifted a golden beaker to pour the offering
of wine to his father's ghost and nodded to me
to call for silence.
"Quiet, Achaeans!" I shouted,
"Silence in the ranks!" and instantly a hush
fell upon the army and he began to pray:
"Great ghost of my father Achilles, receive
this offering I pour to charm your spirit up.
Rise and drink this gift we give to you,
this virgin's fresh blood. Be gracious to us:
set free our ships and loose our anchor-ropes.
Grant to us all our day of coming home,
grant us all to come home safe from Troy!"
So he prayed, and the army with him.
      Then
grasping his sword by its golden hilt, he slipped it
from the sheath, and made a sign to the soldiers
to seize her. But she spoke first:
      "Wait, you Greeks
who sacked my city! Of my own free will I die.
Let no man touch me. I offer my throat
willingly to the sword. I will not flinch.
But let me be free for now. Let me die free.
I am of royal blood, and I scorn to die
the death of a slave."
      "Free her!" the army roared,
and Agamemnon ordered his men to let her go.
The instant they released their hold, she grasped her robes
at the shoulder and ripped them open down the sides
as far as the waist, exposing her naked breasts,
bare and lovely like a sculptured goddess.
Then she sank, kneeling on the ground, and spoke
her most heroic words:
      "Strike, captain.
Here is my breast. Will you stab there?
Or in the neck? Here is my throat, bared
for your blow."
      Torn between pity and duty,
Achilles' son stood hesitating, and then

slashed her throat with the edge of his sword. The blood
gushed out, and she fell, dying, to the ground,
but even as she dropped, managed to fall somehow
with grace, modestly hiding what should be hidden
from men's eyes.
      The execution finished,
the soldiers set to work. Some scattered leaves
upon her corpse, while others brought branches
of pine and heaped her pyre. Those who shirked
found themselves abused by the rest.
      "You loafers,"
they shouted, "how can you stand there empty-handed,
doing nothing? Where's your present for the girl?
When did you ever see greater courage
than that?"

Source: Euripides, *Hecuba.* Translated by W. Arrowsmith. *The Complete Greek Tragedies,* ed. by R. Grene and R. Lattimore. Chicago: University of Chicago Press, 1958, *Euripides* III: 31–33 (= lines 517–88).

DOCUMENT 15
Euripides on the Foolishness of War

In the Trojan Women, Euripides returned to the theme of war and its destructiveness. While he plainly referred to the sufferings of women in war, he also examined the reasons for fighting wars in the first place. In the following passage, Euripides notes the foolishness of the Trojan War, how it was fought for the sake of a single woman, and how thousands died for a woman of rather loose ways who went off of her own free will. Euripides also speaks eloquently of the Trojans—the enemies—who died defending their native land, who were buried by their families in their own land, while the Greek invaders died unmourned by their families and would rest forever in a foreign land far from home. At a time when many Athenians were faced with this reality—fighting and dying far from home, whose cremated remains were brought back in little caskets—Euripides' words must have struck a number of those in audience hard. In the passage that follows, the speaker is Hekuba's daughter Kassandra, and this provides Euripides with further irony—Kassandra was the prophetess who spoke the truth but who was never believed.

O Mother, star of my hair with flowers of victory.
I know you would not have it happen thus; and yet
this is a king I marry; then be glad; escort
the bride. Oh, thrust her strongly on. If Loxias [Apollo]
is Loxias still, the Achaeans' pride, great Agamemnon
has won a wife more fatal than ever Helen was.
Since I will kill him; and avenge my brothers' blood
and my father's in the desolation of his house.
But I leave this in silence and sing not now the ax
to drop against my throat and other throats than mine,
the agony of the mother murdered, brought to pass
from our marriage rites, and Atreus' house made desolate.
I am ridden by God's curse still, yet I will step so far
out of my frenzy as to show this city's fate
is blessed beside the Achaeans'. For one woman's sake,
one act of love, these hunted Helen down and threw
thousands of lives away. Their general—clever man—
in the name of a vile woman cut his darling down,
gave up for a brother the sweetness of children in his house,
all to bring back that brother's wife, a woman who went
of her free will, not caught in constraint of violence.
The Achaeans came beside Scamander's banks, and died
day after day, though none sought to wrench their land from them
nor their own towering cities. Those the War God caught
never saw their sons again, nor were they laid to rest
decently in winding sheets by their wives' hands, but lie
buried in alien ground; while all went wrong at home
as the widows perished, and barren couples raised and nursed
the children of others, no survivor left to tend
the tombs, and what is left there, with blood sacrificed.
For such success as this congratulate the Greeks.
No, but the shame is better left in silence, for fear
my singing voice become the voice of wretchedness.
The Trojans have that glory which is loveliest:
they died for their own country. So the bodies of all
who took the spears were carried home in loving hands,
brought, in the land of their fathers, to the embrace of earth
and buried becomingly as the rite fell due. The rest,
those Phrygians who escaped death in battle, day by day
came home to happiness the Achaeans could not know;
their wives, their children. Then was Hector's fate so sad?

You think so. Listen to the truth. He is dead and gone
surely, but with reputation, as a valiant man.
How could this be, except for the Achaeans' coming?
Had they held back, none might have known how great he was.
The bride of Paris was the daughter of Zeus. Had he
not married her, fame in our house would sleep in silence still.
Though surely the wise man will forever shrink from war,
yet if war come, the hero's death will lay a wreath
not lustreless on the city. The coward alone brings shame.
Let no more tears fall, Mother, for our land, nor for
this marriage I make; it is by marriage that I bring
to destruction those whom you and I have hated most.

Source: Euripides, *Trojan Women*. Translated by R. Lattimore. *The Complete Greek Tragedies*, ed. by R. Grene and R. Lattimore. Chicago: University of Chicago Press, 1958, *Euripides* III: 140–41 (= lines 353–405).

DOCUMENT 16
The Character of Sokrates

Sokrates was clearly an unusual individual. He possessed an extraordinary character that allowed him to ignore the discomforts of military life, cold weather, and camp jealousies. Such things as these he simply ignored. He was also physically courageous. In the passage cited here from his Symposium, *Plato reproduces the story Alkibiades no doubt told of the Athenian retreat after the battle of Delion (in this translation Delium) where the Thebans inflicted a crushing defeat of the Athenians who, as Plato/Alkibiades relates here, ran from the battlefield in disorder—most everyone, that is, except Sokrates. This one simply started off for home as if he was going out for a walk and by this bold display of courage intimidated any would-be attackers. The Laches Plato/Alkibiades mentions as Sokrates' companion in the retreat is the Athenian general Laches, one of the prominent generals of the Peloponnesian War until his death in battle at Mantineia in 418. When Plato wrote his dialogue* Laches *(an early or "Sokratic" dialogue, written perhaps in the 370s* B.C.E.*), which examines the idea of courage, "General" Laches and "Private" Sokrates would figure prominently in the discussion.*

It was after these events had occurred that we served together in the Athenian campaign against Potidaia and shared the same mess there.

The first thing to note is that he put up with the rigours of warfare better than me—better than everyone else, in fact. When we were cut off, and forced to do without food, as sometimes happens on campaign, no one came near him in putting up with this. But on the other hand when we had a feast, he was best able to enjoy it. For instance, though reluctant to drink, when he was forced to, he beat us all at it. The most amazing thing of all is that no one has ever seen Socrates drunk. I think you'll see proof of this shortly.

Also when it came to putting up with winter (the winters there are terrible), his endurance was remarkable. On one occasion there was such a bitter frost that no one went outside, or if they did, they wrapped themselves up with clothes in the most amazing way and tied on extra pieces of felt or sheepskin over their boots. But Socrates went out in this weather wearing the same outdoor cloak he's usually worn before, and he made better progress over the ice in his bare feet than the rest of us did in boots. The soldiers regarded him with suspicion, thinking he was looking down on them.

So much for that incident; but "what the stout-hearted man did and endured next" on campaign there is well worth hearing. One morning he started thinking about a problem and stood there considering it, and when he didn't make progress with it he didn't give up but kept there standing there examining it. When it got to midday, people noticed him and said to each other in amazement that Socrates had been standing there thinking about something since dawn. In the end, when it was evening, some of the Ionians, after they'd had dinner, brought their bedding outside (it was summer then), partly to sleep in the cool, partly to keep an eye on Socrates to see if he would go on standing there through the night too. He stood there till it was dawn and the sun came up; then he greeted the sun with a prayer and went away.

If you'd like to know what he was like in battle—here it's right for me to repay a debt to him. During the battle after which the generals awarded me the prize of bravery, it was Socrates, no one else, who rescued me. He wasn't prepared to leave me when I was wounded and so he saved my life as well as my armour and weapons. I actually told the generals to award the prize of bravery on that occasion to you, Socrates. This is a point on which you can't criticize me or say that I'm lying. But when the generals wanted to award the prize to me, influenced by my social status, you yourself were keener than the generals that I should receive it.

Here's another thing, gentleman. Socrates was a sight worth seeing when the army made a disorderly retreat from Delium [i.e., Delion, 424]. It turned out that I was serving in the cavalry there while he was a hoplite. People had scattered by then in all directions, and he was retreating together with Laches. As it happened, I was near by, and when I saw them I encouraged them at once, and told them I wouldn't leave them behind. I was better able to watch Socrates there than at Potidaia (because I was on horseback I was less worried about my safety), and the first thing that struck me was how much more self-possessed he was than Laches. Next, I noticed that he was walking along there, just as he does here in Athens—to use your phrase, Aristophanes—"swaggering and looking from side to side." He was calmly looking out both for friends and enemies, and it was obvious to everyone even from a long distance that if anyone tackled this man, he would put up tough resistance. That was how he and his companion got safely away. Generally, people don't tackle those who show this kind of attitude in combat; they prefer those who are in headlong flight.

Source: Plato, *The Symposium*. Translated by C. Gill. London: Penguin Books, 1999, pp. 59–61 (= 219E–221B).

DOCUMENT 17
Aristophanes on Sokrates

In Clouds, Aristophanes tells the story of Strepsiades, an Athenian farmer, whose son Pheidippides has pushed him deep into debt in pursuit of expensive aristocratic activities. To fend off creditors, Strepsiades schemes to send his son to Sokrates' school in the hope that he will learn the new rhetoric and so be able to cheat his creditors of what he owes. The experiment fails as Pheidippides is horrified at the thought of joining pale-skinned, barefoot thinkers like Sokrates and then facing his aristocratic buddies. Abandoned by his son, Strepsiades enrolls only to flunk, but manages at last to persuade his son to take lessons from Sokrates. Pheidippides excels at his new lessons, and when he meets his father delivers a devastating critique of the old poetry, Aeschylus, in favor of Euripides, much to his father's dismay. To show further how far from the norm he has strayed under Sokrates' instruction, Pheidippides beats his father and then threatens to beat his mother too. Strepsiades now sees the error of his ways and returns to Sokrates' school, which he burns down, driving Sokrates away.

This may be good, clean fun, as some scholars suggest (e.g., W.K.C. Guthrie, Socrates [Cambridge 1971], p. 55), referring to traditions that Sokrates himself was amused at Aristophanes' depiction of him. While this reading is possible, it is as likely that it did Sokrates harm. He was also ridiculed in at least three other plays. Taken together, this suggests that while a number of people in Athens found him an odd character and somewhat amusing, others perceived his teachings as perversive and a threat to community values. The passage here relates the battle of the two Logics, Right, representing Aristophanes' vision of the "good old days," and Wrong, which conveys the amoral attitudes of intellectuals like the Sophists and, by extension, Sokrates. Their squabbling over whose knowledge is superior has been interrupted by the chorus, which asks them to demonstrate in a contest who really is the better. The stakes are high as the loser's form of education will be banished. In the end, Right Logic loses the debate. He admits that all "lawyers" (literally informers, individuals who often contrived charges against enemies in order to win influence and money), the tragic poets, and politicians, and even the whole audience, are made up of convicted adulterers, the public punishment for which was severe: a radish shoved up the anus, the pubic hair singed with hot ash (those described as having been "Probed" at the end of the selection here). The comedy is at once brutal and also revealing of the nature of Athenian society and culture.

Chorus: And who will put in his claim to begin?
Wrong Logic: If he wishes, he may: I kindly give way:
And out of his arguments quickly will I
Draw facts and devices to adorn the reply
Wherewith I will shoot him and smite him and refute him.
And at last if a word from his mouth be heard
My sayings like fierce savage hornets shall pierce
His forehead and eyes,
Till in fear and distraction he yields and he—dies!
Chorus: With thoughts and words and maxims pondered well
Now then in confidence let both begin:
Try which his rival can in speech excel:
Try which this perilous wordy war can win,
Which all my votaries' hopes are fondly centered in.
O you who were born our fathers to adorn
With characters blameless and fair,

Say on what you please, say on and to these
Your glorious Nature declare.
Right Logic: To hear then prepare of the Discipline rare
Which flourished in Athens of old
When Honor and Truth were in fashion with youth
And sobriety bloomed on our shore;
First of all the old rule was preserved in our school
That "boys should be seen and not heard:"
And then to the home of the Harpist would come
Decorous in action and word
All the lads of one town, though snow peppered down
In spite of all wind and weather:
And they sang an old song as they paced it along,
Not shambling with thighs glued together:
"O the dread shout of War how it peals from afar,"
or "Pallas the Stormer adore,"
To some manly old air all simple and bare
Which their fathers had chanted before.
And should anyone dare the tune to impair
And with intricate twistings to fill,
Such as Phrynis is fain, and his long-winded train,
Perversely to quaver and trill,
Many stripes would he feel in return for his zeal,
As to genuine Music a foe.
And every one's thigh was forward and high
As they sat to be drilled in a row,
So that nothing the while indecent or vile
The eye of a stranger might meet;
And then with their hand they would smooth down the sand
Whenever they rose from their seat,
To leave not a trace of themselves in the place
For a vigilant lover to view.
They never would soil their persons with oil
But were inartificial and true.
Nor tempered their throat to a soft mincing note
And sighs to their lovers addressed:
Nor laid themselves out, as they strutted about,
To the wanton desires of the rest:
Nor would anyone dare such stimulant fare
As the head of the radish to wish: nor to make over bold with the food of old,
The anise, and parsley, and fish:

Nor dainties to quaff, nor giggle and laugh,
Nor foot within foot to enfold.
Wrong Logic: Oh, this smells very strong of some musty old song,
And crickets mounted in gold;
And slaughter of beasts, and old-fashioned feasts!
Right Logic: Yet these are the precepts which taught
The heroes of old to be hardy and bold,
And the men who at Marathon fought!
But now must the lad from his boyhood be clad
In a Man's all-enveloping cloak
So that, oft the Panathenaea returns,
I feel myself ready to choke
When the dancers go by with their shields to their thigh, not caring for Pallas
    a jot.
You therefore, young man, choose me while you can;
Cast in with my Method your lot;
And then you shall learn the market place to spurn,
And from dissolute baths to abstain,
And fashions impure and shameful abjure,
And scorners repel with disdain:
And rise from your chair if an elder be there,
And respectfully give him your place,
And with love and with fear your parents revere,
And shrink from the brand of Disgrace,
And deep in your breast be the Image impressed
Of Modesty, simple and true,
Nor resort any more to a dancing-girl's door,
Nor glance at the harlotry crew,
Lest at length by the blow of the Apple they throw
From the hopes of your Manhood you fall.
Nor dare to reply when your father is nigh,
Nor "musty old Japhet" to call
In your malice and rage that Sacred Old Age
Which lovingly cherished your youth.
Wrong Logic: Yes, yes, my young friend, if you to him attend,
By Bacchus I swear of a truth
You will scarce with the sons of Hippocrates vie,
As a mama's boy known even there!
Right Logic: But then you'll excel in the games you love well,
All blooming, athletic and fair:
Not learning to prate as your idlers debate

With marvellous prickly dispute,
Nor dragged into court day by day to make sport
In some small disagreable suit:
But you will below to the Academy go,
And under the olives contend
With your chaplet of reed, in a contest of speed
With some excellent rival and friend:
All fragrant with woodbine and peaceful content,
And the leaf which the lime blossoms fling,
When the plane whispers love to the elm in the grove
In the beautiful season of Spring.

    If then you'll obey and do what I say,
    And follow with me the more excellent way,
    your chest shall be white, your skin shall be bright,
    Your arms shall be tight, your tongue shall be
    Slight,
    and everything else shall be proper and right.
    But if you pursue what men nowadays do,
    You will have, to begin, a cold pallid skin,
    Arms small and chest weak, tongue practiced to
    Speak,
    Special laws very long, and the symptoms all
    Strong
    Which show that your life is licentious and wrong.
    And your mind he'll prepare so that foul to be fair
    And fair to be foul you shall always declare;
    And you'll find yourself soon, if you listen to him,
    With the filth of Antimachus filled to the brim!
Chorus: O glorious Sage! With loveliest Wisdom teeming!
Sweet on your words does ancient Virtue rest!
Thrice happy they who watched your youth's bright
Beaming!
You of the vaunted genius, do your best;
This man has gained applause: his Wisdom
Stands confessed.
And you with clever words and thoughts must needs
Your case adorn
Else he will surely win the day, and you retreat with
Scorn.
Wrong Logic: Oh, you say so? Why I have been
Half-burst; I do so long

To overthrow his arguments
With arguments more strong.
I am the Wrong Logic? True:
These Schoolmen call me so,
Simply because I was the first
Of all mankind to show
How old established rules and laws
Might contradicted be:
And this as you may guess, is worth
A pile of money to me,
To take the feebler cause, and yet
To win the disputation.
And mark me now, how I'll confute
His boasted Education!
You said that always from warm baths
The striplings must abstain:
Why must he? On what grounds do you
Of these warm baths complain?
Right Logic: Why, it's the worst thing possible,
It quite weakens a man.
Wrong Logic: Hold on: I've got you round the waist:
And first: of all the sons of Zeus
Which think you was the best?
Which was the manliest? Which endured
More toils than all the rest?
Right Logic: Well, I suppose Heracles
Was bravest and most bold.
Wrong Logic: And are the baths of Heracles
So wonderfully cold? [= Thermopylai, the "hot gates/baths"]
Aha! You blame warm baths, I think
Right Logic: This, this is what they say:
This is the stuff our precious youths
Are chattering all the day!
This is what makes them haunt the baths,
And shun the manlier Games!
Wrong Logic: Well then, we'll take the market place next:
I praise it, and he blames.
But if it was so bad, do you think
old Homer would have made
Nestor and all his worthies ply
A real forensic trade?

Well: then he says a young man's tongue
Should always idle be:
I say it should be used of course:
So there we disagree.
And next he says you must be a virgin.
A most preposterous plan!
Come, tell me did you ever know
One single blessed man
Gain the least good by virginity?
Come, prove I'm wrong: make haste.
Right Logic: Yes, many, many. Peleus gained
a sword by being virginal.
Wrong Logic: A sword indeed! A wondrous reward
The unlucky fool obtained.
Hyperbolos the lamp-maker:
Has many a talent gained
By knavish tricks which I have taught:
But not a sword, no, no!
Right Logic: Then Peleus did to his virginal life
The bed of Thetis owe.
Wrong Logic: And then she cut and ran away!
For nothing so engages
A woman's heart as forward warmth,
Old shred of those dark ages!
For take this virginity, young man:
Sift it inside and out:
Count all the pleasures, all the joys,
It bids you live without:
No kind of dames, no kind of games,
No laughing, feasting, drinking,
Why, life itself is little worth
Without these joys, I'm thinking.
Well, I must notice now the wants
By Nature's self implanted;
You love, seduce, you can't help that,
You're caught, convicted. Granted.
You're done for; you can't say one word:
While if you follow me
Indulge your genius, laugh, and drink,
Hold nothing base to be.
Why if you're in adultery caught,

Your pleas will still be ample:
You've done no wrong, you'll say, and then
Bring Zeus as your example.
He fell before the wondrous powers
By Love and Beauty wielded:
And how can you, the Mortal, stand,
Where He, the Immortal, yielded?
Right Logic: Yes, but suppose in spite of all,
He must be wedged and sanded.
Won't he be probed, or else can you
Prevent it? Now be candid.
Wrong Logic: And what's the damage if it should be so?
Right Logic: What greater damage can the young man know?
Wrong Logic: What will you do, if this dispute I win?
Right Logic: I'll be for ever silent.
Wrong Logic: Good, begin. The Lawyer: from whence do they come?
Right Logic: From probed adulterers.
Wrong Logic: I agree.
The tragic poets: where are they from?
Right Logic: From probed adulterers.
Wrong Logic: And the politicians: what class of men?
Right Logic: All probed adulterers.
Wrong Logic: Right again.
You feel your error, I'll engage,
But look once more around the stage,
Survey the audience, which they be,
Probed or not Probed?
Right Logic: I see, I see.
Wrong Logic: Well, give me your verdict.
Right Logic: It must go
For probed adulterers: him I know,
And him, and him: the Probed are most.
Wrong Logic: How stand we then?
Right Logic: We've lost.
You homosexuals, take my robe!
Your words have won, to you I run
To live and die with glorious Probe!

Source: Aristophanes, *Clouds*. Translated by B. B. Rogers. Loeb Classical Library. London: William Heinemann, 1924, pp. 351–67 (= lines 940–1104); slightly adapted by L. Tritle.

DOCUMENT 18
Sokrates Defends Himself

In the defense speech that Plato gives Sokrates in the Apology *(another early or "Sokratic" dialogue of c. 370s B.C.E.), a speech likely based on what Plato recalled Sokrates said as well as some other relevant points Plato may have added, Sokrates' strength of character is revealed. His defiance of both the mob of Athenians calling for the deaths of the generals in 406 after, ironically, the fleet's victory at Arginusai, and that of the Thirty Tyrants, shows that Sokrates possessed great personal courage. But his arguments also demonstrate great respect and submission to the laws that governed the Athenians. Notice in the following passage Sokrates' statement that he had always followed the dictates of the law and had never gone against them—as the majority of Athenians wanted to do in convicting and then executing the generals in 406 and as the Thirty did in 404/3. Sokrates also argues that he did not have students, never took money for supposed lessons, and was willing (and did) speak to anyone, rich or poor, aristocratic or not, who would listen to him, contrary to what his prosecutors Anytos and Meletos would have the jury believe. These remarks amount to Sokrates' efforts to distance himself from the personalities and activities of Alkibiades, Kritias, and Kharmides, all reputedly his protégés, who had brought so much grief to Athens and who, so many believed, must have been directed by someone. Here Sokrates states his case for individual responsibility, a lesson that is timeless.*

The only office which I have ever held in our city, gentlemen, was when I was elected to the Council [of 500]. It so happened that our group was acting as the executive when you decided that the ten commanders who had failed to rescue the men who were lost in the naval engagement [Arginusai] should be tried *en bloc*; which was illegal, as you all recognized later. On this occasion I was the only member of the executive who insisted that you should not act unconstitutionally, and voted against the proposal; and although your leaders were all ready to denounce and arrest me, and you were all urging them on at the top of your voices, I thought that it was my duty to face it out on the side of the law and justice rather than support you, through fear of prison or death, in your wrong decision.

This happened while we were still under a democracy. When the oligarchy came into power, the Thirty Tyrants in their turn summoned me and four others to the Tholos [Council chambers] and instructed us to go and fetch Leon of Salamis from his home for execution. This was of course only one of many instances in which they issued such instructions, their object being to implicate as many people as possible in their wickedness. On this occasion, however, I again made it clear not by my words but by my actions that death did not matter to me at all (if that is not too strong an expression); but that it mattered all the world to me that I should not do nothing wrong or wicked. Powerful as it was, that government did not terrify me into doing a wrong action; when we went out of the Tholos the other four went off to Salamis and arrested Leon, and I went home. I should probably have been put to death for this, if the government had not fallen soon afterwards; there are plenty of people who will testify to these statements.

Do you suppose that I should have lived as long as I have if I had moved in the sphere of public life, and conducting myself in that sphere like an honourable man, had always upheld the cause of right, and conscientiously set this end above all other things? Not by a very long way, gentlemen; neither would any other man. You will find that throughout my life I have been consistent in any public duties that I have performed, and the same also in my personal dealings: I have never countenanced any action that was incompatible with justice on the part of any person, including those whom some people maliciously call my pupils. I have never set up as any man's teacher; but if anyone, young or old, is eager to hear me conversing and carrying out my private mission, I never grudge him the opportunity; nor do I charge a fee for talking to him, and refuse to talk without one; I am ready to answer questions for rich and poor alike, and I am equally ready if anyone prefers to listen to me and answer my questions. If any given one of these people becomes a good citizen or a bad one, I cannot fairly be held responsible, since I have never promised or imparted any teaching to anybody; and if anyone asserts that he has ever learned or heard from me privately anything which was not open to everyone else, you may be quite sure that he is not telling the truth.

Source: Plato, *The Last Days of Socrates*. Translated by Hugh Tredennick. London: Penguin Books, 1954, pp. 66–67 (= *Apology* 31D–33B).

DOCUMENT 19
Women on War

In his comedy Lysistrata, *Aristophanes includes a scene in which Lysistrata and the chorus of women confront an Athenian magistrate on their way to seize the acropolis. As the two sides battle, the poet brings out several issues for the audience (again largely of men) to consider: the war's futility as well as its waste, an implicit critique of the democracy and the way in which the Athenian men have been doing things, and the place of women in society. At the beginning of the passage cited here, the women approach the acropolis because it is also the equivalent of a bank—some years before under Perikles' direction the Athenians had established an "iron fund" to be used for emergencies, and Thucydides (8.15.1) reports that this was opened after the Sicilian disaster.*

The passage is also of interest for its account of women discussing political issues with their husbands, who can only bluster—quoting Hektor in Homer's Iliad *(Iliad 6. 492)—that war is man's affair! Skeptics may doubt the authenticity of these lines, but their truth seems essential for the humor to work.*

Magistrate: Foremost and first I would wish to inquire of them,
What is this silly disturbance about? Why have you ventured to seize the Acropolis,
Locking the gates and keeping us out?

Lysistrata: Keeping the silver securely in custody,
Lest for its sake you continue the war.

Magistrate: What, is the war for the sake of the silver, then?

Lysistrata: Yes; and all other disputes that there are.
Why is Peisander for ever embroiling us,
Why do the rest of the officers feel
Always a pleasure in strife and disturbances?
Simply to gain an occasion to steal.
Act as they please for the future, the treasury
Never a penny shall yield them, I swear.

Magistrate: How, may I ask, will you hinder their getting it?

Lysistrata: We will ourselves be the Treasurers now.

Magistrate: You, women, you be the Treasurers?

Lysistrata: Certainly.
Oh, you think us unable perhaps?
Are we not skilled in domestic economy,
Do we not manage the household finance?

Magistrate: O but that's different.

Lysistrata: How is it different?

Magistrate: This is required for the fighting my dear.

Lysistrata: Well, but the fighting itself isn't necessary.

Magistrate: How could we be saved otherwise?

Lysistrata: We will save you.

Magistrate: You will save us?

Lysistrata: Yes, we will!

Magistrate: You blockheaded woman!

Lysistrata: You seem all upset.
Nevertheless we will do as we promise you.

Magistrate: That would be a terrible shame, by Demeter.

Lysistrata: It must be done, that's all.

Magistrate: Such awful oppression never,
Never in the past did I bear.

Lysistrata: You must be saved, that's all there is to it.

Magistrate: But how if I wish it not?

Lysistrata: That will but make our resolve the completer.

Magistrate: Fools! What on earth can possess you to meddle with
Matters of war, and matters of peace?

Lysistrata: Well, I will tell you the reason.

Magistrate: And quickly,
Or else you'll regret it.

Lysistrata: Then listen, and stop
Clutching and clenching your fingers so angrily;
Keep yourself calm.

Magistrate: Hanged if I can;
Such is the rage that I feel at your disrespect.

Woman: Then it is *you* that will regret it, my man.

Magistrate: Croak your own fate, you ill-omened old hag.
(To Lysistrata) You be the spokeswoman, lady.

Lysistrata: I will.
Think. . . .
All the long years when the hopeless war dragged along,
We, unassuming, forgotten in quiet,
Endured without question, endured in our loneliness all
Your incessant child's antics and riot.
Our lips we kept tied, though aching with silence, though
Well all the while in our silence we knew
How wretchedly everything still was progressing by listening
Dumbly the day long to you.
For always at home you continued discussing the war and
Its politics loudly, and we
Sometimes would ask you, our hearts deep with sorrowing,
Though we spoke lightly, though happy to see,
What's to be inscribed on the side of the treaty-stone?
What, dear, was said in the Assembly today
Mind your own business, he'd answer me growingly, hold
your tongue, woman, or else go away.
And so I would.

Woman: I'd not be silent for any man
Living on earth, no, not I!

Magistrate: Not for a staff?

Lysistrata: Well, so I did nothing but
Sit in the house, feeling dreary, and sigh,
While ever some fresh tale of decisions more foolish
By far and presaging disaster.
Then I would say to him, O, my dear husband, why still do
They rush on destruction the faster?
At which he would look at me sideways, exclaiming,
Keep to your web and your shuttle your care,
Or for some hours hence your cheeks will be sore and hot;
Leave this alone, war is Man's sole affair!

Magistrate: By Zeus, what a man of fine sense, he is.

Source: Aristophanes, *Lysistrata*. Translated by B. B. Rogers. Loeb Classical Library. London: William Heinemann, 1924, pp. 49–53 (= lines 486–520); slightly adapted by L. Tritle.

GLOSSARY

Attika: The region surrounding and including the city of Athens in central Greece. Boiotia and its dominant city Thebes lies to the northwest, the large island of Euboia with its many *poleis*, or city-states (see **Polis**), lies to the northeast.

Cleruch(s): Sometimes translated as "soldier-farmers." These were Athenian citizens who received grants of land outside of Athens as a form of social welfare—those receiving land sometimes came from the lowest social-economic group (called *thetes*). The cleruchs held their land in return for military service and provided the Athenians with an additional military force. Establishing settlements of these was a policy of imperial Athens and something that symbolized Athenian power.

Delian League: The alliance created by Athens after the Persian Wars and after Sparta yielded leadership of the Greeks to Athens in 478/7. Apollo's island home of Delos became the center for the alliance and was the site of the league treasury until 454, when it was moved to Athens. Originally, the larger allied states contributed ships and crews to military operations (e.g., Samos, Lesbos, Khios), while the smaller paid tribute—monetary payments—assessed and collected by Athens. Those whom the Athenians once recognized as allies came to be regarded, as Aristophanes makes plain in his plays, as "subjects" as the alliance became the Athenian Empire.

Helot(s): The slave-like inhabitants of Sparta. The helots outnumbered their Spartan masters approximately 9:1. This was a constant worry to the Spartan elite (Spartiates), or "equals" (*homoioi*), who feared that the helots might rebel at any moment (which they did on occasion). The helots were different from slaves, however, in that they lived in their own communities and so enjoyed family life, which traditional slaves did not. During the Peloponnesian War, the Spartans recruited soldiers from the helots, who were later emancipated and recognized as *neodamodeis*, or "new men" (literally "new of the people").

Hoplite: The core of the armies that fought the Peloponnesian War. These were citizen militias composed of heavy infantry, or hoplites. Hoplite derives from the Greek word *hoplon*, the large (about three feet across) shield that soldiers carried into battle for protection (on the left arm) along with a seven- or eight-foot spear (in the right hand). For personal protection, soldiers also wore a bronze helmet of various styles (remarkably light) that afforded some protection. Some soldiers also wore greaves (bronze shin guards) and a breastplate, though this item appears to have become unpopular, perhaps because it slowed men down. Increasingly during the fifth century and especially through the Peloponnesian War, hoplites fought alongside lighter armed troops called peltasts who carried even lighter equipment but more weapons, and other specialty troops such as slingers and archers. The Athenian general Demosthenes was one commander who achieved some fame (e.g., at Pylos) in combining these different types of troops (though his luck ran out in Sicily, 413).

Oligarchy: Meaning "rule by the few." Oligarchy at the time of the Peloponnesian War was an ancient and still practiced political form among the Greeks. Its opposite is democracy, or "people-power."

Peloponnese/Peloponnesos: The southernmost part of Greece (below the Isthmos) where Sparta was located, in the south-central area around the Eurotas River valley. To the northeast of Sparta lay its powerful rival Argos, situated in such a way as to block Spartan movement into Attika and northern Greece.

Peloponnesian League: The alliance led by Sparta, founded in the later part of the sixth century. The name is a modern convenience, being known in antiquity as the "Lakedaimonians (Spartans) and their allies," the latter being not all Peloponnesian. The term *league* is again a modern idea. The "allies" were only allied to Sparta and in times of peace could be found fighting each other. It was only to Sparta that the allies swore oaths of allegiance, and in return Sparta pledged to aid an ally attacked by a third party. In a league assembly it was "one state, one vote," and the Spartans could ignore an inconvenient allied vote. Sparta always held the command and prescribed the numbers of men each ally was to contribute to a campaign. The Spartans moved to transform the league into an empire after the victory over Athens in 404. In the fourth century, as Spartan power declined, so too did the league, which dissolved in 366 upon the suggestion of Corinth, always the most powerful of the "allies."

Polis: Usually translated as "city-state." *Polis* is a concept more modern than ancient. The term refers to a self-governing community (in which the idea of "government" is also a modern anachronism) that controls the surrounding area—for example, Athens over Attika—and which is free from external authority. A community that was not autonomous (= self-governing) in Greek eyes was not free. Control over the surrounding rural area allowed a town or city to flourish, as the rural population supplied the food that the townspeople would consume, while the townspeople would produce goods and services for those in the country.

Strategos: The Greek word for "general" (cf. *strategy*). In Athens, ten generals (pl., *strategoi*) were elected every year directly by the citizens (i.e., as opposed to the usual selection by lot for other officials), and it was these men who commanded the armies and navies sent out on military campaigns. Athenian generals, however, possessed political authority and privilege as well (they could call a meeting of the council, for example), and could, as the example of Perikles shows, occupy a position of leadership within the democracy.

Trireme: The basic warship of the classical age. The trireme was a long fighting ship rowed by 170 oarsmen. There was an additional group of marines and other sailors on board, but the principal weapon was a large bronze ram at the front, and the object was to steer this into another warship, disable and/or sink it. A ship that was rammed would not sink immediately—the vessel's wood construction usually kept a damaged ship afloat for some time before it finally sank. Triremes were costly, and in democratic Athens, well-to-do citizens demonstrated their civic pride and wealth by paying for a ship's maintenance for a year.

ANNOTATED BIBLIOGRAPHY

Print Sources

The Greeks Speak—Primary Accounts of the War

Aristophanes

Aristophanes. *Four Comedies. Lysistrata, The Frogs, The Birds, Ladies' Day*. Translated by Dudley Fitts. New York: Harcourt, Brace, Jovanovich, 1957. A lively translation that succeeds in bringing to life the flavor of Aristophanic comedy—funny, obscene, and thought provoking all at once.

————. *The Knights, Peace, The Birds, The Assemblywomen, Wealth*. Translated by David Barret and Alan H. Sommerstein. London: Penguin, 1978. Lively translations of a selection of Aristophanes' plays (there is no new translation of all the plays), which provide a wealth of information about Athens and Greece during the war.

Dover, Kenneth J. *Aristophanic Comedy*. Berkeley: University of California Press, 1972. A basic introduction to the plays, with brief outlines and discussions of the topics raised by Aristophanes.

Ehrenberg, Victor. *The People of Aristophanes: A Sociology of Old Attic Comedy*. New York: Schocken Books, 1962. An older study but one that remains of use for its analysis of the different types of people represented by Aristophanes in his plays.

MacDowell, Douglas M. *Aristophanes and Athens: An Introduction to the Plays*. Oxford: Oxford University Press, 1995. A recent work that provides readable introductions to the plays and their historical context.

Winkler, John J., and Zeitlin, Froma I., eds. *Nothing to Do with Dionysos? Athenian Drama in Its Social Context.* Princeton, NJ: Princeton University Press, 1990. A collection of articles that explores the connections between the theater in Athens and society. This is a stimulating study but is most suitable for advanced students.

Euripides

Euripides. *The Complete Plays.* 5 vols. Edited by D. Grene and R. Lattimore. Translated by D. Grene, R. Lattimore, et al. Chicago, IL: University of Chicago Press, 1959. The surviving plays presented in clear and readable translations that also include the line numbers for reference to the Greek texts. Euripides' dramas are key documents to understanding the intellectual climate of late fifth-century Athens and Greece.

Croally, N. T. *Euripidean Polemic: The Trojan Women and the Function of Tragedy.* Cambridge: Cambridge University Press, 1994. A close study of one of Euripides' "war plays," as well as the nature of Attic tragedy.

Gregory, Justina. *Euripides and the Instruction of the Athenians.* Ann Arbor: University of Michigan Press, 1991. A useful work that explores the political nature of Euripides, his dramas, and Attic tragedy.

Plato

Plato. *The Last Days of Socrates.* Translated by Hugh Tredennick with an Introduction. London: Penguin Books, 1954. The essential early "Sokratic" dialogues, but with the *Phaido*, ostensibly the conversation held by Sokrates in jail the final day of his life.

————. *The Symposium.* Translated by Christopher Gill. London: Penguin Books, 1999. An important early dialogue of Plato's in that it provides valuable information for the life of Sokrates as well as the nature of intellectual life in Athens at the end of the fifth century.

Plato and Aristophanes. *Four Texts on Socrates: Plato's Euthypho, Apology, and Crito and Aristophanes' Clouds.* Translated with Notes by Thomas G. West and Grace S. West. Introduction by T. G. West. Ithaca, NY: Cornell University Press, 1984. This is a useful edition to key early "Sokratic" dialogues that make possible the reconstruction of the life of Sokrates; helpful notes explain many points that might otherwise confuse beginning students.

Plutarch

Plutarch. *Greek Lives.* Translated by Robin Waterfield. With an Introduction and Notes by Philip A. Stadter. Oxford: Oxford University Press, 1998. A newer translation than that of I. Scott-Kilvert (see below), it provides a clear and modern rendering of Plutarch that students can easily follow.

————. *On Sparta*. Translated with Introduction and Notes by Richard J. A. Talbert. London: Penguin Books, 1988. Plutarch's wide reading led him to traditions outside Athens, including those surrounding Sparta. Talbert's edition, accessible to all students, brings together various famous sayings of the Spartans as well as an account of their customs and ways that, while attributed to Xenophon, was probably the work of another, now unknown author.

————. *The Rise and Fall of Athens*. Translated with Introduction by Ian Scott-Kilvert. London: Penguin Books, 1960. A readable translation that provides life accounts of key personalities of the war, Perikles, Nikias, Alkibiades, and Lysander.

Russell, D. A. *Plutarch*. New York: Charles Scribner's Sons, 1973. An engaging introduction to the nature of Plutarch's *Lives* that beginning students could follow without difficulty.

Scardigli, Barbara, ed. *Essays of Plutarch's Lives*. Oxford: Clarendon Press, 1995. A work for more advanced students, this volume includes a still-valuable essay on the *Life of Alkibiades* by D. A. Russell.

Stadter, Philip A. *A Commentary on Plutarch's Pericles*. Chapel Hill: University of North Carolina Press, 1989. A work for more advanced students, this study examines the historical traditions for Perikles and the *Life* that Plutarch provides.

————, ed. *Plutarch and the Historical Tradition*. London: Routledge, 1992. Similar to Scardigli's collection of essays, this volume includes essays on Plutarch's use of Thucydides and the *Life of Lysander*, both of use for study of the Peloponnesian War.

Sophocles

Sophocles. *The Complete Plays*. 2 volumes. Edited by D. Grene and R. Lattimore. Translated by D. Grene et al. Chicago, IL: University of Chicago Press, 1959. Sophocles' dramas complement those of Euripides, and several of them including *Oedipus the King* and *Philoctetes* are written in the context of the Peloponnesian War.

Segal, Charles. *Sophocles' Tragic World: Divinity, Nature, Society*. Cambridge, MA: Harvard University Press, 1995. A scholarly treatment of Sophocles and one for more advanced students.

Thucydides

Thucydides. *The History of the Peloponnesian War.* Translated by Rex Warner. With Introduction and Notes by M. I. Finley. London: Penguin Books, 1954, 1972. Another readily available translation (with introduction and notes) of Thucydides' *History.* This edition is particularly useful to beginning students because of the Cartwright commentary (see reference above).

————. *On Justice, Power, and Human Nature: Selections from the History of the Peloponnesian War.* Edited and translated by Paul Woodruff. Indianapolis, IN: Hackett Publishing Company, 1993. A selection of passages from Thucydides focusing on key themes, along with a helpful and extensive introduction.

————. *The Peloponnesian War.* Translated with Introduction and Notes by Steven Lattimore. Indianapolis, IN: Hackett Publishing Company, 1998. A recent translation that gives the reader the feel for Thucydides' language, and yet is clear and easy to understand.

Adcock, Frank E. *Thucydides and His History.* Cambridge: Cambridge University Press, 1963. An older study of the historian, but one still valuable as well as accessible to beginning students.

Cartwright, David. *A Historical Commentary on Thucydides: A Companion to Rex Warner's Penguin Translation.* Ann Arbor: University of Michigan Press, 1997. Many of the references to places and people in Thucydides' account of the war will be unknown or obscure to beginning students, but this commentary (accompanied by an introduction) will do much to explain them.

Cawkwell, George. *Thucydides and the Peloponnesian War.* London and New York: Routledge, 1997. An accessible account of Thucydides and the war he recorded for nonspecialists, this work examines how and what Thucydides wrote. Brief accounts of major figures such as Perikles and Alkibiades as well as his views on the Athenian empire make this a useful introductory study.

Connor, W. Robert. *Thucydides.* Princeton, NJ: Princeton University Press, 1984. A more scholarly treatment of Thucydides, but one that more advanced students could use.

Finley, John H., Jr. *Thucydides.* Cambridge, MA: Harvard University Press, 1942. An older introduction to Thucydides but still useful, especially to beginning students.

Hornblower, Simon. *Thucydides*. Baltimore, MD: Johns Hopkins University Press, 1987. A general study of Thucydides, but a readable one that sheds much light on his technique and approach in writing about the war.

Luginbill, Robert D. *Thucydides on War and National Character*. Boulder, CO: Westview Press, 1999. A readable study of the historian that all students would find useful.

Orwin, Clifford. *The Humanity of Thucydides*. Princeton, NJ: Princeton University Press, 1994. A close study of the historian by a political scientist who brings the perspective of his discipline to Thucydides' account of war and politics.

Pelling, Christopher. *Literary Texts and the Greek Historian*. London: Routledge, 2000. A readable discussion of Thucydides and other writers active during the war.

Xenophon

Aristotle and Xenophon. *On Democracy and Oligarchy*. Translations with Introductions and Commentary by J. M. Moore. Berkeley: University of California Press, 1983. This work includes an account of Athenian political life ascribed to the "Old Oligarch" and that of the Spartans written by an unknown author circa 400. Both works are important to understanding the nature of institutions in these two states.

Xenophon. *A History of My Times*. Translated with an Introduction and Notes by Rex Warner. London: Penguin Books, 1966. Thucydides' *History* was unfinished at his death circa 400, but later Xenophon completed his account of the war in the first two books of his history titled *Hellenica*, or "Greek Affairs."

———. *Memoirs of Socrates and the Symposium*. Translated with an Introduction by Hugh Tredennick. London: Penguin Books, 1970. Xenophon represents the non-Platonic tradition for the study of Sokrates. Xenophon has often been criticized for his simplicity, but his testimony remains important for Sokratic studies.

———. *The Persian Expedition*. Translated by Rex Warner. With Introduction and Notes by George Cawkwell. London: Penguin Books, 1972. The end of the Peloponnesian War caused many problems in the Greek world, and this work by Xenophon reveals one—unemployed soldiers with nothing else to do but fight. *The Persian Expedition* (in Greek, *Anabasis*, or "March Up Country") is also exciting to read.

Anderson, J. K. *Xenophon*. New York: Charles Scribner's Sons, 1974. A general study of this important author and one accessible to beginning students.

General Studies of Greek History

Cartledge, Paul. *The Greeks: Crucible of Civilization*. New York: TV Books, 2000. The companion book to the television program of the same name (see below), this work includes very accessible accounts for beginners of Perikles, Aspasia, and Sokrates.

Davies, J. K. *Democracy and Classical Greece*. Atlantic Highlands, NJ: Humanities Press, 1978. An introductory work to classical Greek history including the era of the Peloponnesian War. While a stimulating study, it might be challenging to beginning students.

Garland, Robert. *Daily Life of the Ancient Greeks*. Westport, CT: Greenwood Press, 1998. A general introduction to Greek society and culture and one written to be accessible to beginning students. It includes sections on war as well as lifestyles of both men and women.

Green, Peter. *Ancient Greece: An Illustrated History*. London: Thames & Hudson, 1973. An older and general introduction to ancient Greek history, but one that beginning students could use profitably.

Osborne, Robin, ed. *Classical Greece, 500–323 BC*. In *The Short Oxford History of Europe*, ed. by T.C.W. Blanning. Oxford: Oxford University Press, 2000. A broad introduction to the study of classical Greece touching directly on the era of the Peloponnesian War. It might be a little challenging for beginning students.

———. *Classical Landscape with Figures: The Ancient Greek City and Its Countryside*. London: George Philip, 1987. An overview of classical Greece that focuses on the city and its relation to the countryside, including discussions as well on war and politics. It would be especially useful for more advanced students.

Sowerby, Robin. *The Greeks: An Introduction to Their Culture*. London: Routledge, 1995. A broad introduction to Greek history, literature, and philosophy. Being more advanced than that of Peter Green noted above, it would be helpful to beginning college students.

Taplin, Oliver. *Greek Fire*. London: Jonathan Cape, 1989. A series of essays that explore the nature of Greek culture and society from Homeric times on, while touching significantly on the fifth century and the war. Also available is a film series of the same title.

Vivante, Bella. *Events That Changed Ancient Greece*. Westport, CT: Greenwood Press, 2002. An acclaimed introductory text to ancient Greece well suited for beginning students. It includes a chapter on the Peloponnesian War.

General Histories of the Peloponnesian War

Henderson, Bernard W. *The Great War between Athens and Sparta*. London: Macmillan, 1927. An older study, but one long regarded as the standard work on the war.

Kagan, Donald. *The Peloponnesian War*. New York: Viking, 2003. The author of four separate studies of the Peloponnesian War (see next section, "Battles and Campaigns"), Donald Kagan has now summarized the war in one volume. While still adhering to a Thucydidean narrative, Kagan provides a reliable guide to the course of the conflict.

Powell, Anton. *Athens and Sparta: Constructing Greek Political and Social History from 478 B.C.* London: Routledge, 1988. A valuable study in that it brings together Athens and Sparta, following the defeat of the Persians and leading up to the great war of 431–404.

Samons, Loren J., III, ed. *Athenian Democracy and Imperialism*. Boston, MA: Houghton Mifflin Company, 1998. A useful work that brings together extracts of primary sources and modern scholarship to provide an introduction to the problems surrounding Athens, its democracy, and imperial actions and policies.

Battles and Campaigns

de Souza, Philip. *The Peloponnesian War, 421–404 BC*. Oxford: Osprey, 2002. A lavishly illustrated account of the war in its middle and end phases. Readable and accessible to all students.

Green, Peter. *Armada from Athens*. New York: Doubleday & Company, 1970. A readable and even exciting study of the Athenian campaign to conquer Sicily that ended in disastrous defeat. A good place to begin in studying this crucial campaign of the war.

Kagan, Donald. *The Archidamian War*. Ithaca, NY: Cornell University Press, 1974. The third volume in Kagan's study of the war, covering the Archidamian or so-called Ten Year's War, 431–421.

———. *The Fall of the Athenian Empire*. Ithaca, NY: Cornell University Press, 1987. The final volume in Kagan's study, which treats the period after the Sicilian Expedition to the surrender of Athens in 404.

————. *The Outbreak of the Peloponnesian War*. Ithaca, NY: Cornell University Press, 1969. The first volume in Kagan's study, which examines how the war broke out and related topics such as the rise of the Athenian Empire.

————. *The Peace of Nicias and the Sicilian Expedition*. Ithaca, NY: Cornell University Press, 1981. The second in Kagan's study, which investigates the negotiations ending the Archidamian War and background to the Athenian Expedition to Sicily and its defeat.

Wilson, J. B. *Pylos 425 B.C. A Historical and Topographical Study of Thucydides' Account of the Campaign*. Warminster: Aris & Phillips, 1979. A scholarly treatment of Thucydides' account of this crucial campaign, yet one that also explains the Athenian's incredible victory.

Woodhouse, W. J. *King Agis of Sparta and His Campaign in Arkadia in 418 B.C.: A Chapter in the History of the Art of War among the Greeks*. Oxford: Clarendon Press, 1933 (reprint edition, New York: AMS Press, 1978). While an older work certainly, it provides a close look at the battle of Mantineia, the battle Thucydides described as being the biggest fought by the Greeks in "a very long time" (Thucydides 5.74.1).

Athens' Defeat and "Lysander's Peace"

Krentz, Peter. *The Thirty at Athens*. Ithaca, NY: Cornell University Press, 1982. A study of the oligarchs who inflicted such terror on Athens after the war and how the Athenians managed to throw them out.

Strauss, Barry S. *Athens after the Peloponnesian War: Class, Faction and Policy 403–386 B.C.* London: Croom Helm, 1986. A work that examines the aftermath of war on Athens and its gradual recovery.

Wolpert, Andrew. *Remembering Defeat: Civil War and Civic Memory in Ancient Athens*. Madison: University of Wisconsin Press, 2002. A new discussion, but not for beginning students, of how the Athenians restored democracy upon the expulsion of the Thirty Tyrants and in the process constructed a collective memory of the event.

The Conduct of War

Hanson, Victor, ed. *Hoplites. The Classical Greek Battle Experience*. London: Routledge, 1991. A study of the nature of Greek warfare by leading scholars.

————. *Warfare and Agriculture in Classical Greece*. Revised edition. Berkeley: University of California Press, 1998. A study of the military techniques used by the Greeks and the impact of war on the land.

————. *The Western Way of War: Infantry Battle in Classical Greece.* New York: Alfred A. Knopf, 1989. An investigation into the nature of Greek warfare.

Roisman, Joseph. *The General Demosthenes and His Use of Military Surprise. Historia Einzelschrift 78.* Stuttgart: Franz Steiner Verlag, 1993. An analysis of the tactics used by a leading Athenian military commander, executed in Sicily when the Athenian Expedition collapsed in disaster.

Tritle, Lawrence A. *From Melos to My Lai: War and Survival.* London: Routledge 2000. A comparative investigation into the impact of war's trauma in both ancient Greece and Vietnam.

Van Wees, Hans, ed. *War and Violence in Ancient Greece.* London and Swansea: Duckworth and the Classical Press of Wales, 2000. A new study of the conduct of Greek warfare that takes into account the nature of the violence and resulting trauma.

Warry, John. *Warfare in the Classical World.* Norman: University of Oklahoma Press, 1995. While examining all periods in both Greek and Roman history, this work includes significant treatment of the conduct of the Peloponnesian War. Numerous illustrations and color plates make this a useful introduction to the nature of Greek warfare.

Athens in the War

Boedeker, Deborah, and Raaflaub, Kurt, eds. *Democracy, Empire, and the Arts in Fifth-Century Athens.* Cambridge, MA: Harvard University Press, 1998. A collection of papers (a little advanced, but many are accessible to students) that examines cultural and intellectual issues in Athens and Greece during the war.

Munn, Mark. *The School of History: Athens in the Age of Socrates.* Berkeley: University of California Press, 2000. A recent scholarly examination of Athens at the end of the war and of the political upheavals that led to the death of Sokrates.

Strauss, Barry S. *Fathers and Sons in Athens: Ideology and Society in the Era of the Peloponnesian War.* Princeton, NJ: Princeton University Press, 1993. A study of the impact of the war on the fathers and sons who fought it.

Sparta in the War

Cartledge, Paul. *Sparta and Lakonia: A Regional History 1300–362 BC.* London: Routledge & Kegan Paul, 1979. A study of Sparta and its neighbors, including several chapters focusing on the war as well as Spartan institutions.

————. *Spartan Reflections*. Berkeley: University of California Press, 2001. A republication of articles by a leading historian of ancient Greece and Sparta in particular. Some of the articles tend to be rather technical and so might be a bit overwhelming to beginning students.

Sekunda, Nicholas V. *The Spartans*. Oxford: Osprey, 1998. A lavishly illustrated account of the Spartans that brings to life their austere militaristic life.

Whitby, Michael, ed. *Sparta*. London: Routledge, 2002. A collection of articles (some more recent than others) representing recent scholarship on ancient Sparta. Outstanding scholarship but might be difficult for beginning students.

States Other Than Athens and Sparta in the War

Borza, Eugene N. *In the Shadow of Olympus: The Emergence of Macedon*. Princeton, NJ: Princeton University Press, 1990. A general introduction to the kingdom of Macedonia. This study also relates developments in the northern Greek world during the war in readable fashion.

Buck, Robert J. *A History of Boeotia*. Edmonton: University of Alberta Press, 1979. A general treatment of this critical region of Greece that in the fourth century would be known as the "dancing floor of Ares," the Greek god of war. It includes a chapter discussion on events in the fifth century and would complement Demand's study noted next.

Demand, Nancy. *Thebes in the Fifth Century: Heracles Resurgent*. London: Routledge & Kegan Paul, 1982. A useful introduction to the leading state of central Greece.

Finley, Moses I. *Ancient Sicily to the Arab Conquest*. New York: The Viking Press, 1968. A general history of the island. This work includes a chapter discussion on the fifth-century history, including events during the Peloponnesian War, that is accessible to beginning students.

Gorman, Vanessa B. *Miletos, the Ornament of Ionia: A History of the City to 400 B.C.E.* Ann Arbor: University of Michigan Press, 2001. A recent study of the eastern Greek world and its most important city that pulls together findings from archaeological discoveries as well as literary evidence. It includes a discussion of Miletos' role in the Peloponnesian War. More appropriate for advanced students than beginning.

Legon, Ronald P. *Megara: The Political History of a Greek City-State to 336 B.C.* Ithaca, NY: Cornell University Press, 1981. Situated between Athens and

Sparta, Megara was a hostage to the power politics practiced by both. This study introduces the student to the world outside Athens and Sparta.

Salmon, J. B. *Wealthy Corinth: A History of the City to 338 B.C.* Oxford: Clarendon Press, 1984. A full account of the history and economics of this important city, which played a key role in the outbreak of the war.

Tomlinson, R. A. *Argos and the Argolid: From the End of the Bronze Age to the Roman Occupation.* London: Routledge & Kegan Paul, 1972. The great rival of Sparta in the Peloponnese, Argos played a part-time but sometimes pivotal role in the Peloponnesian War. While a general study of Argos, this work recounts Argos' role and political developments in the fifth century.

The War's Personalities

Burn, A. R. *Pericles and Athens.* London: Macmillan Company, 1948. An older study of Perikles but one written in an engaging manner accessible to students.

Ellis, Walter. *Alcibiades.* London: Routledge, 1989. A brief but accessible introduction to the famous Athenian who did such great harm and good to his city.

Forde, Steven. *The Ambition to Rule: Alcibiades and the Politics of Imperialism in Thucydides.* Ithaca, NY: Cornell University Press, 1989. A close study of those parts of Thucydides, especially his book eight, in which Alkibiades figures prominently.

Kagan, Donald. *Pericles of Athens and the Birth of Democracy: The Triumph of Vision in Leadership.* New York: Simon & Schuster, 1991. The four-volume history of the Peloponnesian War written by Donald Kagan provides the standard scholarly treatment of the war. This volume on Perikles represents an accessible introduction to this key figure in the origins of the war to all readers.

Podlecki, Anthony. *Perikles and His Circle.* London: Routledge, 1998. A newer study of Perikles and those around him, and their place in the Athenian democracy.

Westlake, H. D. *Individuals in Thucydides.* Cambridge: Cambridge University Press, 1968. A helpful introduction to twelve of the most important individuals mentioned in Thucydides, including the Athenians Perikles, Kleon, and Nikias, and the Spartans Archidamos and Brasidas.

Sokrates, the Sophists, and Greek Philosophy

de Romilly, Jacqueline. *The Great Sophists in Periclean Athens*. Oxford: Clarendon Press, 1992. A more recent study of these early Greek thinkers than Guthrie's (see reference below), this investigation examines the Sophists in relation to their time in the Athens of Perikles.

Farrar, Cynthia. *The Origins of Democratic Thinking: The Invention of Politics in Classical Athens*. Cambridge: Cambridge University Press, 1988. Not only a study of the democratic idea in classical Greece, but also one that relates the intellectual climate. While a challenge for beginning students, it would be useful to more advanced students.

Finley, Moses I. *Aspects of Antiquity*. Revised edition. London: Penguin, 1977. Finley's essay on "Socrates and Athens" provides a readable and accessible account for beginning students of how Sokrates came to be tried.

Guthrie, W.K.C. *Socrates*. Cambridge: Cambridge University Press, 1971. A selection of this leading scholar's study *A History of Greek Philosophy* (Cambridge: Cambridge University Press, 1969); his discussion of Sokrates is accessible to all students.

———. *The Sophists*. Cambridge: Cambridge University Press, 1971. From the same study as this scholar's work on Greek philosophy, his account of the Sophists complements that of Sokrates.

Solmsen, Friedrich. *Intellectual Experiments of the Greek Enlightenment*. Princeton, NJ: Princeton University Press, 1975. A valuable study of the nature of thought in the later fifth century, but not for beginning students.

Stone, I. F. *The Trial of Socrates*. Boston, MA: Little, Brown & Co., 1988. A popular account of the trial of Sokrates by another amateur interested in politics.

Taylor, Alfred E. *Socrates*. Boston, MA: Beacon Press, 1951. First published in 1932, this is an older but brief and well-written introduction to Sokrates and his life.

Art and Culture

Boardman, John. *Greek Art*. London: Thames & Hudson, 1985. A general introduction to the topic of Greek art and one accessible to beginning students.

———, ed. *The Oxford History of Classical Art*. Oxford: Oxford University Press, 1993. A general introduction to the art of both Greece and Rome, the essays in this volume (and the many illustrations) successfully provide the general reader with a helpful overview of the topic.

Meier, Christian. *The Political Art of Greek Tragedy.* Translated by Andrew Webber. Baltimore, MD: Johns Hopkins University Press, 1993. A study of Greek tragedy that places it in the context of political life in Athens.

Osborne, Robin. *Archaic and Classical Greek Art.* Oxford: Oxford University Press, 1998. Superbly illustrated (by black-and-white and color plates), this work brings together the nature of art and the society that produced it. It is, however, not for beginning students who would be better off starting with Pollitt's *Art and Experience in Classical Greece* (see next entry).

Pollitt, J. J. *Art and Experience in Classical Greece.* Cambridge: Cambridge University Press, 1972. An important work that has influenced that of other art historians and those investigating the art produced in the classical Greek world. It is accessible to even beginning students.

Women in an Age of War

Fantham, Elaine, et al. *Women in the Classical World: Image and Text.* New York: Oxford University Press, 1994. While addressing the subject of women in all eras of the classical age of Greece and Rome, this work provides several essays related directly to the Peloponnesian War era in Athens and Sparta.

Henry, Madeleine M. *Prisoner of History: Aspasia of Miletus and Her Biographical Tradition.* New York: Oxford University Press, 1995. A successful investigation that rescues Aspasia from myth and brings her to life.

Just, Roger. *Women in Athenian Law and Life.* London: Routledge, 1989. A useful introduction to the problems associated with studying women in antiquity, but one that also provides helpful background information for the Peloponnesian War era.

Keuls, Eva. *The Reign of the Phallus: Sexual Politics in Ancient Athens.* Berkeley: University of California Press, 1985. A richly illustrated study of Athenian women in a man's world. More suitable for advanced than beginning students.

Lacey, W. K. *The Family in Classical Greece.* Ithaca, NY: Cornell University Press, 1968. A general study of the Greek family, naturally including women, that draws much of its evidence from the fifth-century era of the Peloponnesian War.

Pomeroy, Sarah B. *Spartan Women*. Oxford: Oxford University Press, 2002. A new study of the roles of women in the militaristic state that was classical Sparta.

Films and Electronic Resources

Documentary Films

Greek Fire (video in five parts). Revel Guest for Arts and Entertainment, 1990. A stimulating look at Greek culture and society including the nature of democracy, philosophy, and the idea and nature of war.

The Greeks: Crucible of Civilization (PBS Home Video, two parts). Atlantic Productions in association with PBS and Devillier Donegan Enterprises, 1999. The video version of Paul Cartledge's *The Greeks* (see entry under "General Studies of Greek History"), this film introduces the general public to Greek history with dramatizations of famous personalities including Perikles and Sokrates. It is a useful tool for beginning students.

Electronic Resources

The following web sites were active at the time this bibliography was written.

www.perseus.tufts.edu This site provides students with access to many different types of resources including translations of most Greek texts—even basic ones such as Thucydides, the dramatists, and Plato. Other useful resources such as guides to museum collections are also available.

www.ualberta.ca Titled the "Peloponnesian War," this site provides an on-line account of the war that would be useful especially to beginning students wanting a broad overview.

www.laconia.org Designed by a group calling itself "Laconian Professionals," this site provides a general account of the Peloponnesian War.

www.xenophongi.org Assembled by a group of Xenophon admirers, this site, as the two preceding, provides a general account of the Peloponnesian War.

www.ablemedia.com Designed by the Classics Technology Center, this site provides a more detailed account of the Peloponnesian War, giving a much broader background both in historical narrative and in cultural and intellectual developments.

www.warhorseim.com Author Kurt Kuhlmann has provided a detailed commentary on the Peloponnesian War that is generally reliable.

Modern Fiction and the Peloponnesian War

Caldwell, Taylor. *Glory and the Lightning*. New York: Doubleday, 1974. A novel that portrays the historical and famous relationship of Perikles and Aspasia, written by a well-known novelist.

Dimont, Madelon. *Darling Pericles*. New York: Atheneum, 1972. Another treatment of the famous love affair of Perikles and Aspasia.

Kotselas, John. *Socrates in New York*. New York: Athena Publishing, 1998. A discussion of eternal philosophic issues by Sokrates and three modern men that conveys the universal problems that Sokrates attempted to bring to the attention of his own contemporaries.

Pressfield, Steven. *Tides of War: A Novel of Alcibiades and the Peloponnesian War*. New York: Doubleday, 2000. In 1989 Pressfield wrote *Gates of Fire*, a historical novel about the Spartan stand at Thermopylai in 480 (New York: Doubleday). Pressfield has read a good deal of the primary sources, and this enables him to write authentically. While his stories remain modern fiction, they successfully convey the flavor of ancient times. Pressfield also wrote *The Legend of Bagger Vance* and is an entertaining author.

Renault, Mary. *Last of the Wine*. New York: Random House, 1956 (reprinted New York: Vintage Books, 2001). Famous for such historical novels as *Fire from Heaven* and *The Persian Boy* (both about Alexander the Great), Mary Renault presents a Peloponnesian War story in *Last of the Wine*. Its hero, a young Athenian named Alexias, comes of age during the war and meets such famous personalities as Sokrates and gets caught up in other events at the war's end in Athens.

Shakespeare, William. *Timon of Athens*. Edited by H. J. Oliver, in the Arden Edition of the *Works of William Shakespeare*, R. Proudfoot, A. Thompson, D. S. Kasten, general eds. London: Methuen & Co., 1959. Shakespeare's play of Timon the Athenian is set in the era of the Peloponnesian War. Shakespeare found the idea for this play in Plutarch's *Life of Antony* (70), and while Timon seems nearly a legendary figure, there seems some basis for his existence as comedies by Aristophanes and Plato (the comic poet, not the philosopher) refer to him. Ironically, the Shakespearean drama *Pericles* is not about the famous Perikles of the Peloponnesian War but one of a later date.

Twose, Anna. *The Lion of Athens*. London: Chatto & Windus, 1976. Another historical novel that takes as its subject the relationship of Perikles and Aspasia.

INDEX

About the Author

LAWRENCE TRITLE is Professor of History at Loyola Marymount University, Los Angeles, CA. He is the author of *From Melos to My Lai: War and Survival* (2000) and *The Greek World in the Fourth Century BC: From the Fall of the Athenian Empire to the Successors of Alexander* (1997).